# THE INDOOR
# PEOPLE'S
# NATURE

I0042447

THE INDOOR PEOPLE'S NATURE
*Anthropology on the Move Towards an Ecologised World*
© 2025 Cecilie Rubow and Aarhus University Press

Translated from the Danish edition
INDENDØRSMENNESKETS NATUR, 2022

Cover and graphic design: Jakob Helmer
Typeset with: Canela Text & Freight

ISBN: 978 87 7597 257 9
ISBN: 978 87 7597 995 0 (e-pdf)
ISBN: 978 87 7597 996 7 (epub)

Published with the financial support of:
Institute of Anthropology, Copenhagen University
Jorck's Foundation
Danish Art Foundation

**Statens
Kunstfond**

Photo pp. 6–7: Anne-Li Engstrom
Photo p. 266: Susanne Borup
Other photos: Cecilie Rubow

Aarhus University Press
Helsingforsgade 25, DK-8200 Aarhus N
unipress@unipress.au.dk
aarhusuniversitypress.dk

CECILIE RUBOW

# THE INDOOR PEOPLE'S NATURE

## Anthropology on the Move Towards an Ecologised World

Translated by
Tam McTurk

AARHUS UNIVERSITY PRESS

# contents

natures

It all started with me just going out. My first port of call was the beach – in the eyes of most Danes, the very epitome of "good" nature. Nothing quite beats being buffeted by the wind, gazing out at the horizon, walking on the sand and bathing in the light.

I am one of the indoor people. I grew up in an ordinary house and hung out in schools, shopping centres and gyms. Once a year, when the family went hunting for mushrooms in the woods or skiing in the mountains, we were "doing nature". In summer, we'd drive past fields, unsure whether they were rye or wheat, and marvelling every year at how yellow rapeseed is. A walk in the woods never lasted long. We'd be back in the house pretty sharpish. A couple of hours of nature, perhaps in a boat on the fjord, was fine as a quick break from real life, but not strictly speaking necessary. Not like going to school.

Later on, I doubted whether I had ever actually been *out in nature*. Virtually all Danish forests are managed. How natural is it, really, to keep felling trees and planting new ones in straight rows? Or to follow the trail left by a snowmobile in a national park? Maybe that's why, when I looked out the window, I could only tell big birds from small ones. When I ventured outdoors, I found it all a bit disorienting. Often, I'd worry it would bore me, that I might miss out on something. For me, home has always been indoors, so I've never felt entirely at ease in the big outdoors. I don't know enough about other species and how they live. I've no idea where clean tap water comes from. Or the material in my t-shirt or the components in my mobile phone, not to mention how electricity makes it into plugs and devices. I know even less about how any of these are connected with other creatures, including other people, who might also need them.

That's what growing up in the modern world was like. And was supposed to be. Never worrying about where tap water or petrol came from was great for the consumer and a rational goal for utility companies. It was the principle behind every shop of any size. You didn't need to know where things came from. All of the steps between source and commodity were invisible. This is how much of nature disappeared from our consciousness. This is how much of nature disappeared into the goods we consume.

At the height of my indoor life, I decided I would go in search of nature.

## return of the natures

Nature has all but disappeared from the life of the indoor person. If you divide a day into 100 × 15 minutes (it's 96, but let's keep the mental arithmetic simple), how many of them do you spend indoors? If every quarter of an hour equals 1%, on how many winter days does the time you spend outdoors creep above 10%? The question is based on my own experience. Spending so much time indoors is something new in human history. And it's not just down to the weather in northern Europe. How much time do you spend outdoors in the summer? And in which outdoors?

We spend so little time living in nature and know so little about it that we refer to all sorts of indoor things as "natural". The advertising industry uses the word for everything – from milk cartons and anoraks to potted plants and cruise ships. They're all great for nature lovers, apparently. For the indoor person, nature seems to have vanished but still be everywhere. It gets so complicated when a word describes so many things. Should we stop using it? Some scientists have given that serious consideration, but the idea has never really caught on. I think it's a response borne of frustration, a bit like smashing a plate in a tantrum. We can't blame the word for everything. We have to work with it.

One day, after I had begun to wonder where nature really was and noticed how often it popped up in conversations, on TV, and in scientific reports about its state, it struck me the subject was ripe for an anthropological study.

But where should I go to find it? To keep things manageable, I had to narrow my focus. I decided to start by looking for what the Danes consider the epitome of nature – the best nature, the version least likely to be described as culture. The idea was to establish a baseline for the study before moving on to more complex settings.

I work in the centre of Copenhagen, by the Lakes. In some places, they look a bit like a river, but they are in fact five basins supplied with water by a river excavated and thoroughly regulated by humans. I moved into the office many moons ago and used to take a photo of the view every day. When I finally made a collage with them, I realised how much this urban space changed colour and character with the seasons and time of day. In the summer, big chestnut trees filled almost the whole picture. In winter, wisps of snow swept across black ice. At night, the neon signs on the north side drew my attention to the depth of the darkness. A constant stream of cars passes below the window. When I'm sitting in one of them, I always like to observe and ponder the square spaces around the Lakes. These are carefully designed and constructed spaces, with wide expanses, full of life and colour. Humans settle and set up home here. So do ants and birds. Humans have created their own landscapes and transformed them beyond recognition.

When I take my bike to work, I don't have to stray from paved cycle paths. When I take the train, I have to walk less than a mile in total. Our entire infrastructure is based on not spending much time outside. I often imagine what the Lakes looked like centuries ago, before somebody dug up Ladegårdsåen to supply fresh water to the city, and what this space would have looked like had the long-since-abandoned plans for a 12-lane motorway come to fruition. I was born in the mid-1960s when dreams like that were common. For my parents, modern life was there for the taking – a house, kids, two incomes. The national and local infrastructure facilitated a childhood spent in kindergarten, school, sports halls, cinemas and the sweet shop on the corner. Kids had their own rooms. The most modern homes had a garage – the car, too, spent most of its time indoors. In the modern world, nature is a kind of pastime. A place "you don't belong".

As mentioned, the beach was my first port of call. A strange choice for a scientific study, perhaps, but as a scientist and indoor person, I had a bit of an "in" here. Admittedly, I'd never been a great fan of the beach in summer and had always found the combination of sand, salt, sun and wind tiresome, even on brief visits. However, I started to change my mind about beaches during a research project in the Pacific. I was particularly taken with one on a lagoon – possibly one of the best beaches in the world from a tourist's point of view. Screaming turquoise meets chalk-white, not overcrowded, set on a lush and accessible coast, but also increasingly vulnerable to pollution and erosion. The threats seemed to come from near (inadequate sewers and lack of coastal protection) and far (acidification of the oceans, rising sea temperatures and increasingly ferocious cyclones).

The people who lived around and off the lagoon saw fish stocks diminish, sand turn brown, reefs disintegrate and thick algae explode in the warm season. I learned about coastal sand budgets, fish species, rising sea levels, storms, nitrates, sea gods, fish traps and how to channel grief over a devastated beach into collective action. The locals couldn't save the lagoon overnight, but they began studying its condition to learn more about its creatures, stories and biological processes, as well as their own

11

potential to influence them. The endeavour ended up changing themselves. They learned how closely their lives were interwoven with the lagoon, and how it was affected by what they did on land. At the time, they couldn't always figure out what caused what – but today, I would say that they "ecologised" their relationship to the lagoon because they no longer thought of nature purely as something else, something out there.

## in the field

In terms of distance, the fieldwork didn't take me very far from my desk, my view of the Lakes, and the lecture theatres and classrooms. Anthropologists used to spend months sailing overseas to carry out fieldwork. Back then, people thought the more far-flung the destination, the stranger the local habits would be – an idea dropped when it became clear everybody has their own culture, and it's impossible to rank them in terms of "strangeness". What yardstick would we use – theirs or ours? Instead, the job of the anthropologist became to elaborate on the idea of what it means to be human.

And so it was, on a chilly day in March, that I set off to do fieldwork on the north coast of Zealand, where I met some of the winter beach people. At the time, the government was advocating a small number of projects to develop the coastal zone. One involved extending the beach west of the harbour in Gilleleje by removing an industrial site, building a hotel partially embedded in new dunes, a long pier with winter bathing facilities and what the planners called a "nature room".

It piqued my interest that the project would be an exception to the rules for the coastal zone – an attempt to *optimise* the beach by adding "more" nature. The project described the nature room as having floor-to-ceiling windows that would provide an "unrestricted panoramic view", represented by an illustration of a woman and child – wearing what I would call an overdressed indoor outfit– gazing out across a calm blue sea towards the cliffs of the rugged Kullen promontory on the coast of Sweden.[2]

It was a fascinating image. Was this the perfect way for the modern indoor person to experience nature? They were inside, behind thick glass, but had the ultimate open view of the water, sky and distant horizon. A single sailing boat suggested a recreational environment. No container ships, fishing boats or ferries.

In the end, the New Nordic Coast project floundered on local protests – particularly by fishermen, whose livelihood it threatened. But the vision of experiencing nature from indoors was fascinating. Had the public-private partnership managed to provide the envisaged "knowledge, experimentarium and information about the sea – fishing, nature below the surface",[3] it might even have been good for democracy given that all the good indoor sea views have long since been snapped up on this stretch of coast.

I started the fieldwork on the west beach at Gilleleje, but when the New Nordic Coast project floundered – and I had suspected that the local consultation would reveal fault lines in the form of different ideas about what constitutes good coastal nature – I turned my attention to other parts of the coast. Eventually, I concentrated on the beaches in another coastal town, Tisvildeleje. West of it are the heathlands of Tisvilde Hegn and the protected Melby Overdrev towards Liseleje. To the east is an area densely populated with holiday homes. In the middle, just off the pier, is Lejet. In the 1800s, this cluster of dwellings formed a small fishing village. Now, the area is a magnet for a demographic variously dubbed "Copenhageners", "the elite" or, somewhat sneeringly, "hipsters". Still, everyone agrees it's a beauty spot. The beaches are long, white and ideal for walking and swimming. According to the Danish Nature Agency, the forest and heath comprise a mixture of habitats – green and white sandy landscapes, dunes, oak thickets, tall beech trees, lakes and plantations of Scots pine amid rolling hills.

The journey from the University of Copenhagen to North Zealand is neither long nor spectacular. People often think of the anthropologist as a man in the tropics, dressed in linens, wearing a pith helmet and carrying a notebook, imperiously seeking out natives to describe their strange habits and customs. It's a far cry from what I was doing. For one thing, it's cold. And what's strange about going to the beach?

I conducted my first interview on Gilleleje Beach in March 2017. It was with a retired gentleman, a former civil servant, who told me he went for a walk on the beach every day. The whole situation, approaching a stranger on the beach, felt awkward. I don't like phoning strangers, either. Being apprehensive about speaking to people is a bit of a drawback for an anthropologist – and occasionally turn out not to be a totally unfounded fear. I left it to chance and just approached the first person I saw. I didn't get the man's name, nor those of the other beachgoers I chanced upon. The plan was that these partially improvised interviews would broaden my horizons before I started to identify the people who would make particularly interesting subjects *and* might be willing to have longer conversations about questions I didn't yet know I would want to ask.

The man told me that the most fascinating thing on the beach was the "shwooshing" sound of the pebbles rolling in the waves. The way he said it, emphasised by an outward sweeping gesture with one of his hands, made me listen for the pebbles moving underfoot. Collectively, thousands of them create an almost impenetrably dense sound, which is then interrupted by the next wave. "But it's better when the stones are bigger, like those further along the beach," he added. He told me how he observed the power of the sea in different weather, and that these forces are so strong we would be better served letting the coast do its own thing rather than trying to protect it with granite and concrete: "The sea always wins in the end." I had the distinct impression that his daily walk on the beach with his excitable little dog was far more than an ingrained habit.

In the past, I had encountered all sorts of people – family, friends, colleagues, people at social gatherings and voices on the radio – who told me how much they loved spending time outdoors and how much good nature did them. But as I gave it more thought, I realised none of these conversations had brought me any closer to what it was that these people were looking for, or what they found out there. The realisation confirmed my suspicion that the subject was ripe for an anthropological study of the ideas we take for granted. Not that we should expect insights to be served up on a plate – the things we take for granted tend to guard their secrets. The wind was getting colder. I asked the man to tell me more about his daily practice of following the sun, the wind directions and how the storms transport sand and seawater. He hesitated and reiterated the obvious point: that he went to the beach every day because it was "nice and invigorating". Hmmm.

Sheltering from the wind, I wrote field notes and recorded the sound of the shifting pebbles, and his brief concluding remark reminded me that not everything can or should be translated into words – even though it was my job to make them stretch a little further. The next quick interview brought me a little closer to the intensity of people's experiences on the beach. Conversations with people from very different backgrounds – on weekdays, the North Zealand coast is populated primarily by highly educated people, artists, pensioners and the self-employed – showed that the benefit they derived from walks on the beach and gazing at the horizon reminded them of a kind of religion. In Europe, people have been sanctifying nature for centuries,[4] but these acts have often been obscured by other, more powerful cultural currents that have instead tended to use, process and alter nature beyond recognition.

Beachgoers called walking on the coastline a "meditation on finiteness and infinity"; or "sacred and elevated". They said it's "almost magical to come out of the forest and see the beach open up"; that "there's nothing more life-affirming than sitting by the water and watching the sunset"; "you forget time and place and feel incredibly small"; "nature is my god, if I have one"; "an evening at the beach can be almost otherworldly, like heaven has come to Earth"; that the beach is "somewhere you become one with the universe"; and that the view of the sea can "awaken a primordial feeling of happiness".

I always began these short, random interviews with an open question about what a walk on the beach meant to them, for example, "Do you mind if I ask what brings you out here?" I also experimented with different ways of introducing myself: "I work at the University of Copenhagen and am researching the Danes' relationship with nature" – or, less neutrally, "… the Danes' *love* of nature". In follow-up interviews and conversations with people to whom I had been referred because they were known to be particularly engrossed in the beach, sea and sky, we started talking about the "love of", "interest in" or "fascination with" nature.

Nature lovers showed me that magic works in many different ways on the beach and its hinterland. I will start by telling you about Liv, the Green Lady.

# the world by the window

Liv Tvermoes sat in the first-floor bay window of the last house on the street called Ved Stranden in Tisvildeleje, gazing attentively at the sunset. An hour earlier, she had spotted the first hint of it on the frame of the kitchen door downstairs. That was her sign. She carried her plate up the narrow staircase, ate her carefully prepared meal, and spent the next few hours looking out the window.

A month on, my project was beginning to take shape and feel like anthropological fieldwork. I had reached out to some local people, who offered to help. Before long, several of them mentioned Liv, but I didn't visit her for months, which gave me time to gather enough background knowledge to discuss local matters with her.

Liv looked out at the sea and sky every evening. One day, years ago, she turned off her TV and decided not to spend any more time on that. Liv was in her nineties. Her movements were calm, she seemed patient and imperturbable, and she sprinkled our conversations with an enthusiasm for the wondrous beauty of the world – not least just outside her window.

The first time I sought out Liv, she said she was glad I'd come. A friend was visiting that day, helping in the garden, but she took the time to sit down with me on the bench under the gable and outline her life in Tisvildeleje. She had first come here as a child after her father had been prescribed fresh air for health reasons. At first, the family stayed in a boarding house every summer. Eventually, they bought one of the first holiday homes in the town, which she had to sell later on. Since retiring from her job as a secretary at the US Embassy in Copenhagen, Liv had been lucky enough to live in this little house with its narrow kitchenette and a living room with space for a table, couch, grandfather clock and some chairs. The upstairs room housed her bed and a desk and had a sea view. The next time I came, she told me we could talk about nature and how she lived with it every day. She made it very clear to me that this was an important story.

Around town, Liv was known as "the Green Lady" because she always dressed in shades of the colour. Her house, too, was mostly green – the cushions, the chest of drawers in the hall, the grandfather clock, the coats hanging on hooks – with occasional touches of white, grey and beige. The reason behind her fondness for green had faded into the mists of time, and Liv made do with telling me in passing that it was just a habit now. It wasn't a statement. There was no particular reason. Green just worked. Liv was enthusiastic about all things organic and sustainable, grieved over the scale of climate change and implored me not to "skip newspaper articles about the climate – you mustn't!" But we didn't talk about that much.

She said she had "woken up" after reading about environmental problems and did her bit, including sorting her rubbish for recycling. Liv seldom ate meat, and even then only chicken. She rarely travelled further than the 12 kilometres to Helsinge and openly acknowledged her limited range and influence. Liv also knew she didn't have long left, so her focus was on living right there, in her little house by the sea, conserving her strength. She fervently hoped it would be right there, by the sea, that she would draw her dying breath.

Liv seemed to find it natural to take ownership of "our project", as she called it. She knew full well that I had much to learn and thought it perfectly reasonable that an anthropologist should seek her out. In fact, she would have liked to have been an anthropologist herself. It was fascinating, she thought, as were local and natural history – which she now mostly studied in detail from her window. She had become a delicate flower and could no longer walk to the beach, swim, cycle in the woods, lie on the forest floor and enjoy the wildflowers. "But it doesn't matter," she said. She remembered it all.

We talked at length about what she saw out of her window – we always returned to that – and I tried to see it through Liv's eyes. For example, she would look at the clouds to see if the next grey one would bring rain. She would observe the light and the patterns on the water. Later in the evening, when the sun dipped below the horizon, she eagerly awaited what she called "the important phase", to see whether clouds would appear on which deep-red hues could spread.

We didn't just talk about what Liv saw out the window. We also talked about the act of "seeing" – how it could be a particularly intense and rewarding state of being. Sometimes, unusual phenomena popped up, about which she would wonder for years. But they weren't necessarily any more important than her thoughtful daily observation of the sea and sky.

## three natures

Is "nature" best defined as that which remains untouched by human hand, everything that isn't "culture"? Is it more accurate to say that human beings have always lived in the middle of nature and, crucially, that the most important thing about nature is that we manage and change it to shape our surroundings? Or is nature best understood by our inseparable entanglement with it and with all kinds of other beings? In everyday speech, we switch effortlessly between all three meanings.[5]

Liv was firmly rooted in all three natures. She especially loved the sea outside the window, just as it was – untouched by human hand. I will call this type of nature the *first nature*.

She also loved the local environment that had emerged around the first fishermen's cottages and the natural surroundings that her predecessors in the town had changed and cultivated and from which they benefitted. The beach, the forest and the fields outside her window are all part of what I call the *second nature*, which is neither untouched by nor completely entangled with humans, the latter of which constitutes the *third nature* (nature-culture).[6] I will expand upon the distinctions between the three natures – concepts that are woven through the fabric of this book. They form a thread that binds the stories I want to share from my fieldwork and act as a kind of linguistic scaffolding that enables me to tell the story of how I went out in search of nature.

My story is about how it is important for the indoor person to know the difference between the three natures and that we can't do without any of them. In this book, my aim is to interpret the three *through* each other and to explore what nature lovers, environmentalists and climate activists can teach the indoor person. Interpreting these concepts through each other endows them with meaning by emphasising the differences, but it also means they never stand completely alone. Concepts are simplifications of that which in practice is more complex and, as I will show, tangible phenomena in the world and social situations involve all three natures, albeit to varying degrees.

Definitions of concepts often make for somewhat arduous reading. It's a bit like having to move all your furniture before you paint a wall, and just as tedious. But it's equally important to tidy up before you write, so you can start to use language in a new way. Concepts provide simple tools we combine to describe more complicated patterns. The examples I use to define my concepts stem from fieldwork, during which I listened to how modern Danes use the word "nature", and from a long research tradition that has explored different concepts of it.[7]

In terms of landscape, the epitome of the *first nature* for the indoor person is usually the great outdoors – the wilderness of northern Scandinavia or the forests and some of the coastline in Denmark – which we see as untouched by human hand, as truly wild places, pure nature. When it's windy on the west coast of Jutland, the beach becomes a churning mishmash of water, salt and sand, and all you hear is the wind and the sea. It's wild. There is nothing for it but to observe, lean into the blast, and dress appropriately. This is nature as it is in the wilderness – no internet, no visible infrastructure, no roads, houses or bridges. When you lift your gaze to look in certain directions, it's easy to imagine the landscape has looked like this for hundreds of years. In this sense, the first nature is defined by a lack of human involvement. It is something in its own right. It is nature unbound – so much so that the indoor person can only cope with short bursts. But it's not that simple.

Areas and phenomena other than the wilderness are also seen as proper outdoor nature. People with gardens shape them and significantly influence what they look like, but how trees grow leaves and drop fruit is out of their hands. If you go for a walk in a park or along the side of a field in which everything looks well-kept and trimmed, you might think it is first nature. No matter how much humans intervene, the plants in these places have their own nature. Chloroplasts, roots and stems do their own thing. So, whenever we look at something green, whether it's a plant nursery, a park or a cemetery, we think of it as nature. Natural materials are also used in everything with which we, as indoor people, surround ourselves, and in the same way that human beings contain aspects of first nature – in our bodies, senses and the things to which we pay attention. The question of what

21

is identified as first nature may shift depending on its quality and the importance accorded to it as first nature, but untouched nature as a concept always reflects the idea that humankind has not fully illuminated, mastered or domesticated the world.

The qualities of the *second nature* are most evident in built-up and farming landscapes, where it is clear nature isn't solely its own work or just raw materials. All over Denmark, landscapes have been profoundly changed by agriculture, forestry and urban development.[8] Despite how long ploughs, livestock, the saw and industrial machinery have been around, Danes still talk about forests, parks, gardens and open landscapes as nature – knowing full well that these parts of the landscape are not completely untouched by human hand. We take this human influence on nature for granted. The crunchy cauliflower you grow in your garden to eat – provided the larvae don't get in there first – is cultivated flora, distantly related to the grey-green sea kale with thick, wavy leaves found on even the most stony of Danish beaches. Likewise, traces of human activity are seen in the oldest forests, lakes and streams, as well as in the open landscape, with its fields and heaths. Humans have "surrounded" themselves with a world that they have made habitable.[9] You could say that landscapes understood in this way are events.[10] They are constantly coming into being, rather than existing as untouched things, objects or beings out there. Whereas first nature is defined by the absence of a human or cultural imprint, second nature is defined by human processing, which is clear not only in its results but also in the way we habitually interact with nature. To harvest crops, spot a bird or use a computer, we need special skills and routine practices. In that sense, it is not only humans who have a second nature and use it to create homes for themselves – all living creatures do that when they forage and nest in each other's habitats.

The *third nature*, the absolutely entangled nature-culture,[11] is seen in the lasting mark humankind has made on the planet, including on everything we call human. As a concept, it doesn't restrict our understanding of nature to something at its most proper only when untouched by human hand, or the kind of nature that we cultivate and manage. The third concept differs from the first because it doesn't focus on the *difference* between the human and the natural; and from the second because it doesn't focus on the role played by humans in creating and managing nature. Instead, the concept of the third nature reflects all the connections and entanglements between humans and nature that lead to us also understanding humankind as nature-culture. The qualities of the third nature are evident in complex ecosystems, in which humans are so thoroughly entangled with plants, animals and minerals that we often overlook each other's contributions. As such, from a third-nature perspective, it makes no sense to say that the things with which we surround ourselves indoors are not nature-culture, too. The food we eat, the raw materials processed into steel, concrete and fibre-optic cables – all the elements that make up our infrastructure – come from nature and don't stop being nature just because something else is added. In recent decades, in the sciences and beyond, we have paid more attention to these connections and to how the *apparent* separation between humans and other species often turns out to be a form of collaboration. The political attention paid to pollution, the extinction of species and climate change[12] means that there is more widespread acknowledgement of our responsibility to understand and develop ways of living in *co-operation* with ecosystems.

As concepts, the three types of "nature" are contradictory, yet the qualities they point toward can all inform the ways we "world".[13] Even apparent wildernesses are not uniquely pristine and wild. Somebody has been there. Witness the empty beer cans, salmon farms, queues of mountaineers at the base camp on Mount Everest, or that, on closer inspection, even the bluest skies are dirty. Wildernesses and nature reserves are managed, as has been made abundantly clear in recent political debates about open landscapes in Denmark. In the same way, cultivated land is not just the result of human endeavour, but consists of various half-frames generated in cooperation between humans and their surroundings. Humans play an active role in the world, but so do seeds, pesticides, water and bolt guns – they all have their part to play. We *world* along with our surroundings.

Given the word "nature" has so many meanings, how can we work with it? Throughout the rest of the book, the three concepts of nature function as linguistic scaffolding, and I return to them in each chapter. However, the points I want to make are most clearly illuminated when some life is added to the scaffolding. And with that, let's return to Liv.

## meeting the world halfway

On one visit, Liv talked about how the sound of the waves changed throughout the year and how she also studied the length of the shadows.

"Fascinating, eh?" she went on, "A lot of important stuff goes on in nature."

When she moved into her little house by the sea, Liv had felt anxious about leaving her home a little further inland. In particular, she wasn't keen to leave behind the warm doorstep from which she watched the sunsets – first, as a child, with her parents and sisters, and later alone. Now the beach, the ocean, was just below her window.

"I felt as if the waves were coming for me, weren't they, *damn it*? And then, one day, I said, 'Come on then!' And since then, I haven't been afraid at all. One time, I was sleeping when a storm hit. In the morning, I couldn't see out the windows. They were covered in salt and sand. But I slept well." Perhaps Liv wouldn't mind being compared with Saint-Exupéry's Little Prince, who befriends a fox by patiently moving closer and closer to it.

Although Liv spent most of her day indoors and could no longer go to the shops or pick daisies, it was obvious that I was far more of an indoor person than she was. As an inveterate indoor type, I had long since lost any connection to the landscape, which was a distant "out there", but Liv spent the day conversing with the chestnut tree outside the front door, tending the herbs in the wooden box and defending her beach roses against the Danish Nature Agency's insistence that they are invasive and harmful. It was as if her breathing was in sync with the constantly shifting sea.

"Today, a blackbird with food in its mouth came and wanted to talk to me," she would say. Or, "When the first snowdrops came, I pulled on my big wellies and went out with an old spade. They had to be brought in!" Or, "You can keep looking for as long as you like, as long as something says 'thank you'." Or, "When in nature, you have everything." Liv often spoke in short sentences. She knew how to make the most of a small house and did the same with words. Neither the house nor her sentences felt cramped.

After one interview – on a clear day in February – I went down to the beach. We'd had a nice chat, but it left me feeling a bit down. The slight breeze wasn't breathing much life into the beach, which felt cold, lifeless and never-ending. The water was dark blue, dotted with ripples, like a still-life painting. It was as if the contrast between Liv's way of living by the sea and the way I was standing there right then grew in my mind. How would I ever get rid of my "indoorsness", as she had? There's no such word, of course. But that's how I felt. I felt very distant, out of step with the colours, the salt water and the seagulls, the species of which I still couldn't tell apart, whose names I hadn't learnt. My inner monologue was in full flow: "You're a human being without surroundings." I wrapped my arms around my chest, but it didn't warm me up.

I grew up by Mariager Fjord in Jutland. My inner sense of the place lives on, albeit painfully, because that particular fjord has since succumbed to deoxygenation. In 1997, fish were found floating belly-up on the surface for miles around, and people reported a putrid stench. In the intervening years, my sense of landscapes, other than urban ones, has been, at best, weak and fleeting. Although I now love my garden and, like many others of my generation, I have travelled to indescribably fascinating destinations on five continents. There I was, standing on the beach, unable to get any closer to nature. That afternoon, I felt as if the beach didn't want me to come any closer, as if it was rejecting me. In truth, of course, it was me who had cut myself off. I sensed, with startling clarity, what I had long suspected – that I had no friends among the other species, that the wind, water and sand were just swirling around me in lifeless movements.

I decided to practise actively looking at the sky whenever possible and agreed with Liv that I would drive up to Tisvildeleje one evening to watch "her" sunset. She insisted I did it on my own. I'd hoped she would be my guide, my "informant", but she left me alone in the garden – on a green chair with green and white cushions, of course.

"I believe it's a kind of religion for all of us," she told me afterwards. "You should watch the sun setting because it has always been beautiful. But not everyone takes it all in."

It was a quiet, clear evening with few clouds, as a warm day in early June drew to a close. It felt a little awkward. Sunsets are hard. We've all seen too many bad paintings poorly attempt to replicate one. I started writing notes about the garden and what Liv had said, just to feel I was doing something. Then, I walked around the garden for a while and looked down at the beach where some young people were hanging out. I sat back down and wondered whether Liv was sitting up in her bay window, what she could see from there, what thoughts and "dreams", as she called them, she could see playing out from her vantage point. Important dreams, I could tell, ones in which Liv felt truly present and alive.

As ten o'clock approached, I was intensely focused on the colours of the water, which changed gradually as the sun went from pale yellow to orange. Blue, black and silver flickered, followed by gold. A few slightly bigger waves, swells perchance, smeared the surface with new white stripes, roaring and undulating in my ears, first to the left of the garden, then to the right. Birds flew overhead. The clouds drifted by, vapour trails gleaming high above in the blue of the sky. All sorts were happening at the same time. The vista was ever-changing. I couldn't possibly focus on both the kaleidoscopic sea and the insects buzzing in the hedge.

It all became a bit much. For Liv, paying attention to it was like a slow, steady breath – a far cry from my breathless sundown. Speaking about her taxi trips to Helsinge, she described the interaction between the senses and the outside world: "It's as if the fields welcome you." I asked about this feeling as a form of "connectedness". Liv found the word a bit too onerous and mystifying, as if it implied, as I understood her, a previously established connection. She said it was more like an encounter, "where you meet it part-way [...] There has to be a soul that opens up as well." The landscape can't do it all for you.

Liv pops up again in the following chapters. She wasn't my only teacher during my fieldwork. Compared to the other beachgoers and the birdwatchers, botanists, environmentalists and climate activists I met later on, she wasn't always the most pedagogic, either. At times, she'd be impatient if I asked her to expand on something she had already said. Some of her statements were a bit cryptic: "There are colours, everywhere. The colours are always there." Another time, gesturing towards the window, she said: "The old tree. The reef. And the window. It's all connected." As we talked, she tried to show me connections between phenomena I sometimes had difficulty grasping in our conversations. But she also advised, in a typically Liv statement, "You need to take it and make it your own," so I had to see if I could learn something.

For months, Liv had been trying to find the lyrics to a tune, but could only remember a few words from one of the verses. She was delighted when I finally tracked it down. It turned out to be "Lette bølge, når du blåner" (When the Light Wave Turns Blue) by Johan L. Heiberg, from 1829. Liv had sung it in school, and could only remember fragments.

"It fits our project well," she said. She would think, slowly, about the poem over the next few days.

> Gentle wave! As you turn blue,
> Transparent, bright and clear,
> To Heaven's colours turn you,
> As you have no colour here.
> Heaven never, just impersonated

Rests in your deep embrace,
Never is your longing sated,
It is eternal like the loss you face.

Wave! When at your clearest I find,
Your water heaven doth imitate
Ach! Your longing the heart it does remind
Of what fate doth separate.
Heart! You ought not to complain!
Even nature feels loss the same;
Console yourself with what doth remain
Only an image and a name.

I never did hear what Liv made of the poem. She was sceptical about Christianity, of which she "understood not a jot" – including the idea of an afterlife, on which she refused, therefore, to comment. If we interpret the poem's longing for heaven as an example of classical Christian metaphysics, I find it difficult to reconcile these lines with Liv's relationship to the sea and the light. I think she would have paid less attention to the lack of colour than to how the colours, the light and the water, the wave and the sky are always entangled – in the living world – and how we can be left with a longing to "take it all in" precisely because we don't always live in life's embrace. In that sense, everything Liv said reflected her striving to embrace and live with the relationships that "fate", our existences, also "separate".

Liv had refused treatment at the hospital in Hillerød several times. I didn't get the chance to show her what I had learned before her final day in the little house by the sea. I didn't get to talk about the three natures with her, or how, to me, she was one of the few people who breathed intensely through all three of them. She admired the sea out there for its own beauty and strength and sought its qualities every day. She had found her home, with sea, window and reef protected from the weather. Liv worked with the sea, just as the sea works with the light. She couldn't detach herself from it, just as she had become part of the beach, the forest and the history of the town.

"Lie in the water for five minutes. Don't swim, breathe. You'll be born again." Liv couldn't hold the sea at arm's length. She didn't just enjoy the sunset as a beautiful picture. Liv was *in* the picture and saw how it all began again every day. She constantly wanted to be closer to the colours, to bathe in them, to feel the wind, become part of the movements, and engage with them in a spirit of love and respect. She did so not without a tinge of misanthropy and a critique of overconsumption and self-conceit, and not without being aware of her own limitations.

I have since come across another fragment of a poem that fits our project. The American poet Alice Fulton wrote these lines in "Cascade Experiment":

> [...] we have to meet the universe halfway.
> Nothing will unfold for us unless we move toward what
> looks to us like nothing: faith is a cascade.
> The sky's high solid is anything
> but, the sun going under hasn't
> budged [...]

There sat Liv, as I see it, in her bay window on a rotating globe in the universe, earthling as she was, aware of "meeting the universe halfway".[14]

# ecologising the world

In the modern world, it makes sense to keep nature and culture apart – just as it has made sense to study religion, economics and gender in isolation. Modernity is the idea that differences matter more than connections. In the modern world, the differences between women and men define gender. Differences between nature and culture define the world. Differences between the religious and the secular define politics. And so on. I call it "the History of Big Differences".[15] As a result, modern people are in the greatest need of the first and second concepts of nature. They need nature as something outside of themselves, something to admire from afar – in many cases, something we need to protect ourselves against and, to an increasing degree, something we have cultivated as useful surroundings.

Across scientific disciplines, research has argued that the History of Big Differences is a product of Enlightenment rationalism[16] and has never been the whole story, and I agree with those who argue that it *ought* not to be the whole story. In a negative sense, climate change is the most compelling example of how people and the planet are inexorably entangled and how the modern world order is under pressure. Humans and all of our domesticated species put enormous strain on natural resources.[17]

The biodiversity crisis suggests too little space is left for nature as the great untouched (with lots of the quality of the first nature), and climate change adds a lack of care for our surroundings (the quality of the second nature) to the picture, not to mention insufficient attention to all of the planet's interconnections (the quality of the third nature). The Anthropocene Epoch,[18] in which human activities trigger global changes in the state of the Earth, is the dark side of the third nature.

Although volcanic eruptions, sunspots and other phenomena are also part of the scientific explanation for climate change, carbon dioxide can no longer be understood purely as an isolated chemical, as an element in photosynthesis, or as an emission from burning wood and other waste. $CO_2$ has become a scale in itself, one by which to measure your activities. $CO_2$ has become a new form of nature in the realm of politics, a component of personal choices and crucial ways of worlding responsibly. For people who think a lot about climate change and want to contribute to a more sustainable future, this makes $CO_2$ just as much a part of nature as birds in flight and electricity generated by Norwegian rivers. As such, we can perceive and refer to it as a chemical compound out there (first nature); *and* as part of the cycle of life that the global community should manage responsibly (second nature); *and* as part of a cycle with which we have already long since been intertwined, via our skin and hair, and deep down in our lungs (third nature). Depending on which nature we focus our attention on, the ecology changes.

So, when I went out looking for nature, I also found something else. I started on the beach, moved on to the woods and heath, and then returned home, heading back to the city. In none of those places did I find only one nature. Instead, I found a world entangled in people's thoughts and everyday lives. Did I find nature at all? Gazing out over the water or peering under a rock, feeling the soil under my nails, examining every component of my bike? In my search for nature, I was accompanied by nature lovers, environmentalists and climate activists – and by animals, plants, cameras, books, seeds, colleagues and students. The story I want to tell encompasses all of these elements. It's a much bigger and more complex story than a binary distinction between nature and culture conveys.

Ecology is one of those words we ought to use much more. In Denmark, it is mainly used to describe organic goods that meet certain standards for how they were produced (e.g. without pesticides) and is associated with certain forms of animal ethics. However, more far-reaching understandings of the word are gaining ground and being applied to living connections in the world. In this book, I use "ecology" to talk about ways to world that involve the three natures.

I will also go down the noun-as-verb path and say we *ecologise* in different ways. The French anthropologist and philosopher Bruno Latour takes the same approach when he advocates for an ecologisation of politics. He understands the term as the opposite of "modernisation", which rests heavily on the first concept of nature.[19] Modernity saw the environment as a special area within politics. Interest groups took care of "nature" as if it were something separate. Perhaps we can already see a ecologisation in European politics, where it is difficult for parties to survive if the green transition isn't a key part of their policy agenda. Can we also move towards it in our everyday lives? Are our lives becoming ecologised in such a way that the indoor person can no longer pretend the outdoors is none of their business? Is the outdoors also becoming ecologised, with new solutions for how people can inhabit the world without turning everything into surroundings for them to use?

As an indoor person, I have followed nature lovers, environmentalists and climate activists to learn how they ecologise when they look out of their windows, spend time on the beach and in the forest, watch birds, live with plants, monitor the nature they love, mourn the extinction of species and try to develop responsible communities. Throughout these stories, the qualities of the three natures emerge – and ecologise – in surprising and inspiring ways.

# to beach

"People just aren't used to talking about it," Peter's mum said in the car on the way to an event at our kids' class was holding. She had just told me that she's been coming to the North Sea several times a year, all her life. "The emptiness," she repeated several times. "That's what's great about the beach. You can be alone. [...] Yeah, there are plenty of great places around Copenhagen, but no real nature, not like in Jutland."

In the far west of Denmark, the beach is so big you can drive a car on it, the sea so wild you have to look out for riptides, children have to learn to swim and the wind is so strong it feels like it blows right through you. In icy winters, the sea contorts itself into strange shapes. When I dug a little deeper into the question of the wind and the water ("What's it like to be buffeted by the wind?"), I was met with a hesitation and uncertainty.

"It's hard to explain what happens on the beach." You have felt the salt wind so many times that it's got under your skin. You can see the sand, horizon and grey-green lyme grass in your mind's eye, feel them between your fingers, crunch them between your teeth – they "get right into your soul". But how do you explain something like that? I ask if there are any animals on the beach. "No, there aren't. The good thing is that there are *none*."

## beach and repeat

Nikolaj Vendersen is tall and thin, maybe even downright bony – and, as he puts it, the "dry" type. "Do you get what I mean? I like being dry, and the beach helps give me that dryness." He's an academic, has been visiting Tisvildeleje all his life and bit by bit I get the impression he has built up a deeply ritualised approach to how he "*beaches*". The verb is mine, incidentally, to convey how Nikolaj doesn't seem to regard the beach as just a place, or something we can reduce to a noun. The beach is something he *does*, and he was unusually explicit in the way he described how it has literally helped shape his body, his tough "dryness", and how the sun changes him at the cellular level. He monitors these changes closely. The beach also helps shape his mind. I don't know how he had prepared for my visit, but his response to the question "What do you do on the beach?" was direct. We cycled from Holløse to Tisvildeleje, along the steep hillsides, stopping at several of the stairways down to the beach to look out over the water while Nikolaj explained that he comes to the beach twice a day – for a morning run and an afternoon walk.

Before the morning run, he puts down a towel at "his" groyne, a particularly good bathing spot because the water is so green, the shade you sometimes see on rocky coasts in southern Europe. He then runs towards Tisvildeleje, down to Hyrdebakken, up and down the stairs five times, a total of approximately 700 steps, and then back again. He might pass about 20 people and loves the way they greet each other with a "good morning" and the odd quick comment. He runs, is hardened and takes on colour.

The afternoon walk is just as much of a ritual. He sets off on his bike but continues on foot to Brantebjerg or Lille Kulgab. He finds this part of the beach, after the pier, which has no groynes or other forms of coastal protection, irresistibly beautiful. He wonders why so few people go there. Even on hot days. It's so close to Copenhagen. But not everybody loves the beach as much as he does. He has met neighbours who have had a holiday home there for a year without once venturing onto the beach: "They ask me how I got down there. They've just been sitting on a deck for a whole year!"

In the afternoon, it's a crucial part of the ritual that he walks towards the sun and the line it makes on the water. That's why he does it. If he notices birds at all, it's usually the song of the lark as it takes off from behind the dunes before swooping back down to its nest. He walks alone, an inner monologue running about all the things he wants to say and the ones he should have said – but didn't – in meetings, speeches and conversations. All the while, the sun, wind and the horizon are all there, as well as details like the "incredibly beautiful black rocks" used to make the groynes. If I understand Nikolaj correctly, spending time on the beach is less about observation, and more about imprinting the surroundings on him. He is less of a person who *faces* the landscape and enjoys the view than one who surrenders himself to it.

"And then there's the wind, which caresses you. The older I get, the more I understand the importance of that." We looked out at the silvery water to the west. "When I reach my turning point, I stop, face the sun and think: 'With all this light, there's nothing to fear. As long as you have light in you, you'll be fine.' I tell myself not to forget this. But I do. I don't think my body remembers the light, so I have to repeat the walk again and again. If there's anything religious about my approach to the beach, it's that need for repetition."

All the people I've met on shorelines beach in their own distinctive way. A lot of them find it inspiring to walk their dog there and might not do it otherwise. Some walk every day, others go on a long drive once a week and combine a walk with a dip or a spot of birdwatching. Some are particularly interested in the ever-changing colours of the sky and water. Some look for stones or can't help but hope to find a lump of amber. Some hanker most after the almost meditative state they reach while walking on the beach, others see it as an opportunity for a more focused conversation with themselves. Almost all are captivated by the horizon, that line through the landscape that only really exists as a contrast between land and sea, and which also seems to run all the way through our lives. What's out there, on the other side? More of the same? Is it the scale of the universe you get a sense of, or is it infinity, the primordial soup of everything? The question extends into the personal, too: What is infinite in my life? Where do I begin and end? I've heard many answers, but regardless of what the horizon means to people – freedom, meaning, possibility, hope, energy, an affirmation of life or grandeur – the line is fascinating in itself.

As we stood at one of the steep staircases down to the beach, Nikolaj pointed out that from where we were standing, at Tisvildeleje, you can see the round horizon between Kullen to the east and Sjællands Odde to the west. He stressed the word "round", and I saw how up here, from this height, the sea appeared to be curved, like the globe. The depth perspective made me feel a little dizzy. I couldn't quite grasp how I had never noticed this before. "In the middle – and *you* can see it because unlike me you have your glasses on," says Nikolaj, "is Hesselø. From here, you can watch the sun all summer and know exactly where it's going to set. At Hesselø at midsummer, and then further and further to the west."

He had been using the same stairs down to the beach for decades. This particular summer they had been fenced off, with two planks nailed across them blocking access. A sign warns: "Danger. Keep out. Tisvilde Coastal Protection." It's a good 20 metres down, with thickets of sea buckthorn and beach rose on either side. "Be careful!" says another sign. "Onshore winds can cause an outgoing current." Six or seven steps have been removed at the top and bottom. Nikolaj recounts the complicated dispute and subsequent deadlock that arose when the local council decided it would no longer maintain the stairs. Responsibility for them, and for the path to them from Holløselund Strandvej, reverted to the landowner – who refused to pay for maintenance or compensation for anyone injured on them. Subsequent negotiations between several landowners' associations to set up a "staircase guild" collapsed and led to lawsuits. Nikolaj likes to speak his mind. His thoughts are not new, nor is there any sign he'll run out of them any time soon. In recent years, a similar dispute has raged between groups that support the annual music festival *Musik i Lejet* and all of the activities associated with it, and those who feel the event places an unreasonable burden on the whole area, including its residents, the forest and town.

"These stairs lead down to the beach," says Nikolaj. "I know them. I've always used them. They're *my* stairs. When I was a boy, before the stairs, we'd lower ourselves down by rope. Of course, somebody else owns them, but they're mine, too. It's a disaster I can't use them anymore." I asked him how he gets down to the beach now. He told me he uses stairs further to the east, at a small public spot, "but it's a completely different beach; it's not like here". Not only are there more pebbles there, it is, I sense, a completely different world, one that pales in comparison, one devoid of history.

Beach person incarnate that he is, Nikolaj is also an expert in intense summer sunbathing, which he learned from his mother: First the back, then the front and then one side at a time. He soaks up the heat and slips into a state halfway between awake and asleep. Other beachgoers report similar semi-comatose states, while the winter bathers often focus more on how the shock of the cold is like a revelation, and that when they re-emerge the spreading warmth feels like getting their life back, feeling fresh – "almost like being born again".

## nature and romanticism

According to literary historian Jan Rosiek, writers discovered the place to which Peter's mother and Nikolaj keep returning, the wide-open expanses of empty beach, between 1750 and 1840. The French would call it *"rivage"*, the coastal area that includes the surf, shore and dunes. In most contexts, "beach" works well enough in English and everybody understands what it means. Having said that, just a few generations ago, the locals in Tisvildeleje used the Danish word usually translated as "beach" (*strand*) to refer to the stretch of water where fishermen worked in open, 18-foot boats. In the 16th century, the settlement on the site, which housed 12 fishermen, was called Saltebodsleje. In those days, it was their place, but 200 years later, drifting sands enveloped the area, and only two buildings survived.[2] It was also the sand's place. By the early 20th century, long after the sand had stopped drifting, Tisvilde Hegn was planted. The first summer guests holidayed in the fishermen's cottages, while the families slept in outbuildings. A big seaside hotel was built, the first plots for holiday homes were parcelled out, and campers pitched tents in the spot now occupied by the car park and the Nature Room. Beach huts sprang up – some stationary, others small tents on wheels that were pushed down to the water's edge. In other words, the "beach" was moving further inland.

In romantic literature and visual art, *rivage* is a territory that encapsulates the "confrontation"[3] with nature, as something unspoiled, in contrast to urban and industrial landscapes. In Denmark, this "territory" constitutes the most common form of relatively untouched nature. By the early 19th century, so many trees had been felled that forests accounted for only 2–3% of the Danish landmass.[4] The towns and cities, especially Copenhagen, were becoming densely populated. In the absence

41

of mountains, plains, big forests and marshes, the coasts and beaches were the most expansive landscape the country had to offer. Whereas European Romanticism had previously been fascinated by the remote harshness of the desert and the rugged brutality of the mountains, fascination with the beach better reflected the qualities of the Danish landscape. Painters, poets and authors sought out the windswept coast (and the few remaining forests) in pursuit of the epitome of "Danish nature", of landscapes imbued with historical, spiritual and national depth. Landscapes became places to which city-dwellers flocked in order to feel overwhelmed. In its earliest form, which emerged in the 18th century, tourism was the art of selecting, framing and representing scenic views. The mountains were considered forbidding, chaotic and sterile, until generations of nobles, priests and teachers had their eyes opened to the notion of picturesque scenery on their grand tours of classical Southern Europe. They started seeking out places in Denmark with aesthetic qualities capable of opening not only their eyes, but also the gate to their souls – and in doing so, set their minds free.[5]

For any indoor person seeking to understand where the ideas they have about nature come from, there is no avoiding Romantic literature. Without Romanticism, we wouldn't frequent beaches the way we do nowadays. We wouldn't think of meadows as glimpses of paradise. Danish museums are full of idyllic landscape paintings. In this excerpt from the short story "Eneboeren på Bolbjerg" (The Bolbjerg Hermit, 1834), Steen Steensen Blicher describes a scenic vista in Jutland:

> And should an artist ever manage to reproduce this beautiful, uniquely Danish scenery, he will find the large meadows enlivened by tame and wild animals and thus

be able to imbue his painting with a true appearance of heavenly peace and tranquillity.[6]

Johan Thomas Lundbye, who painted landscapes in West and North Zealand in the 1830s and 1840s, wrote in his diary about how, inspired by the German romantic giants Hegel and Goethe, he sought "Nature's yearning sigh for redemption", and asked himself what it meant:

> I do not understand it, but I long to understand this thought. I see the strange, the great, in the calm and seriousness of nature – like tones from a huge harp, which I do not understand. They resonate deep within me, and the same tones should also resonate in my images. I love them, yes, these notes are my dearest pleasure, and they evoke absence and longing, for what I do not know myself![7]

Lundbye then writes that even the wisest of people encounter barriers to understanding nature. It is the great riddle "to which the Lord has given no one the key". Instead, the senses can be nourished by the awe-inspiring, and through daydreaming we can lose ourselves in pleasurable visions.

In the Romantic 19th-century worldview, the beach embodied the idea of the sublime, an encounter with the wild and surprising. At least, that's how the Central and Southern European avant-garde saw it, and their ideas eventually made their way to Scandinavia and North Zealand. Tourist associations and local historians proudly recall the philosopher Søren Kierkegaard's trip to Gilleleje and the surrounding area in 1835 to view "the romantic *situations*". In his journals, Kierkegaard wrote about how he found places, especially at Gildbjerg near Gilleleje, where he could fall into a reverie and open his soul in a contemplative manner to everything he had seen so far, and all that hopefully lay ahead:

> In the heart of nature, where a person, free from life's often nauseating air, breathes more freely, here the soul opens willingly to every noble impression. Here one comes out nature's master, but he also feels that something higher is manifested in nature, something he must bow down before; he feels a need to surrender to this power that rules it all.[8]

The excerpt illustrates the epitome of the modern man, who has installed himself, under God, as lord of the other creatures, and yet also finds something higher in nature. Kierkegaard's silent longing is not quite as humble as that of Lundbye. As his journals clearly show, this feeling of greatness and necessity is fleeting. Kierkegaard soon abandons his hope of finding truth in nature. Searching for the sublime in North Zealand probably made him feel at once big and small. At the same time, he sneers at how these places are sentimentalised,[9] as noted by the theologian Joakim Garff in *Søren Kierkegaard: A Biography*. He finds himself running about looking for "romantic situations", before realising "that nature is nothing, that nature always refers the observer back to himself and to his cultural framework".[10] Hence the cultural expectation of finding greatness in North Zealand. It is not something tourist brochures bother to mention these days.

Pure Romanticism has always been the preserve of the privileged indoor person. The longing for nature as mental and physical recreation is strongest among city-dwellers, particularly the more affluent. For two centuries, horses, trains and cars have shuttled city-dwellers out to encounter nature. The stereotype of

Romanticism so strong that it quickly fragmented, and can never quite be put back together again. In Thorkild Bjørnvig's poem "På stranden" (On the Beach),[11] 150 years later, the observer returns to the sea and stands alone on the beach:

> A waft of dry seaweed hit me.
> The smallest pebble I gathered
> and gazed at, was the centre of space,
> its coloured rings ran through my fingers,
> through the air, away from the island, to the edge of vision
> and the outline of Jutland. And the beach I walked on
> in its remoteness became one with a line:
> The horizon itself – was now in me – for Jutlanders to see,
> and now, right now, for the low April sun.

The pebble, worn smooth by the millennia, creates a connection with the hand, and then with the expanse of the beach. The observer's gaze then lands on the remote coast of Jutland, meets the mirror of the sea and horizon and looks back at their *own* beach. The observer is then amused to see themselves, via the other people – the Jutlanders, gazing longingly towards their horizon – and via the Sun, on whose horizon lies the Earth.

These two brief glimpses of how Kierkegaard and Bjørnvig saw the beach represent narratives about the ebb and flow of Romanticism. Following the Romanticism of the Golden Age, God disappeared from the great outdoors, and people only saw themselves in the things that absorbed them and their cultural habits. Great religious sensitivities and trembling awe had fragmented.

In the 19th century, urban expansion in many areas north of Copenhagen was so dense and rapid that the Danish Society for Nature Conservation was formed in 1911, partly as an offshoot of a campaign to guarantee public access to the coast outside

Dyrehaven, a park at one of the royal hunting lodges. In the decades after the Second World War, whole swathes of Zealand's north coast were parcelled out for holiday homes. A mosaic of settlements sprang up, reflecting both the city dwellers' longing to get "out", and the local authorities and contractors' more or less successful attempts to navigate the labyrinth of regulations and exemptions from the various beach-protection laws and create a suitable infrastructure and attractive environment. Now, despite the monumental scale of all this construction work and the nose-to-tail traffic on Friday afternoons and at the start of every holiday as Copenhageners escape to their holiday homes – or "go to the country", as it used to be known – the beaches still seem to be more or less free of humans.

I met one beach person who recalled standing "stark naked on the beach on a quiet evening and feeling like a god", but that was an exception. Most of the narratives lacked this high Romantic tone. Not do they echo the sense of mastery of nature Kierkegaard expressed before the consensus became that global ecological crises demonstrate the opposite. Both the beach and the mind are strewn with countless broken shards, yet the grandeur of the beach has not vanished totally.[12] Romanticism has not been vanquished from advertising either. The indoor person still seeks good views, no less insatiably than Kierkegaard, but the tone has changed and is no longer the mellifluous sound of Lundbye's harp.

Whenever I asked someone what they thought was the best thing about the beach, they would mention the lack of people. The summer beach with rows of parked cars by the North Sea, sunbathing, picnics, parties in the dunes – even swimming for the winter types – all pale in comparison to a walk on the beach with nobody else around, or at worst just a few others doing the same, slipping past each other like shadows or with the curtest of greetings. There are striking similarities between the struggles to preserve empty coasts today and last century, and the joy of beaching still has much to offer the senses: wide-open spaces, wind, sea, sand, seaweed and ever-changing light. Standing up in the dunes, sliding down the sand, stumbling across pebbles, walking along the shore with the horizon in your eyes and seaweed up your nose, the wind swirling around your ears and pummelling your body – you can still stand here in the middle of space, sense the limit of your reach and abandon yourself to the power of the beach.

## the landscape and the amplitude of the empty

The modern concept of "landscape" emerged in the 15th century. At least that's when the word first appeared in the European languages. The idea of the panoramic view really came into its own in 17th-century painting, and it seems to be generally accepted that the artists' and bourgeoisie's search for the great outdoors, which would continue for centuries to come, represents an attempt to redress the alienation from nature that city life entails, by promoting the attraction of landscapes as a balm for the soul. In the 19th and 20th centuries, the emphasis was on the aesthetic qualities of the landscape and the freely enjoyable view, which presupposes that you are not working: "So the terrains of nature are not landscapes in themselves. They only become so when they are framed by the distinctive and panoramic optics that an idle person, typically a city dweller, brings along as part of his or her cultural baggage when venturing out for trips into the great wide open – what is appropriately called 'the free' in Germanic languages."[13] Today, researchers stress the special impact of walking on physical and mental health, albeit with greater or lesser enthusiasm and more or less of an evidence base.[14]

Views from cliffs, dunes, holiday homes and beaches, out over the sea and along the coast, towards the shimmering horizon, have served a symbolic function as a mirror for the soul in countless variations of architecture, poetry and painting. When we talk about the beach in romantic terms, we are talking as much about ourselves, our inner selves, as we are about seagulls, sand, sea rocket, wind, heavy legs and salt on the wind. As a manifestation of first nature, the very greatest outdoors the Danish landscape has to offer (albeit only half on land), the beach is a different space, far removed from average everyday life, with work, family and other obligations.[15] Rosiek, who wrote about the beach as *rivage*, looks into that aspect when he compares the beach to what the French philosopher Michel Foucault[16] calls *heterotopias*, or "other spaces", which have arisen in modernity. Gardens, museums and theatres are some of the classic "other places" that offer a chance to world through fiction and semi-utopias, rather than completely unattainable new worlds in temporary and semi-ideal places.

When the beach is that empty space, it means no other people are on it. Today, even the fishermen are all but gone. The beach has no houses, roads or masts, and (almost) none of the signs, hedges and tiles that usually plaster built-up areas. The beach is among the emptiest of landscapes, and offers something "completely different" – a free space. On the beach at Melby Overdrev, I met an older man who told me his wife had dementia, and that climbing the dune and walking along the beach for an hour or two was an absolutely essential daily break from the oppressive atmosphere at home. It was, he said, like "taking time off, a breather, spiritual solace". The wind, the sun, the swirling water and the dog impatiently circling us, I realised, gave him the energy, light and bandwidth he needed. He just knew it. It made him feel good every time. "Usually, our focus is narrow," he said.

"Out here, we have a wide-open perspective." I understood from the context that he didn't mean it in a purely topographical *or* spiritual sense, but both at once.

In the classical metaphysics, flowers, trees, birds, the sea, sun and stars all point to God as the creator, who stands outside Creation. In this theological tradition, God is not present in nature, at least not in such a way that by worshipping it you worship God. Or, as it is often formulated, God is no *more* present here than anywhere else. On the other hand, God's omnipresence doesn't mean some places don't channel our thoughts better than others.[17] The sea is one of the more hackneyed metaphors in psalms and hymns – how vast and deep it is, how awe-inspiring the thought that only God can part it. Of course, this is nothing compared to the role of Heaven in Christian poetry, as the home of angels, the afterlife and God the Father. The difference between humans and God is the same as between Earth and Heaven, or time and eternity.[18] On the beach, all of these aspects can merge momentarily. As Blicher wrote in "The Bolbjerg Hermit", "The sea, the wild, the boundless sea, everywhere, as far as the eye can see, without variation, without a resting point for your fitful gaze, until yonder in the distance, where it merges darkly with the sky, like time with eternity."[19]

Despite all the fine imagery in the hymn book, it is striking that none of the beach people I met used distinctly Christian or other kinds of manifestly religious language. At best, they have made use of quasi-religious allusions. For example, Nikolaj noted that the repetitive aspect of his walks constitutes a kind of religious ritual, while the winter and summer bathers compare a dip to a rebirth: "Float for two minutes and you start a new life, it's like an absolution." Some beach people also sum up their experience by describing it as "almost religious" or "almost holy". Similarly, the elderly gent with the impatient dog talks about the

beach – as I have heard people describe Sunday services countless times in previous fieldwork – as a place where life feels particularly full, a place to recharge batteries before returning to
everyday life with renewed hope.

In classical metaphysics, this hope is associated with an im-
material life "on the other side", quite different from the mortal,
finite one on Earth. On the beach, this metaphysical expectation
can be brought to life with the horizon indexing the infinite, the
possible, a form of freedom that will one day reveal itself fully
and completely. For those more attuned to semi-metaphysical
thinking, this other world may already be present in the earthly
one. It's not that it nurtures hope of special transcendental or
supernatural experiences or privileged insight into a world beyond. Nor does the beach offer a glimpse of an afterlife, a life
after death – at least not without also framing this precisely (and
perhaps decisively) as something *imagined*. For such people,
life is magical enough in itself. And the impression life makes
eternal enough.

## susanne's fascination

Susanne Borup was one of five photographers who caught my eye
one day as I made my way down to the beach at Melby Overdrev,
which has become my personal favourite outdoor place. It is a
former shooting range, where the vegetation was kept at bay for
more than a century, and it is now the biggest heathland in Zealand. The flat brown, green and purple heath vibrates with colour
and life, transitioning into more scattered flora as it climbs up
the high dunes, the tops of which offer views of an unspoilt beach
stretching in a six-kilometre arc from Liseleje to Tisvildeleje.

At the large car park in the middle of the heath, the five
photographers were standing in a semicircle, their 600mm

lenses pointing at a bushy tree. Every other Tuesday, Gribskov Photo and Video Club meets to look at each other's work. Every other Thursday, they go on a shoot together. They were looking at a yellowhammer when I interrupted. Earlier that day, they had taken pictures of mushrooms, sandwich terns, black-headed gulls, herring gulls, poppies, butterflies and larks. They explained that they had time to spend in nature now they were retired, but had always had an interest. Susanne said birdwatching makes her "happy – high". When I asked her to tell me more, she said, "at its deepest, it's endorphins – because you can nature yourself out of any problem. You get out into the light and all your problems disappear." She also said she had recently been to the Johannes Larsen Museum, devoted to a Danish painter known for his bird motifs. After seeing his pictures of light-filled landscapes, she "felt almost holy inside for days".

I didn't know what kind of bird a yellowhammer was, but Susanne showed me it on her camera display. That autumn, I joined them on shoots whenever I could make it up from Copenhagen. I wanted to learn to see and move like they did. I brought a camera and a pair of binoculars. It turned out that I wasn't capable of listening, watching, using a camera and taking notes all at the same time. The trips ended up being much more about photography and memorable walks than actually *watching* birds. On other walks with Susanne at the beach, especially at Holløse Bredning, I asked her about what seemed to me to be some highly unusual turns of phrase. What did she mean by "nature yourself out of any problem" and feeling "almost holy inside"?

Susanne is a retired headteacher who lives in Tisvildeleje. She first took an interest in photography at 19, but put it on the back burner for decades while she focused on her education, work and family. These days, she likes to get out with her camera several times a week. Her Facebook page presents a constant stream of images, especially birds, and her external hard drives are home to around 20,000 carefully sorted image files. She also invested in a good colour printer and sometimes exhibits her work. Whenever I've met Susanne, she has been in a good mood, her eyes sparkling and her complexion warmer than the average indoor person for the time of year. But sometimes, when she talked about the great sorrows in her life, including illness and the sudden death of family members, I could sense how that amber tone can be shattered.

Her cat had greeted me. We were looking out the conservatory window at a bird-feeding buffet with a Japanese-inspired house especially for titmice, with fat balls and other contraptions containing peanuts and sunflower seeds, to keep some of the garden's birds in and others out. As we were talking, Susanne spotted titmice, hooded crows, magpies, nuthatches, tree sparrows, robins and many more that she mentioned and I didn't recognise.

In response to my opening question about her fascination with nature, she said, "I think it has to do with nature being bigger than us, so it really is a religious experience. There are many ways of being religious, but something happens to you inside when you worship in whatever way it is you go in for. Nature itself can be the great altar. Religion is a set of teachings about how to be a good person, which must be the purpose of life. Nature teaches you this. Nature is great. So for me, there isn't much of a difference. I don't go to a church regularly, only for the big occasions – baptism, confirmation, weddings and funerals. If people derive pleasure from it at other times, that's great. But in my experience, greed and selfishness flourish as much in the church as anywhere else. But nature never lets you down. It's always there. It always has something to offer. Some people like to walk in the forest, and the trees have a calming effect on them. For me, it's the opposite. I need openness, to see as far as possible. The seashore is great for that. It makes something happen in my body that I can't explain. It's really holy. You can walk and walk, and time and place disappear. I've often found myself sitting somewhere, completely engrossed in whether I'll see a particular bird, thinking 'it usually comes here'. In my excitement, I'll think that half an hour has passed, but it turns out to be 90 minutes. It's a bit Zen. It calms down all the thoughts whirling about in my head, which isn't easy to do. In there, everything is buzzing about. Out there, you find peace. Peace of mind."

She continued, "Club outings are more about community. I don't think any of us expect to take a particularly great photo. Often, the light isn't ideal, and the birds take a dinner break in the middle of the day, so you don't see that many between 10 and 12. And anyway, the ones we want to see usually skedaddle when they hear six cackling humans stomping about. They spot us long before we get a sniff of them. It's really best to do it on your own. You have to be quiet. The other day, it snowed. It was Friday, and I thought, 'I'm going to Ramløse River because there's a kingfisher there.' I saw it from behind, flying over the river, as I approached with my little three-legged chair and camera. I walk a little further, thinking, 'This must be where it lives.' But you never know. I didn't see it again that day. But I sat there and looked for about an hour and a half. I heard a woodpecker above me. I saw a tree creeper – and took a nice picture of it – and a little mouse at the foot of a young tree. I watched and listened. It was starting to thaw, with fluffy snow still lying on the branches. I sat there thinking, 'It doesn't really matter that the kingfisher didn't show up. This is precious.' I think everyone has experienced that, to some extent. Hunters do, and people just walking in the woods. I think the mountain bikers do, too, even if they're moving a bit faster."

# the big nature

Again and again, with the focus on different aspects, I keep being told that on the beach, in nature, even when watching a small bird, you come face to face with "the big", which makes you "small" – and it's a great feeling. I have often asked whether it feels like being recalibrated. Interviewees said it does, in the sense that in everyday life or in society more broadly, we are expected to live up to endless demands and obligations. When that happens, we try to be big – bigger than we are capable of remaining in the long run. We are compelled to perform, succeed, do even better, go the extra mile, and reach out even more to our children, colleagues, the people we care about and those to whom we have obligations. Be a good citizen, take responsibility. Live with your pain because you used your body incorrectly. Overcome your anxiety and discomfort. That's what's so great about being on the beach and other outdoor places. These are places where we can "lose ourselves", forget our troubles and be our true size – absolutely tiny in a vast universe. Some associate this recalibration with calm, meaningfulness, happiness, energy, inspiration and hope; others with a rediscovered wonder and gratitude that the world exists –and that we do, too. "When you're struggling with a problem and go for a walk, you find out it didn't really amount to a hill of beans." I've heard that kind of thing hundreds of times. On the beach, you start to trust that things will be fine. You soak up as much light as you can and fill your lungs with as much fresh air as possible. Some might interpret this positive feeling as merely a release of endorphins. But, as Susanne said, it's more than that. For her, it's a form of eschatology because, as she puts it, "nature will cope". Nature is the first and the last. In that sense, humanity is a small part of a bigger story.

For a long time, during walks on the beach and trips back and forth to my desk, I tried to understand the beach people's experiences as a form of sanctification. It seemed likely to me that even people who are not particularly into religion might still be said to have transcendent experiences.[20] Transcendence is, of course, a notoriously difficult concept. Many of those I have met along the way, in academia and beyond, have advised avoiding it,[21] but I haven't. It provides a practical framework for everything relating to the spiritual, magical and religious. But I have tried to stick to the key questions – *what* is transcended, *when* does transcendence happen, and *how* does it happen?

Even the national church in Denmark, which is Lutheran, pays little heed to classical transcendence, with God as a supernatural force, miracles and an afterlife. On the contrary, the emphasis is on us not elevating ourselves to the same status as God and the belief that love conquers all.[22] The dominant strain in academic theology has no time for either classical metaphysics or transcendence. You will not hear about God as "an otherworldly divine being", the "immovable foundation of everything" or an "immutable source".[23] As one theologian put it, "humankind's emotional life has been looked down upon".[24] Christianity has become secularised,[25] and both emotions and nature has been taken out of religion.[26]

If God, as a different reality *behind* everything, can no longer keep traditional metaphysics going, can nature step in and accommodate new forms of transcendence? Wouldn't that be the perfect horizon for the indoor person? I began to pay attention to how magical moments involved freedom, gratitude and other powerful experiences that go beyond everyday life. The beach has the potential to provide such experiences. They might not be guaranteed but, as Nikolaj put it, you can still seek them out by using specific practices and techniques, such as focusing all your attention on the sun – or, as another Tisvildeleje resident told me, standing naked on a hot summer evening, like a great hunter-gatherer in a world aglow with life. Such practices might also include the more improvised actions of other beach people – standing atop a dune and taking in the whole landscape through the breath, through the skin, or confronting a storm and struggling to remain upright, howling and screaming as big waves crash, and absorbing their power. With the wind on your body, the sun in your eyes, the sand under your feet, beachgoers say you become a more real version of yourself. Your physicality comes alive in interaction with the beach. You are truly present, right here and now. This "here and now", which brings us very close to (and even inside) the body, is far removed from indoor life. Office chairs and sofas are designed to make you feel your body as little as possible, leaving only your head and hands free to work, talk, read or watch endless content. Instead, the beach offers an unequivocal "here and now" that facilitates transcendence via a completely open space, where the line of the horizon plays a dual role as both the border *and* the point of transcendence. Out there is where the mysterious expanse of infinity begins. On the beach are pebbles that rolled here millions of years ago after volcanic eruptions in the mountains to the north, reminders of a primeval time before Denmark was a thing. The wind carries grains of sand that have been ground by the enormous, rolling mill of the sea.

## the forgotten connections

Only later, while reading my notes and transcripts, did it dawn on me that Nikolaj, the older gent with the dog, the winter bathers, Liv and Susanne don't just talk about the beach as some big, other place – in other words, all of the attributes I have previously associated with the first nature. They also talk about the beach as a place with which they feel *connected* and at home. I had come to associate how people experienced beaches *exclusively* with the concept of first nature. My new theory was that I had arrived at that interpretation as a robust indoor person. I hadn't practised enough. Nor had I listened properly. In fact, I was *unable* to listen closely enough. Little by little, I realised that if I let go of the first concept of nature, with its emphasis on *separateness,* as the only framework for my interpretation and instead listened out for the quasi-religious *connections* between people and their environments, then I might coax a different story out of them.[27]

Right from the outset, the interviews had been pointing towards this, towards connections. But I kept overlooking the clues – in the joy Peter's mum felt on the North Sea beach, in the way Nikolaj basked in the light and the way he merged with the stairs and the black rocks in the groynes. Reading my notebooks and transcripts with connections in mind revealed characteristics I associate with the second nature. Admittedly, standing on the beach and looking at the open landscape can be like looking at a picture in a frame – just like looking out of a car window or in its mirrors. High-rise buildings, too, present panoramic expanses. But on the beach, we can also walk into the frame.

## the felt body

The German philosopher Hermann Schmitz contends that it is a simplification to say people have a physical exterior and a spiritual interior. He adds a third "felt"[28] body, which messes with the distinction between body and soul (a binary that might be said to belong to the anthropology of the first nature). In the second nature, humankind is in the middle of the world, never separate from it, the central figure, who inhabits, changes and adapts to the world, makes it their home by emphasising connections with their surroundings. Schmitz's felt body offers an alternative, non-dualistic analysis, which harmonises with the second nature. Similarly, as I will show, his theory of sensing encroaches into the territory of the third nature's entanglements with the world.

As mentioned in the first chapter, cultural analysis needs multiple concepts of nature if it is to understand the different ways in which we world. On a single walk, we can be in many places and times at once, and be influenced by the special qualities of the place, as well as our personal and collective expectations.[29] Visiting the beach on the north coast of Zealand – or any other landscape, for that matter – loving it and knowing how to behave and take it all in requires building up (*worlding*) certain sensitivities over a prolonged period. There is no such thing as a neutral encounter with the world. Begin – again – to be struck by the view from the top of the slope, go down the stairs and meet the landscape in the blackness of the rocks and the strength of the light. Soon afterwards, thoughts of the most recent irritating or fantastic meeting at work or an argument with a neighbour drain away through the feet and the skin, as the sand and wind insist on making their presence felt. As Peter's mum said, it isn't easy to explain what happens on a beach. On the one hand, lots of different things happen; on the other, some of the things we experience are just beyond the reach of words – in the felt body. They become a routine action, as we learn new ways of walking and relating to the landscape.

Schmitz characterises the felt body as "surfaceless" in the way it follows the senses into open spaces. Take, for example, a situation where you enter a room and immediately sense the atmosphere, or step outside and feel, deep inside your body, piercing shafts of reflected light from the sea. Such atmospheres and feelings are the best habitat for the felt body. It is as if the landscape passes through unimpeded, and the sensations are unmediated. According to Schmitz, even if such experiences appear fleeting, even unremarkable, they still imbue our lives with content and direction – both indoors and outdoors. He sees his thinking as a means of identifying and describing spontaneous sensations as valuable per se, not just as a biochemical response to endorphins or a product of the imagination.[30]

Specifically, Schmitz describes the wind, one of the beach's finest qualities, as one of the "half-things" that the felt body detects. In his conceptual universe, half-things are those not best understood as complete, individual objects. The soul, for example, isn't a thing in itself, in the felt body, precisely because it can't have life or dimensions without a relationship to a body. I think the horizon is also a half-thing. It's a relationship between the sky and sea, rather than a "full thing" (as Schmitz terms such individual objects).[31] Many phenomena can be described as both full and half-things, depending on our perspective. For the felt body, the wind on the beach, for example, isn't best described as molecules moving at high speed, or as a whole, discrete thing separate from other things. The feeling of the "wind blowing through you" only happens when somebody feels the wind whistling across their face, fluttering through their hair, pressing against their clothes, whipping up the sand and making ripples on the water. In that sense, the wind is difficult to explain, even as we stand in it. Being "pummelled by the wind" is a moving quality for the felt body, as if body and mind are freed from the skin and allowed to flutter in the wind, hover in it, fight against it, even as the air fills the lungs, oxygenates the blood and it feels as if our vision is becoming clearer. In a situation like that, we can't identify precisely where the wind is. But if we look at a weather app on our phone, we may well be told that it is coming from the north-east and that the strongest gusts are likely to be 18 metres per second, a description closer to a full thing, a component of North Atlantic weather systems.

In this way, the beach and moving around on it unite multiple opposing ways of worlding, which together produce the special sense of presence so valued by beach people. They feel their body is at the centre of the forces that constitute the walk, as if this place were a full thing, a completely different place with clear boundaries and plenty of substance (that is, the first nature). At the same time, there is also an opposite, expanding effect, of being a half-thing, at the centre of the Universe, a body that has learned ways of navigating landscapes (as a surrounding environment, that is, the second nature). Moreover, that body is at once big and small, and is entangled in the light, the wind, the sand (as third nature). So, even when we venture into the great outdoors, which is usually associated with the first nature, we may also encounter the other two.

## the beach's cascade of full things and half-things

"It's a dream. It encompasses what you are. It's here and not," a young guy on the beach at Melby Overdrev told me. As usual, I had asked what he was doing on the beach and what he experienced there. He replied, "Being connected to something bigger than myself. Like meeting something that belongs to itself. The beach is just doing something on its own, and you feel like coming back." He didn't say much more. He seemed a bit shy and kicked the sand awkwardly. But it was enough, even if it wasn't always clear to me what all of his "its" referred. Perhaps it's easy to overthink remarks like these. Maybe a long interview, multiple walks and random tangents would have brought me closer. But now, for me, his ambiguous words serve as a frame for all of the beach people's stories. In one way, the beach is itself, a full thing, something entirely separate; but also a half-thing to which you can connect via practices such as dressing for the elements, protecting the face from the swirling sand, keeping the body warm, and letting your attention dwell on every movement. In this way, the beach is an event[32] in which body and landscape are interwoven.

Schmitz has a special term for this blurred entanglement. He calls it *excorporation*, which he describes as the felt body flowing outwards on the wind, or how it feels "lazing in the sun", or in meditation or mystical experiences of unity with God. Here, writes Schmitz, the self is dissolved into a "transcending into the objectless".[33] The self, which feels uptight in everyday life, can be loosened up, set free to run with the felt body, and end up "beaching" in the literal meaning of the word. It beaches like the cascades of *shwooshing* pebbles. You live in the wholeness of the beach more than in your person *vis-à-vis* the landscape. When you excorporate, you are washed up on the beach like the water.

On the one hand, I would now say that the beach functions as something "other", something in itself. All of the beach people say that the sense of detachment and distance embodied by the beach is like what I call first nature. The beach, in its windy, dry, salty form, with its infinite blend of the hues of the sea, sky and sand, is a distinctive landscape that stands out clearly from the forests, arable land and cities. The few figures walking the shore on the many less warm days of the year slip into the rhythm of the beach, seek out this almost deserted space precisely for a prolonged daily or weekly – or even just holiday – shock of *otherness*, both physical and psychological. In this way, the walk on the beach can, in some interpretations, and at least momentarily, world "the other" – all the light on which your life depends, the nature that never lets you down, that over which you have no dominion because it is so vast, because it is itself. It is a form of transcendence in which, despite the vastness, you forge a connection. Between the living body and the cold sea. Between the soul in the eye and the wet sand.

*On the other hand*, it is as if there is *no* separation – and perhaps there never really was – between the self and world around us; as if the everyday indoor logic diminishes us to primarily being a presence within our clothes. The beach is a manifestation of the dream expressed by Liv and the young man on the beach, as are the forest, the meadow, the heath or the nearest chestnut tree. Here, the differences between people, waves, drifting sands and trees become less stark, and the connections' undulation in the water, the clarity of the light and the veil of the sea mist cohere into something vastly greater. This greatness is not *outside* the world or the present, and can't separate itself into its own distinct form of being (as something purely spiritual or non-material). The primacy of the connection emphasises that there is no *difference* to transcend. Rather, a sense of belonging with the felt half-thing emerges. In this form of metaphysics, you don't have to look far for the connections because they are entangled in the same being – or, as some might say, in the same becoming.

The beach abounds with full things and half-things, which remind us that we, too, are both. We are human beings in the world, faced with the otherness of the beach we are a full thing that can be defined and, in the blurred universe of the beach, we are not defined, not a thing, not a spirit, but a connection – a half-thing. In this way, the beach is a vibrant, semi-magical world, ideal for the indoor person seeking the untouched, which in the beach people's ecology is also often the empty space – by implication, devoid of other people, indeed other *creatures* – and, as such, offers a connection to a huge, sensually fluid universe that vanishes in urban, human, spaces. Well, at least until a bird shows up.

jizz

Stig and Michael raised their heads from the telescope.

"Black kite."

They looked at Steen for the direction.

"At the end of the vapour trail."

Steen pointed north. Stig Toft Madsen, anthropologist and birder, introduced me to bird migration at Hellebæk in April. Birds of prey circled on rising air currents. Some continued towards Sweden.

"Red kite over the V."

I asked Stig where the V was. He pointed at a row of trees by the marsh to the west and adjusted the telescope for me. The bird hovered briefly into view. I concentrated on the forked tail and rust-red plumage.

"Osprey," said Michael. To the north was a small black dot.

"The white breast," he replied, when I asked how he could tell it was an osprey. He was in no doubt. It was the jizz (explanation to follow!). He spent a couple of hours birdwatching that day after work. He made notes on a small pad. If he remembered, he'd enter his observations into the Danish Ornithological Society's database when he got home. After a day at the computer and in meetings, being out here was, he said, "like meditation". He added that there is a "special serenity to birdwatching". He and Stig have met like this many times. Now retired, Stig has lots of birdwatching plans.

About 20 pairs of binoculars are pointing north. Stig tells me that Steen, who is farthest up the hill, has been keeping detailed notes on migrations in April for 40 years. He asks whether I can work out a birder hierarchy. I look at Steen, who undoubtedly seems to be top dog, but then I nod in the direction of "the Monk", who is sitting back in his chair, kitted out with binoculars, telescope and hat, casually oozing authority. I had seen a short TV documentary on the Monk's competition with Rolf

Christensen to spot the most species in Denmark. At the moment, the difference between them is only seven. Jørgen Munck (aka the Monk) writes on Netfugl.dk: "As every ornithologist and reader of the *Guinness Book of Records* knows, I have (probably) been number 1 on the Danish list since at least 1985, and I intend to stay there for many years to come." He further demonstrates his credentials by precisely describing the characteristics of a particularly rare species, and points out that he was the first person to spot 400 recognised species in Denmark when he saw "the Eastern Calandra Lark on Jersig beach in January 2006".[1] Prior to this, I had also read about the Monk in the anthropologist John Liep's article about the legendary competition between the ornithological roughnecks, which described their skill in spotting rare birds, their formidable ability to concentrate and their insistence on remaining undisturbed.[2]

I didn't tell Stig that I had been practising my birdwatcher skills. We didn't really talk much, so he seemed more impressed by my appraisal of the social hierarchy than it deserved. I spent a few hours with Stig and Michael. I've never watched so much before. By the end, I felt as if my whole head was just one big eye.

\* \* \*

Working with the camera on the east beach at Gilleleje, Susanne saw an eider out on the water.

"It's a brown female. Where's *he* then?"

She spotted him further out.

"He's lying down, calling out 'awoo, awoo' and pulling his head back."

Closer to us, there are "herring gulls in their first coat of feathers". There are "black-headed gulls without a chocolate-coloured hood, with a black dot at the ear, red legs, red beak – the legs will turn more and more aubergine in colour […]

"The sun under their wings makes them look pink. It's mesmerising!"

I followed Susanne's movements. Memorised her descriptions. Watched Susanne, watched birds, took notes.

"Look at the craw on that cormorant, look how thick it is, it's digesting something, look at the colour of those feathers, isn't it great?!"

The seagulls were Susanne's first motif when she began to combine her interests in photography and birds – they're easy to snap, after all. She wasn't best pleased when people started calling her the seagull lady. The nickname distorted what she was doing, made her sound like some kind of weirdo, a hermit cut off from the world in pursuit of a passion, rather than someone opening up to a world she'd known as a child, but had lacked the time to think about ever since. Once, while watching a Balanchine ballet performed by androgynous dancers with white sashes and chewing-gum-coloured legs, she was surprised to find herself thinking: "My seagulls!" Of course, the largely unheeded species could be the inspiration for an exquisite ballet.

Her favourite seagull picture is of a herring gull, head under wing, eye razor-sharp in the camera's focus. It takes effort, timing, technique, patience and a good camera to take a great bird photo. You need sharpness, light and movement to make the bird come *alive*. It might be sitting still on a branch, but it's even better if it's in motion. A great photo is one in which the bird, its plumage and colours are just as wonderfully captivating as they were in real life. Susanne told me that when she looks at one of her photos she can remember the precise moment it was taken: "I know exactly how I felt at the time. The light was amazingly beautiful when I took the one with the two butterflies. Up on the heath. Every time I look at the picture, I'm transported back there."

House sparrows, tree sparrows with their pretty cheek patches, blackbirds with their fluffy plumage, lapwings, wagtails, great black-backed gulls, terns, yellowhammers, coots or the penduline tit she managed to snap after several days spent tracking it down. Susanne finds them all "wonderful", "adorable", "exciting" or "beautiful". The cormorant has "delicious liquorice feet", the swallows collecting mud are "irresistible". The insects, too, such as blue broad-bodied darters and other dragonflies, even those with frayed wings, are "marvellously beautiful".

She stores the photographs on external hard drives in a highly organised manner. Her archive of birds (and occasional insects and plants) grows year by year, but Susanne doesn't keep lists or count the species. They are just images of beautiful life forms studied through binoculars and lenses and researched online and on her shelves crammed with ornithology books. Migration routes, changes of plumage, mating times, nest-building techniques, movements – and especially the colours – are all permanently imprinted on Susanne, regardless of species. It's as if she tastes the details, as if the archive were a form of synaesthetic factory in which the pathways of the senses constantly criss-cross, bringing new life, adding richness all the time – rarities and the absolute commonplace side by side. I don't quite understand why the black-throated loon is Susanne's favourite bird, and I sense finding out would mean taking a trip to the lake in Sweden where she observes it every year – the lake that holds on to "a piece of her soul", as she puts it. Perhaps she might whisper the tale of her pent-up grief there in the silence of twilight.

* * *

Bo Johansen indicated a tree in Tisvilde Hegn that he had been observing for a few days, along with his photographer friend Jacob Michelsen. Jacob was already there, in a camouflage tent. Bo told me that two black woodpeckers were getting their chicks ready to fly. The two experienced birdwatchers had been exchanging notes for some time. For the past few days, I had been part of an SMS chat with Jacob. On 30 May, he wrote:

"Arrived 05.45, set up and concealed 05.50, he feeds 05.58 three chicks, 2 x male and 1 x female, chicks hanging out/ screaming 06.20, he feeds 06.55, he feeds again 07.35, she feeds 07.40, she pecks excitedly in dry pine 07.44, photographer arrives from NW and walks under the nesting tree 07.46, commotion afterwards from the adults, male woodpecker moves around and pecks while the photographer quietly walks around 07.53, he feeds again 08.55, she feeds 09.00, male + female close to the nest without feeding 09.35, chicks very quiet 09.45, rain starts 09.50, Bo arrives 10.30, unrest and adult woodpeckers hesitate, he feeds 10.55, a little break in the rain and more light 11.05, he feeds + cleans the nest 11.17, he feeds 12.17, he feeds 13.00, she feeds 13.38 (slow-motion landing), he feeds 15.20, I leave the area 16.00, all 3 chicks still in the nest hole."[3]

A few days later, the parents were flying to the nest every 10–20 minutes. We stood half under a pine tree and chatted while we waited for them to come back. At one point, Bo suddenly and dramatically turned his upper body, his eyes and ears following the bird's approach from behind, above us and slightly to the right. He had heard its wings flapping before it came into view and followed it with his eyes long before I noticed anything.

Earlier that spring, one early April day, Bo and I went to Melby Overdrev to look for the European stonechat, another of his long-standing interests. I had studied it on the Danish ornithologists' database (DOFbasen) and memorised the rusty red underside and the male's black head and throat, but wasn't sure I would be able to tell it apart from a bullfinch or chaffinch without help. I *wanted* to, but kept finding the language of plumage and behaviour didn't really gel with my fleeting glimpses.

When I arrived, Bo was already immersed in his "obs". His way of using binoculars – always at hand, frequently at his eye, allowing him to rapidly shift focus from near to far – together with his vast inner catalogue of images of shapes, movements and sounds, meant that he was constantly spotting species: shrike, nightjar, woodlark, chaffinch, redpoll. Even when Bo pointed out the birds, my senses seemed to be in slow motion. About four out of every five times he identifies a bird in the forest, it's by sound.

On this particular trip, Bo told me about the dingy skipper butterfly and other rare insects, such as the blood droplet burnet; about the wrynecks and the bird box project he was working on to encourage them to breed in this precise spot. He talked about the various difficulties involved: the wryneck feeds on certain ants, great spotted woodpeckers and great tits sometimes squat in the boxes, and humans – interested or indifferent – don't always allow wrynecks the peace and quiet they need. So Bo and a photographer keep some nests secret.

Bo's specialism is the black woodpecker. About 30–40 years ago, when he was a student, he spent his free time ringing black woodpecker chicks and observing their behaviour, calls and songs: beak thrusts, wing shakes, the flight call *tick-tick-tick-tick-tick-tick*, the perching call *kyik-kyik*, their drumming and much more. Later, for a while, he was a full-blooded twitcher, known as Kilometer-Bo because he would jump into his car as soon as he got wind of a new species on Birdalarm. On one occasion, he and a friend drove 18 hours to see a trumpeter bullfinch. He

71

has spotted 280 bird species in Denmark in a single year, 230 in North Zealand alone and has logged over 55,000 sightings (an extremely high number) in the DOF archive.

Bo describes himself as an avid collector, not only of birds but also of butterflies, orchids, binoculars, stamps, antiques, amber and certain types of paintings. He can't resist a "camouflaged hunt", and likens it to a kind of "primal instinct". He just has to get out, get going, keep going, immerse himself, meet other people with similar interests, others who might be interested in joining him on a trip, help journalists and filmmakers, get some fresh air, keep moving – all on top of meetings with the Danish Nature Agency and working with DOF on bird counts, etc.

We walked for almost five hours. It was 4°C, and we were still no more than 300 metres away from the cars. Bo spotted three or four stonechats in the distance. Back at the cars, still cold, I saw a small bird fly out of a bush. I pointed at it, unsure of what I had seen. It was gone. Then it popped up again, and I saw something whitish and reddish on its chest. Could it be the European stonechat – and much closer than any of the others had been? It *was*. Bo picked up the telescope, adjusted it. The bird was foraging, and I saw it for up to about ten seconds. Did the reddish colour tend towards orange? We talked about that. It sat down and wagged its black tail. Gone. Then the female emerged, lighter in colour. Gone again.

\* \* \*

Birte Andersen took me out to see waders, her speciality. On the way to the dunes at Ølsemagle, she asked a birdwatcher sitting on a small wooden bridge over a stream whether there was anything to see. He wasn't forthcoming. Soon after, our chat petered out, too. Birte scanned the sky, lake, reeds. She walked briskly towards the northern tip of the isthmus, expecting to find a big flock off to the west. We slowed down. Birte explained we should tread softly, get as close as possible without spooking them. We left the path, no longer "going for a walk". We were half-creeping, with a gait perhaps best associated with hunting, playing hide and seek, or unwanted guests trying to make themselves invisible. We tried to approach the multi-coloured flock of birds on their terms. The change was more dramatic than I had dreamt. I usually walk briskly and combine the time I spend outdoors with my need for exercise. Now, the centre had shifted, and a current passed through my body, reminiscent of an unforeseen and vulnerable infatuation, a suddenly heightened awareness that made my eyes sharper and filled my world with the sound of hundreds of birds. A soup of half-recognised sounds, which I would never be able to translate, became the centre of the world. Flocks took off in synchronised choreographies, long-legged waders skittered, ducks dived.

Birte found a good vantage point and decided this far and no further. She set up her telescope and began scanning the shimmering, flapping group of birds in the shallow water and on the cackling sandbanks. She looked up and to the north, which was now behind us. A woman and a man were approaching. They turned their heads, chatting to each other. The birds darting around the water's edge in front of them took flight as they came closer. "Pretty annoying that they don't look where they're going," Birte snarled. Soon after, the couple turned around. A Caspian tern took to the air. Birte had it in her sights. She showed me. Its distinctive red beak was pointing downwards, which she said meant it was hunting. "Shiny black hood," she said. White feathers gradually darkening to black at the tip of its distinctly rounded wings. Birte swapped the telescope for her camera and started taking pictures. I focused on seeing as much as possible.

Birte started birdwatching years ago following a stressful period in her work as a church minister. She needed to get away from the books she had to read, the meetings, the conversations, the seemingly endless chores. They were meaningful tasks (mostly), but there were simply too many of them. Her husband Jon – a college lecturer – and their two children began making trips to Sweden to look for birds of prey. Later, they expanded the repertoire to other locations and birds. Jon and one of the sons liked to draw, Birte and the other son took photos. Many years into their shared interest, Jon suffered a brain haemorrhage, which affected his language and mobility. But the birds are still in him.

## ways to bird, forest, beach, cycle

Studying birdwatchers was not part of my original project design, but seizing the opportunity to follow unforeseen leads and happenstance is an inherent part of the anthropological fieldwork tradition. This particular detour helped me understand how the Norwegian anthropologist Michael Hundeide became so engrossed in his work with birdwatchers, and how his nearly 500-page PhD thesis turns on its head the "nature experiences, knowledge acquisition and natural history enthusiasm" of ornithology as a hobby.[4] In the past, I might have ignored birders and twitchers – tacitly accepting that they need to tread carefully when pursuing their passion, and even have to put up with condescension, because outsiders often find it hard to see what's so fascinating about watching birds. I take it all back now. Even though I certainly don't have the perceptual abilities, patience or propensity for the type of absorption demonstrated by the ones I've met, their enthusiasm was contagious. I'm still hoping to see the kingfisher down by the river, to recognise the song of the robin before sunrise, and to identify birds of prey by their wings – it turns out that not all of them are buzzards after all.

Hundeide divides the modern quest for closeness to nature into three categories. The first is thrill-seeking, which he defines as the pursuit of transcendent, ecstatic experiences characterised by adrenaline rushes and mastering extreme forms of nature. The second is curiosity and the urge to do research; while the third consists of a search for surroundings characterised by harmony, silence and a sense of connection and belonging. As my fieldwork shows, there are an astonishing number of ways to birdwatch. Susanne preferred slow, patient, daily observation in familiar surroundings, supplemented by opportunities to take photos of local birds in other places while on holiday. Bo was at times intensely competitive in his hunger for sightings of rare species, but it didn't mean he took no joy in long, quiet and repeated sightings. In other words, the individual can accommodate multiple combinations of Hundeide's three categories.

From the first trip, and before I knew about the different approaches they use, I looked out for unspoken aspects of how birdwatchers moved and the details they emphasised. I observed different ways of walking, in terms of pace and rhythm, how they used their eyes and the other senses, as well as their moods and all sorts of more diffuse ways of sensing landscapes in more silent registers. I presumed it would be difficult to register such movements and sensations. Before I started, I went on trips with people I already knew to practise my observation skills. One morning, for example, I went hunting with my uncle Henrik. We looked at maps, wrapped up warm, found hiding places and crept from one of them to the other. We waited and waited, but no animals showed up. Great, I thought, quietly pleased there would be no shooting. The only animal I've ever hunted was a medium-sized cod off the coast of Bornholm. Henrik, who trained as a teacher before starting his own business, was also notorious for hesitating to shoot. He often found himself stunned to be face-to-face with precisely the animal he had been looking for. On the way back, we talked at length about how hunting is a special language – one that, to Henrik, seemed untranslatable and irreplaceable. When we got back, he told me he was exhausted by my non-stop stream of questions.

The notes from this trip and the following ones comprised a somewhat chaotic assemblage of ideas, quotes, half-analyses and vague hints. But I allowed myself not to be too self-critical and followed up on all sorts of different things. The diversity of the forest offers so many registers of movement, sensing and moods that they collide with each other, and in doing so become apparent over time – resulting in what Henrik calls "big nature experiences".

For example, one day, while cycling with a small group of women, who called themselves "the Snails", I was surprised to find myself thinking that mountain biking is more like skiing than anything else. At first, it was just a quirky, random observation that arose partly from my many skiing trips. Mountain biking turned out to be quite the balancing act. We rode along narrow forest paths, slowed down on the straights, slogged up hills, and – as instructed – kept our "arse well back" on the way down, which produced almost the same gliding sensation and shifting sense of inertia that is so mesmerising when skiing. Along any given 100-metre section of track, the landscape around you constantly changes, offering new angles and perspectives as you glide along. When it's time to work hard, you adapt your breathing. On the steep sections you feel the concentration more deeply in your legs with every metre that passes. Body and hill merge in an interaction felt long afterwards.

Even though I had my cyclocross bike with me, which has impractical handlebars and the wrong suspension for the single track in Tisvilde Hegn, the Snails coaxed me into their rhythm – albeit somewhat slower than their usual one, I sensed. We stopped for a breather at a viewpoint overlooking the sea. We talked about cycling, the times they'd flown over their handlebars, and about forest etiquette. We enjoyed hot drinks, talked about punctures and kit and kept coming back to why they feel the need to don chequered socks and helmets and get out there to work their bikes, bodies and the hills. I learned to alternate between concentrating on a point three metres ahead (to anticipate your next movements) and on my surroundings – the trees, the deer (standing frozen and looking at you), the owl (crossing your path), the smell of wild garlic, the cold, the wind, the light. Like skiing, mountain biking offers a cascade of delights: landscapes, exercise, breaks, silence, appetite, dramatic crashes, technique, fluid smells, abrupt encounters with other creatures, endurance and friendly competition. At its best, just like on the beach, you "excorporate" and merge with the landscape.

That particular day, I had come straight from gruelling talks about the working environment at the University and attempts by external consultants to untangle some tense social threads. The process wasn't going well, to put it mildly, and I mulled over these "co-operation difficulties" as I drove up to the forest, even though I was trying to think about the sea, about Hegnet. It would be trite to say my mood had changed completely afterwards, but it had. It's not easy to pinpoint exactly why. After I made the comparison to skiing, I started to see mountain bikers completely differently than I had as a walker. As they hurry past with varying degrees of good grace, they almost inevitably startle pedestrians, especially mushroom and moss enthusiasts, for whom slowness is the best way to calibrate themselves to the qualities of the landscape. But the mountain bikers also talked about how the forest gave them peace, the space to be and to breathe – to be absorbed by the trees. They, too, felt at one with nature.

There are so many reasons to love the forest, the beach, the heath. So many reasons, qualities and interests that people often discuss whether they are all reconcilable. Every square metre in Denmark seems to be measured, marked, ringfenced and managed with multiple layers of rules and regulations. Even deep in the forest, you can be sure the surroundings are micro-managed and highly regulated. The competition for space is fierce. As my colleague Stine Krøijer puts it: "Trees, too, are political." In fact, the whole forest is political. In collaboration with the Danish Nature Agency in North Zealand, Stine and I conducted a series of interviews with forest users, and found that horse riders, walkers, birdwatchers, the agency's staff and many others all told very different stories about the same place. Some talked about landscapes and how new plans for "rewetting" would make the forest more open and species-rich. Others focused on striking a careful balance between production and the new strategy for unspoilt forests. Everywhere we went, we heard about the importance of keeping horse riders, mountain bikers, black woodpeckers, walkers and orienteers more or less separate.

Hundeide throws himself energetically into a discussion familiar from experiences in the forest and on the beach. Are some types of experience more legitimate than others? Do the thrilling outdoor ones reduce the surroundings to an "aesthetic backdrop"? During the fieldwork, one person I met was an energetic critic of the widespread fascination with the aesthetics of the open horizon. We had talked about wind farms off the coast of West Jutland. I mentioned how much the sight of wind turbines upset some beach people. Those who love the open and empty horizon sometimes protest loudly, no matter how green the energy generated. One particular critic, a fisherman and philosopher, also assured me that he "hated nature experiences". For him, the empty horizon was synonymous with the dangers of being alone at sea. He was keenly interested in the sea, marine life, environmental issues and the potential for sustainable fisheries, but "experiences for the sake of experiences" meant nothing to him. It was a critique of reducing the world to a recreational scenic view – an aestheticisation of the ocean you work *on* and *with* for a living. He had no problem with wind farms. If you want energy, you have to accept it might affect your view.[5]

As per the German sociologist Hartmut Rosa, you might ask: When natural history enthusiasts geek out about spotting species, doesn't it become competition or knowledge for its own sake, tramping around just to tick boxes? When people seek out nature for peace – or fitness – isn't it just a selfish quest for the authentic self? Aren't they really looking at themselves, using nature as little more than a mirror? Are all of these approaches equally legitimate, necessary or desirable? And, for the more pragmatically minded, is there room for us all?

## jizz

Jizz is an ornithological term that refers to identifying a bird at a glance. Patient observations, conscientious reading, the birdwatcher's own photographs and knowledge of bird behaviour coalesce into rapid recognition of species by their "jizz". For veteran bird watchers, it also means in the same instant, or perhaps slightly later, identifying the sex and age of the bird and the different coats of feathers some species develop over the course of a year or a lifetime. When they identify a bird by its jizz, they just *know*. Except, of course, when they're wrong. When the bird is completely new to them, slower methods are called for, studying one feature at a time – or, in special cases, one feather or gene at a time.[6]

Some botanists also talk about plant jizz. When we instantly recognise a plant – the common cowslip, for example – it's because it has worked its way under our skin, as it were. It is a bit like how we recognise a friend in a crowd by the briefest of waves, the particular way they move or their contours, especially ones you expect to see there. The etymology of the word jizz is unclear. It might stem from the military term GISS, meaning "general impression of shape and size", which is used to identify aircraft quickly. Some say it's older than that and was first used when birdwatching became popular in Britain in the 1920s.[7]

The inherently ephemeral nature of the word itself captures the experience of recognising "something" – be it flying creatures, slow-moving plants or the contours, colours, movement and light of landscapes. Liv, for example, hardly knew any birds. She said she didn't really see them. But still, we might say that all summer long she identified evening skies by their jizz. She glanced outside, sat down with her dinner and waited, curious to see if she was right or wrong. Would the sun really light up the clouds? Where would the light come from? How would the red hues spread? The jizz is an ultra-short perception based on a combination of practised skill and surroundings.

If romantic literature, painting and nature 'enthusiasts' stories are to be believed, an overall impression has multiple layers. For example, when long practice and heightened awareness meet the extraordinary – such as an arduous walk, a lucky day, a particularly beautiful sky, a long sought-after bird or a particularly beautiful specimen that presents itself in an unusual way – then the moment of recognition can extend into a process of discovery, in which it is as if time is standing still or, as I will show later, even as if we are in the moment just before time starts.

The bird kingdom offers experiences akin to those on the beach but arguably even more special because of the various species' specific attributes. Countless programmes on TV feature enthusiasts bubbling over with excitement. Morten D.D. Hansen, a museum director and biologist who hosts and contributes to multiple TV and radio shows, is one of the best-known in Denmark. He is famous for his empathetic, passionate and celebratory style, often employing religious concepts to convey intensity and profundity. Both a seemingly ordinary Wednesday in an unassuming field, as spring birds fly overhead, and an extraordinary outing to see migrating birds of prey elicit descriptions of "an almost religious sense of joy and gratitude", of experiencing "Nirvana" and "all-encompassing magic", "the greatest miracles" or "a kind of mass or service". In D.D.'s vast spectrum of "enchantment", birdwatching makes you feel "blessed", "part of a larger community" and "invited to a party".[8] Seeing the first swallow arrive from South Africa in the spring, knowing that the marsh tit has 2,000 hiding places, that the goldcrest catches more than 1,000 insects an hour, or that swifts fly over 300,000 kilometres a year without landing – all of these are reasons to enthuse, as are common or garden beetles, flowers and hoverflies, all of which hint at the most amazing adventures.

Media outlets are awash with stories expressing awe, gratitude and excitement about biodiversity, with an emphasis on the emotional richness of "witnessing" other species' lives. D.D. and the self-proclaimed nature nerds Sebastian Klein and Vicky Knudsen (among others) are highly enthusiastic presences on TV, on radio, on social media, in lectures and in books. On every trip and in every retelling, they seem to reach a new pinnacle of delirium and breathlessness as they experience "the ultimate expression of life and wildness", "the greatest miracles" and "becoming part of a larger community".[9]

During my fieldwork, I came across some wonderful descriptions of cranes' mating dances in southern Sweden, murmurations in southern Jutland and mornings spent lying in wait for a fox staking out a chicken coop. One particularly fine example was the session with Bo, which he himself called one of the best that year. Writing about the black woodpecker's nest, he describes how the male, "with a jackdaw call", flew "over to the female, who invited him to mate, which typically happens on a horizontal branch".[10] These are excerpts from an article in the Danish Ornithological Society's journal *Pandion,* in which Bo details observations of the black woodpeckers over 19 breeding seasons. He writes that, in the end, they didn't mate, and the male resorted "to a classical threatening posture with beak thrusts and shaking wings". I wouldn't be able to describe it that way, of course. But my own moment was still intense. I watched not only Bo's attentive fluttering about as the birds swooped overhead but also their dance on the branch as Bo repeatedly assured me it was a unique moment.

As fascinated as I was by the diversity of the bird enthusiasts' overall impressions – and occasionally those of the beetle people, butterfly lovers and beach nerds – I was just as keen to eavesdrop on the magical moments of everyday life in which sometimes there was an obvious intensity and activity, while at other times very little appeared to be happening. Sometimes, almost nothing.

## focus behind the words

As I left Hellebæk, I had a better understanding of what Michael meant when he said that observing birds of prey on a day like this can be like meditating – even without me knowing exactly what he meant, because there are so many forms of meditation. Many phenomena are indistinct and overlap, but what all forms of meditation and mindfulness have in common is that they seek to still the mind by achieving a vigilant, "neutral state of observation". I've heard many beach people and winter bathers make a similar comparison. Susanne talked about "being in a Zen state", others about "time disappearing", or describing how walking on the beach or birdwatching can lead to "a pleasant, life-affirming calm". Some said this meant they "had no need for a psychologist", others that "a trip to the forest is like taking happy pills" or "you can't peel the smile off my face". Both the beachgoers and the bird enthusiasts frequently emphasise the subtle interplay between intense enthusiasm and quiet joy. The most effusive praise centred around an irresistible calm, brought about by a combination of physical presence and surprising observations.

It takes time to achieve a state of "almost nothing". Susanne, for example, talked about the long periods spent sitting completely motionless with her camera. After a while, she might hear a bird, follow it with her ears around the bushes, glimpse it briefly, and then note that it seems to either forget her or consider her part of the background and approaches her – getting so close that the camera is just resting in her hands as the bird comes fully into focus. Then, it's a matter of staying in focus and holding the camera still as she follows it around. It's difficult when the bird is in the crosshairs. The camera is quite heavy, the long lens makes it difficult to balance, and she has to alternate between watching the bird with and without it. Susanne was intrigued by how she had become accustomed to following the birds and had learned to switch rapidly between short- and long-distance observation. One day, after we talked about the elasticity of the eyes, which allows us to shift our focus and is not improved by staring at a screen all day, I was at a creepy-crawly macro event on the heath with a group of insect people, when I realised that I had new eyes. After hours spent watching photographers squirming and crawling to get a close-up of tiny lives, I spotted an insect – a 14- or 16-spotted ladybird, just 20 cm from my nose. My gaze then panned across the waving grasses – I saw all of them individually – to a group of trees with thousands of glittering leaves, before one of the beetle people drew my attention to a lapwing, suspended in the air, its detail razor-sharp. In that sequence of events, it was as if I was no longer short-sighted; as if my sense of sight had been enhanced, achieving a clarity and a zoom capability normally reserved for high-end cameras. Surprised and excited, I told Susanne about it, and she said "yes, yes – we can actually see like that. In fact, many people don't even know how to use their eyes."

It takes two good eyes to spot birds unless they're having a snack at a feeder or we're counting ducks in the park. Birds are flighty – literally – but in the context of birdwatching, this is a very challenging quality, one that really puts the senses to the test. The English anthropologist Tim Ingold recently noted how animals, plants and landscapes can have different qualities (he called them affordances),[11] that encourage particular practices and experiences to a greater or lesser extent. From a human perspective, therefore, stones, butterflies and St John's wort all have different qualities. Ingold suggests that instead of seeing beings and things as something in themselves, out there, as something perceived from a distance and separately, as "inside the head" or in the body, we see that their "affordances" express that the beings concerned gather information based on how they interact with what they encounter. For example, the surfaces, hardness, shape, nutritional content or fragility of some things invite certain actions rather than others. For humans, flat stones are great for skimming across water; butterflies are good at hiding, but you can learn to find them; and the red dots on the petals of the St John's wort smudge between your fingers and turn schnapps a bright colour. The qualities in our surroundings allow for certain activities and exclude others or make them inappropriate. For example, you can't skim plants on the water or brush your teeth with stones. As mentioned, we can meet things and beings halfway. The point is to stress how the experience depends on *the action*, on the way in which we meet the world.[12]

When we crawl around like Birte, turn like Bo or handle our binoculars and camera with practised agility, what we experience is at the end of these actions. Experiences don't just happen – even the big ones. The world isn't just out there. We have to meet and experience it. Doing so takes knowledge, practice, tools, timing and co-operation. Watching birds in their own territory isn't like going to the zoo. Free birds don't sell you tickets for the show. We have to seek them out. Some of them may be lured to feeding stations, but we otherwise have to put ourselves in the right situations to see them – often only for a split second. We need to be totally ready, totally focused. It might be a matter of just seconds. We have to act in order to experience the birds and eventually know them by their jizz. The beauty of the term jizz is that it expresses the brief encounter between birdwatcher and bird. And that is all there is in terms of perception, mere moments. Going to the zoo is also an action, but the quality of the enclosures means we can take as much time as we want with our untrained senses, easily stack moments on top of each other, and quickly observe our fill.

Birds are great at just popping up out of nowhere. We wait and look to the sky for birds of prey, preferably from a vantage point with good visibility, near their coastal migration routes. Studying the sky for hours on end makes us aware of updrafts – something only glider pilots usually notice. Birds of prey use them to gain altitude. Spend time on a good coastal outcrop, on a day with the right wind, and flocks of chaffinches will suddenly appear out of the sky. The sandwich tern will emerge from the sea. The penduline tit will turn up, seemingly out of nowhere, on the way to its newly built nest. Geese suddenly make large patterns across the sky. Formation after formation. At night, migrations are audible. Suddenly, the overwintering great tits have guests at the feeder.

Bird people look up, mostly. Much of the time without seeing anything. They're waiting for the next bird. They are completely in their eyes, in their ears. Reading the signs. Assessing the possibilities. The wind, the heat, the activity at a nest, birdsong, other birdwatchers, other pairs of binoculars. There's nothing – until suddenly, and often very briefly, a bird appears, and all of their concentration is focused on it. Maybe just for a split second, during which they identify the species on the jizz. Maybe they only see it out of the corner of their eye while waiting for the next one. Hours can pass without anything happening. Or at least nothing special. On the big spring migration days, flocks of birds keep appearing out of the blue, all of them heading to Sweden. It's as if our ears and eyes expand as we watch, as if our perception is becoming attuned to their qualities: their speed, colours, patterns and sounds, an overwhelming variation with a certain degree of regularity and an infinite depth of detail, which varies from species to species, depending on gender and age. We have to be truly present.

On my first many excursions, I found the silence of the birdwatchers difficult, because I didn't know what I was looking at. Over time, I learned a little more. Sometimes, I felt immersed in the silent work with the senses, and I experienced the feelings others had told me about. It's as if you become invisible, time disappears and this is all there is: a kite, nothing, a blue tit, nothing, nothing, a parrot crossbill. Armed with binoculars or a camera, birds come so close we can distinguish the subtle nuances in the colours, see what they have in their beaks, how the wind puffs up their feathers. Sometimes, we see one of them looking back at us. Such moments can be unfathomable. We know the bird usually sees us long before we see it – but what does it see? What happens when our eyes meet? What kind of connection is it, so brief, that to them we seem to be in slow motion? "It looked at us!", "I took a photo of the seagull just as it looked at me", exclaim excited twitchers after fleeting encounters. Hunters, too, talk about the moments when animals look at them – and they either let it go or shoot. In moments like that, I am told, there's an invisible elastic, a feedback loop, a presence, something beyond words, hard to fathom and inherently good, intense moments crackling with life, joy and enthusiasm. The birds, the animals, don't just exist, they are constantly foraging, calling, being watchful and changing plumage. To be truly with them, even for a split second or a series of them, depends absolutely on our ability to be present. Whether we're hiding and waiting, or just lucky, a moment such as this is an encounter, an action.

Bird photographers delete almost every picture they take once they get home. Susanne saves maybe four out of 150, edits them slightly according to strict guidelines, adds a title to each image and archives it. Then, she talks to her husband, Eskild, about them, prints some of them out, leaves them out on display for a while, posts some on Facebook, makes postcards, discusses them with other birders, and occasionally exhibits some of them along with other local photographers. Her process turns the many walks on Hilløse Bredning, by the coast, in Hegnet and on Overdrevet into a vast catalogue of moments she can revisit in the days and years to come, recalling the feathers, colours, feet and movements and – as she puts it – the situation in which she took the picture. Her photography becomes a cascade of temporalities – sensations of different durations, moments, presence, memories – stacked one on top of another. All of this can be done in silence. And that, I sensed, is one of the really great qualities. How much of these moments are beyond words?

## the imagery

*Tick-tick-tick-tick-tick-tick-tick* is the flight call of the black woodpecker. The male eider goes *awoo awoo*. The chiffchaff says *chiff chaff* (of course). There are many shades of yellow feathers. The "flying door", the white-tailed eagle, has the largest wings.

Ornithological lingo is full of onomatopoetic words and characteristics that call for comparisons. How do you determine the shapes of birds' wings when they never stop moving? Take the chiffchaff, whose name echoes the short version of its call. The Danish wildlife database *Naturbasen* provides much more comprehensive information about how it sounds, but others emphasise the resemblance to the sound of a leaking tap: *drip-drip-drip-drip-drip-drip*.

These attempts to use words to describe birdsong perhaps make more sense once we've heard the song many times, once we are able to match it to the transcript and accept the translation. We can also represent the calls visually, using sonograms or spectrograms, so we can "see" the sound waves and compare and memorise the song, the way we do with sheet music. It is said that some birdwatchers practise the songs and calls throughout winter so they don't forget them. That's how they can walk along a riverbank and hear 42 species in a single day – or visit a popular lake and record 87.

The question of whether birdsong and other animal sounds are a form of language is controversial. Does it make sense to compare birdsong and calls to human language, or is it a completely different way of communicating? And what do we understand by communication in the animal kingdom, especially when it comes to the silent language: the colours, movements and shapes?

The American anthropologist Eduardo Kohn analyses the language of the Ecuadorian Amazon forest and the Runa people who live there.[13] He does so via the lens of the philosopher Charles Sanders Peirce's theory of language, which consists of three different layers. He calls the first symbolic, in the sense that the connection between expression and content is an agreed convention. The word "song" refers to the sound you recognise as the blackbird's call, but is itself a random sound, one that emerged along with thousands of others in your specific language. The situation is slightly different with iconic terms – the second layer of language in Peirce's theory. In such terms, there is greater consistency between content and expression, even though typical dog sounds (*woof-woof*) and bird sounds (*cheep-cheep*) vary between languages. Nonetheless, the purpose of these terms is to mimic the sound they reproduce. The key point here is to note the *similarity* between the actual sound of the chiffchaff, and the sound of the word that describes it. In a visual context, an iconic image is one that *looks like* what it represents. For example, a pine tree can be accurately drawn in detail, or we can draw a shape recognisable as one. Pierce's third type of sign is called indexical, i.e. it refers to something to which it is *connected*. If you hear the song of the chiffchaff, it indicates the presence of the species, even if you can't see one. The sound is directly connected to the bird, it originates from there, just as smoke indicates the presence of a fire. By "signs", we don't just mean human beings' spoken and written language. Broadly speaking, only humans use symbolic language, but we share the other two types with all other creatures. In fact, some animals do use elements of symbolic language. Chimpanzees can learn to recognise and respond to a certain number of written words or drawn symbols, for example. However, the extent to which this capacity overlaps with human language comprehension is disputed

Snails, bacteria and all sorts of other life forms make extensive use of icons and indexes in their behaviour and communication with their surroundings. Biosemiotics explains how the environment means something to creatures and how they interact with each other – how they *world* in encounters with their surroundings.[14] Woodlice, elephants and birds of prey all sense the phenomena that are particularly meaningful to them. Dampness means something special to the woodlouse. If it spends too long somewhere dry, it will die, so it identifies and hones in on dampness rather than sunlight. Plants, on the other hand, reach for the light, as the chlorophyll in their leaves converts solar energy into chemical energy – all through semiotic processes. Biosemiotics understands all living things in this way, as geared for something, not just as DNA-controlled machines, but creatures, bacteria, synapses, feet and roots, clever sign readers and creators in the way they register and interpret light, bacteria, water, fungal spores or whatever else happens to be important for their life processes. It is in the encounter between creatures and their surroundings that life unfolds via these sign processes.

Semiotic language theory also claims that we should not understand symbolic language as completely detached from iconic and indexical forms. While human language is unique, symbolic language only works because it builds on the other two.[15] Our bodies function like those of other species, in that they are constantly engaged in billions of semiotic processes, all based on iconic and indexical signs. The fact that we think in images indicates we are connected to other life forms that do the same. Vision is not the same in all species, and we all register and perceive the world differently, yet we all encounter the world by interpreting and processing signs. "We" in the broad sense, because as you read these words, other parts of you – organs, senses, cells, etc. – are busy reading all sorts of other signs.

In the first instance, Kohn observed that the people with whom he carried out his fieldwork, whose survival depends very much on knowing where to catch animals in the forest and which predators to fear, rely heavily on indices and icons, which they use, as he puts it, "to think the forest". The Runa people know the plants, where they grow, how they look and taste, and what they can be used for, and they know the animals and their habits. In terms of imagery, nocturnal dreams, too, are crucial signs, even the dreams of their dogs – which they interpret based on their movements and noises. All of these serve as signs and images with which to navigate the forest. They pay particular attention to pumas, precisely because they are extremely dangerous. The Runa's animistic worldview, in which other living beings have souls, just as humans do, makes it crucial to share language with them in order to live safely in the forest, to hunt, cultivate and find plants. For an outsider like Kohn, it took a long time – years in the field – to learn the language of the forest enough to start writing about it. Throughout his fieldwork, he carefully recorded the Runa's way of life, noting down conversations, stories of dreams, the practicalities of hunting and the vast knowledge of plants and animals interwoven into their lives.

The focused attention on their surroundings common to birdwatchers, forest people and beachgoers steers my thinking down similar paths to Kohn.[16] He sees imagery as "a form of resonance that is lost when you focus only on the specifically human. This other form of being, which we so badly need today, can be lost".[17] It might be said that Kohn is offering a kind of critique of the indoor person, who is so concentrated on human things that they completely forget the languages of other living creatures. He doesn't just mean it's been a long time since you cared about the woodlice under the flowerpot. Rather, his contention is that our understanding of the language of the enormous kingdom of the forest has been in decline for centuries.

Nevertheless, what Kohn refers to in an interview as a "different kind of being" seems to me still to manifest in the way many people in Denmark behave outdoors. Those at home on the beach and in the forest constantly see signs of life, which themselves are signs of other life. Large grazers, for example, have an impact on local flora – eating some species, leaving others be. You can see it. You can follow their trail. Insects have symbiotic relationships with certain flowers. An easterly wind may mean a bird migration is about to pass this particular promontory. The presence of ants invites wrynecks to nest in certain trees. Some plants with special roots are a sign of certain soil conditions. A high humus content is good for growing certain plants. Measuring instruments and laboratory tests detect the slightest chemical variations, while footprints, scent trails and holes in the bark are signs of other life for the observant.

However, as I've said before, many of us are not awake to these forms of life. We don't register them, or have names for them – perhaps because we haven't learned them, or have forgotten them. We don't think we need them (perhaps, in a sense, we don't) or don't appreciate them (for various reasons). We have retreated behind our windows, where we can't hear or smell the passing fox, who has also moved to the city. We can't expect children to learn about more than a handful of species in school, know their names, behaviour, where and when to find them, or what interests them. In the modern world, preoccupied as it is with the human condition, it isn't necessary. As a teacher, Susanne was an exception, of course. Her classes all had to learn about the five most common seagull species.

Bird people are among the experts on signs of life. A south-easterly wind in April is a sign that large migrations of chaffinches are likely to appear on some north-east coasts in Denmark. A flap of the wings, followed by *tick-tick-tick-tick-tick-tick-tick*, alerts us to the presence of another species. The red feathers on the top of its head confirm it's a black woodpecker. Its wing movements indicate a female is nearby. To take it all in, you need to be fully focused, fully immersed, fully engaged, your senses attuned to bird language. It can completely displace human language, at least temporarily, because our symbols and chatter disturb the birds, and stop us from paying attention to and accessing the other languages.

Bird language takes a long time to learn. I've tried to concentrate on it, but haven't made much progress. For a long time, I found it difficult to tell a blue tit from a great tit. Ridiculous – but what was I supposed to do? The answer, of course, is to spend more time on it. A lot more. Andreas Egelund Christensen is a geographer and ranks high on the twitcher list (although he hadn't yet entered his approximately 430 sightings on any of the official sites). One afternoon, as we watched birds of prey (red kite, lesser spotted eagle, little grey eagle, buzzard, golden eagle, blue hawk, pallid harrier, peregrine falcon) at Flagbakken near

Skagen, he told me that he had memorised all of the European birds by reading about them in *Europas fugle* (Birds of Europe) by the age of seven. He then learnt all their Latin names off by heart, and how to spot them in the wild. He did this weekend after weekend for decades. Alone, with his dad and with friends. He describes his interest in birds as deeply nerdy. He loves to be a geek about the most minute visual differences. And his ears are always on high alert. Using Kohn's terms, he might be said to have refined his iconic and indexical skills by not only being a geek about feathers, but also building on those signs via symbolic human language. Being able to spot granular details, having words to express the small similarities and differences in feathers and behaviour, and having had thousands and millions of birds imprinted on his retina and in his ears, Andreas – like Bo, like Birte, like Susanne and the people on the hill at Hellebæk – registers so infinitely much more than those of us who haven't started learning to speak bird.

When he hears the cranes over the city from his office in the centre of Copenhagen, he opens the windows and basks in the sound. The day we spent on Flagbakken, everyone could see lesser spotted eagles, buzzards and golden eagles, but it still fell to Andreas to confirm what we were looking at, because he was the most fluent in bird.

## the beauty

Rasmus Ejrnæs, a biologist and botanist, has spent years observing birds and plants *and* learning to meditate – and sees great similarities between the two activities. He explains that the non-interference inherent in the act of observation, of simply witnessing things happening, affords access to a sense of meaningfulness. I sought him out after reading many of his books and articles on red-listed species and about his long campaign for more space for "wild nature" in Denmark. I noticed how he often uses quasi-religious terms to describe the joy and wonder he believes is to be found in nature.

I asked if this reflected an interest in religion. Rasmus didn't see it that way. Neither did Andreas – or any of the others. But that *didn't* mean there *weren't* similarities, to put it in a somewhat convoluted way. It *is* tricky to look at what lies behind the History of Big Differences. If we approach the world via the lens of the second and third nature, there is little difference between the religious and the secular, or between the self and the world around us (as described in the previous chapters). Instead, we meet the world halfway. If we're really dedicated, then yes, we can experience the language of nature over and over again.

Andreas told me how, for him, birdwatching alternated between a competition and a wonderful escape from everyday life, how it could leave him feeling mesmerised, infinitesimally small or high as a kite, and how, of course, he saw plenty of similarities with meditation *and* was happy to pay his DOF dues in recognition of the organisation's environmental voice. He shared its concern for the state of the environment, the well-being of the birds and, therefore, the habitats on which they depend.

Andreas finds it easy to elaborate on how the different ways of birdwatching are to some degree aesthetic, meditative, oriented toward natural history and more or less associated with commitment to the environment. In other words, like Rasmus, Bo, Susanne, Liv and many others I met in the field, he transcends Hundeide's categories for closeness to nature. His curiosity, urge to explore and environmental commitment coexist with more ecstatic experiences. We might also say that the bird people relate to their avian subjects with more or less distance (as a species, a population or ticks on a checklist), forgetting themselves to some extent and feeling at one with nature.

Perusing Rasmus's articles, interviews and comments in Facebook groups and other media, I noticed a particular interest in metaphysical questions. What is humankind's place in the world among the other species? What does the Western Christian tradition mean for the way people understand nature? What does "wild nature" offer that is so special? In particular, he rails against the prevailing obsession with *utilising* nature – despite recognising how the extraction and processing of resources is a prerequisite for our own existence. His issue is that this attitude predominates and drowns out all sense of the *beauty* of life. In our conversations, Rasmus has told me, albeit often only in passing, how experiences of nature can be "pre-linguistic", an opportunity "to witness creation". Similarly, in his books and articles, he writes about "how to become a little more peaceful and generous",[18] how a "sense of belonging" can be felt in "spontaneous nature",[19] and that making space for this is itself a "celebration of life"[20] and "its beauty".[21]

In my interviews with Rasmus, I tried to understand the source of his quasi-religious statements, approaching the issue from various angles. The penny finally dropped during the third interview when he summarised it for me.

"At some point. I realised that neutral observation – non-interference – is much the same in both meditation and botany. In a long study, you spend weeks and months observing very small areas and recording everything that grows there. Meditation offers a plethora of ways to calm the mind – focusing attention on your breathing or heart, and doing energy exercises. Similarly, with this kind of pedagogy, you end up doing less and less. Once the head has calmed down, you do less and less until you find yourself doing nothing. You end up in what might be called a natural state. Yes, I know that sounds a bit boring. Nothing is happening, after all, but it is the moment before creation. Creation happens all the time, but when we are completely still, we get closer to the magical moment *before* creation. You can experience this in meditation, where you concentrate on the mind, but I have also noted it when spending a long time training the mind to observe plants and animals. You spend hours registering plants, for example, each and every single one in a field of, say, five by five metres. [...] It's hard to talk about that moment. You might compare it to a shy animal, who's afraid to come out because it's so delicate or so... so subtle, unspeakable or sacred. I don't know how the hell to describe it!"

It has struck me since then that the "moment before creation" was a variation on phrases I've heard from many other beach and forest people, even without them going "out into nature" specifically *in order to* meditate. The meditative aspect is part of it, inseparable from observation and photography. The experience of time standing still, of being invisible, as a floating presence, an imperceptible extension of being both intensely *and* restfully present in the senses. This experience doesn't require references to a special spiritual world, a creator god or mystical forces. Rather, it's as if the moment we excorporate (as Schmitz puts it), we are close to the world just as it is coming into being. We meet the world halfway, and right there – in the objectless transcendence – experience becoming one with the world around us. A world almost indescribable, almost not there, and yet present in everything that is in the process of becoming – like us.

Echoing Rasmus' words quite closely without referring to meditation, a nature guide told me that in particularly pleasant locations – a beautiful clearing, an old hill or next to water – he quite often feels "a special calm, a silence, an atmosphere of what there is, just before it happens – a beginning". I also imagine that Susanne and the beach people were attempting to say something similar, brimming with creation, that they experienced the pause in linear time and given space, which feels like the pulse of the living world – pre-dimensional and more than just human. It might be argued that religions have sought to cultivate moments like these through the ages, but that they also "grow in the wild" – and thrive – in many other places.[22]

In one interview, Rasmus expressed the hope that growing interest in "wild" nature – both politically, in rewilding large, protected areas, and in the nooks and crannies of our cities and people's gardens – means that "we recognise the beautiful nature – the same nature – inside ourselves and discover that much of our existence is unplanned, of no great use, uncontrolled, etc. I think we need to let the wild do its own thing in the world around us." The wild has been trampled underfoot, forgotten, removed. It needs space to unfold with greater diversity. But at the same time, Rasmus says, we need to recognise the non-wild side: "The other part of our existence, the useful and planned part. We shouldn't hate it. We need to love that, too. We have to be able to love both, even if we're *bloody well shaking inside*, right?"

Translated into my terminology, Rasmus thinks the second nature is out of hand in the overzealously managed Danish landscape – the soil has been consumed and cultivated, the animals hunted and domesticated, reducing the world to surroundings for *humankind*. This has made it possible to turn natural riches into objects and has wiped out whole species. Perhaps unintentionally, one outcome is that there are far too few contiguous areas of (relatively) pristine first nature. Without giving other species the opportunity to multiply via all their interdependencies, *humans, humans, humans* – in all our efforts to exploit the environment – can fail to recognise the wild in life and also that, ultimately, we ourselves are nature. It is fascinating and uniquely wild not only to witness and be silently connected to the other creatures, which also come into being in uncontrolled processes of evolution and disruption. As I understand it, this is the aspect of Rasmus' experience that he wants to share with others. He wants us to understand that we breathe in the air that plants breathe out, that insects pollinate plants, that not only would the world be quieter without birds, but also that a world without birds would fundamentally change the landscape – because they spread seeds, connect ecosystems, consume and fertilise. Of course, humankind might survive, says Rasmus, but how poor would life be? How poor is the landscape already? In a country like Denmark, the wild has all but disappeared, with few contiguous areas of biodiversity left. As I will show in the next chapter, these reflections on wild nature – as something both external and internal – led Rasmus to his characterisation of the wild human's nature.

## the indoor person's jizz

Even the most die-hard of indoor people use imagery, of course. It also works in pigsties and department stores. Inside, images are everywhere, indices and icons that refer to or look like something else, icons that resemble something else, but which in this context are largely directed by the symbolic worlds of human language. Children still sit indoors for at least ten years, learning the basic symbols of democracy, urban history, modernity, photosynthesis and arithmetic. The blackboard chalk and computer screen have their own materiality, as do the packed lunch and exam nerves. Ecological semiotics covers everything, not just between the living. It's so interesting and exciting that it's hard to find reasons or time to go outdoors. So much so, as shown in later chapters, that it might not seem relevant to venture out anywhere, because the most important, visible or attention-grabbing nature that Danes seem to encounter in their everyday lives is found indoors.

Kohn asserts that we miss out on something vital if we focus on the specifically human. I think the beach and bird people would agree. How many times have I heard people say that they would die or wither away if they had to live in the city, unable to make regular excursions to the countryside or find breathing space in parks, on the coast, under trees or at a watering hole on a common. They see the built environment as temporary vacuums that have somehow taken on too much of a life of their own. The many symbolic languages people master, share and about which they get excited, can be said, in a sense, to be limited and of a single type, which means we forget to pay attention to the languages of plants, birds and other species.

However, we should be cautious about saying that the full-blooded indoor person isn't just as dependent upon and fascinated by indexical and iconic language as their outdoor counterparts. Otherwise, why would we love going to gigs, the ballet or theatre? Why would we cycle, go plane-spotting, redecorate the living room or even just cross the road? We're surrounded by imagery. But to echo Kohn and his thoughts about the forest, not all imagery is as alive as it is in the moment a bird catches our eye or the male woodpecker feeds his hungry chicks. And it's not everywhere imagery is as vital to life as it is when plants produce the oxygen we breathe, or the big scabious mining bee hunts for the field scabious, upon whose pollen its larvae almost exclusively feed. When we sit behind our windows, as I do now, and rarely look out, preoccupied with the symbolic world, with the products of humankind, how can we connect with the qualities of other species? Qualities we sense via practical involvement? If what we experience is an extension of our actions, then the difference between the bird on the poster and the bird in the bush is radical. It takes a lot of practice to use jizz to identify a bird. Only by practising for a long time do we know how incredibly beautiful a wagtail looks every year.

It's no surprise that human beings are so interested in other humans and that cultural and social spaces have expanded to a degree that seems to overshadow and even threaten and inhibit the life processes of so many other species. However, for most people, it is still an unpleasant, scientifically verified surprise that human ways of worlding have been able to overlook the consequences for other species, and how these consequences affect humans – even indoors. There isn't necessarily any such thing as a safe and secure "indoors" when a hurricane hits the coast and the sea level rises.

One day we may be able to walk into a shopping centre with the same level of equilibrism as the bird people, knowing where all the goods come from, what resources were used to make them, and where they are going next. But to provide that kind of attention and care, we need institutions to support such attention. If we are to know things by their jizz, we need to be more aware that everything is always in the process of being created; that we are not only *in* the world, but also *of* and *with* the world; and that all things and beings make a contribution by being full of life.[23] Maybe we could find the right sneakers, cucumbers, phones, cars and cauliflowers by their jizz, and know where they come from and where the component parts are going – without ignoring anything and without too much killing in the process.

plant blind

Last summer, I entered into a relationship with a plant. It was confusing at first. I had decided it was something I wanted. But what plant, and what kind of relationship? I've had all sorts in the past – a plum tree, potted plants, even a whole kitchen garden, and their life force has always seemed to weave itself into me just as much as all of the ones I've eaten.

It is estimated that plants account for 80% of the Earth's biomass.[1] They bring colour to the outdoor world and pass through hands, pots and the whole family's organisms as we cook with them. If forced to choose between animals and plants, I'm very much a plant person – but, like the majority of my own and subsequent generations, not one who pays much attention. My eulogies sound trite, even those about the bitter flesh of the aubergine and the soft, grey-green sage. It's not that I don't like them, it's just hard to say exactly *what* I like about them.

This ambivalence has left a suspicion of species loneliness.[2] The great outdoors has never been my domain. Animals flee my clumsy gait, and I can't follow ants' trails. The restless energy of animals seems aimless, so I am amazed to hear that the flower growing in the forest near the local supermarket is a wood cow-wheat, which can only be pollinated if ants make off with their seeds, which have an elaioplast, whatever that is. Listening to the nightingale's song on DOFbasen, I'm surprised how much of it consists of guttural hacks in between screeching rhythms. I imagine that if I were left alone with plants and animals for any length of time, I would feel as abandoned as the hapless participants in the TV programme *Alone*.

At one point in my fieldwork, I found myself on Amager Common, a semi-wild and open green space in south-east Copenhagen, on a cold April day, albeit with a touch of warmth in the sun. I met a young man. He was sitting on a bench, listening to loud music and looking out over the green expanse, to "get some vitamin D". It was the second time he'd been to the Common. He liked the fact that "it's more overgrown and authentic, closer to real nature than a park". He told me his mum is a gardener, so he would probably be able to "identify things in a plant nursery", but not the ones in front of him right now. He said that he was considering studying anthropology, and that made me think of recent conversations with a group of students, about how they didn't connect ecological crises with outdoor nature as they knew it in Denmark. What preoccupied them most was social justice – specifically, the fact that climate change mainly affects those who have *not* emitted large amounts of $CO_2$. Secondly, they associated the effects of climate change with floods and forest fires elsewhere in the world. Danish nature was something they associated with days out as kids, agricultural landscapes and breathing spaces like Amager Common, which they visited from time to time.

These students didn't associate Danish landscapes with what I call the third nature, even though as educated young people they knew full well how crops in fields become fodder, fuel and food and are, therefore, completely entangled with their bodies. They also knew that certain Danish coasts are increasingly prone to flooding, and that winters have become warmer, including in their lifetimes. But that wasn't what concerned them most. Our conversations about their everyday lives reflected a different way of thinking, one in which the outdoors, the environment and nature-culture were like three different areas on a map. To them, sites like Amager Common were outdoor nature, places to go on trips. The second nature they focused on consisted of parts of the Global South where changes are particularly detrimental to the environment; while the all-encompassing third nature consisted of $CO_2$, of which the Global North generates far too much.

They presumably spend 97% of their time indoors. I haven't monitored the time the young people or I spend outdoors, as one American study did,[3] but it's not hard to figure out that a 90% indoor person, reportedly the average in Europe, knows little about plants. In Susanne's generation, student teachers were given assignments to create herbaria containing 1–200 plants during their training, whereas now, according to a Danish online magazine, one in five young Danes thinks "the word for plaice, a kind of flatfish, is the name of a bird Less than half recognise an oak leaf; less than a quarter, fireweed.[4] As the article asks, "Can we look after something we don't know anything about?"[5]

Plant blindness is an ancient phenomenon, as illustrated in the medieval *Scala Naturae*. According to Arthur Lovejoy, a philosopher and expert in intellectual history, it dates back even further, to Plato and Aristotle, and constitutes a hierarchy that classifies everything in creation, with God at the top, followed by the angels, the humans, the animals and – second bottom, just above non-living minerals – the plants.[6] On this scale, plants are closer to non-living things than to humans, despite making the biggest contribution to maintaining life on the planet – so much so, in fact, that we could, quite reasonably, turn this hierarchy upside down. Although this system and the built-in assumptions that plants lack both movement and the ability to communicate are antiquated and vigorously refuted by scientists, who nowadays point to the sensory capacities and intelligence of plants,[7] it reflects the confusion that surrounds our encounters with plants. I say "our" here, because I sense that many others share similar feelings of awkwardness. No matter how enthusiastic we are about the ingenious abilities or stupefying beauty of certain types, and how much effort we put in, plants are often hard to reach, which leaves us feeling like outsiders.

## to know a plant

During my fieldwork, I asked how people get to know plants, and I tried to acquire new plant habits. I went on a week-long botany course, bought several plants books and a magnifying glass, and learned about the plant community's morphology, taxonomy and ecology. As part of the course, we went on field trips, observed plants in their habitats, and plucked unknown ones to identify – with "some of us" having to consult reference works. Later on, when out and about, I worked with the flora on beaches, salt meadows, waste ground and roadsides. I also observed various plants over a period of time and collected specimens to imprint their characteristics and names on my mind. With a select few, I tried unfamiliar methods of growing, indoors and out. After these basic exercises in the plant kingdom, I decided to find a single plant and get to know it better.

How do you get to know a plant? Let's say we (I will start with a generalisation) go for a walk and encounter one. Perhaps it's a plant we've seen before – bluebell-like branch, lanceolate stem leaves – but we don't know its name. Or, as has happened to me frequently during intense periods of plant study – the name eludes me, so does the family, even the distinctive characteristics. It just grows there, it *is* there. In that sense, they embody an excess of being, but that doesn't tell us much. Because nothing's happening. At first glance, the plant seems unaffected, while I become shaken – a cocktail of irritation and curiosity. I have to take the next steps. Get my book out. Or use a plant-identifier app on my phone. Other questions spring to mind: What is the relationship between *recognising* and *knowing* a plant? The book (or app) tells me it's a bluebell. Maybe I'll remember it the next time. Have I made any progress? Should I pluck it and take it home to get to know it better? Or not? After all, it might be a rare type. Should I leave it for others to enjoy?

The young man on the bench enjoyed a fine day out among the anonymous plants, without feeling the urge to get to know the trees being battered by the wind, such as the hawthorn and sea buckthorn. But, I have asked myself – partly inspired by some young people who appear later in this book – if I wanted a more *committed* relationship with a plant, how would I go about it?

When the anthropologist John Hartigan was carrying out fieldwork at the botanical garden in Valencia, he was similarly concerned about how little attention he paid to plants.[8] Hartigan is part of an anthropological tradition that no longer focuses on humans as the primary object of study, and recognises animals and plants as ethnographic subjects, a shift in emphasis that entails seeking to describe these forms of life directly, not just via representations, i.e. via the knowledge – or symbols, as Kohn would put it (as per the previous chapter) – that employees and guests of botanical gardens (for example) use when referring to plants.

Hartigan decided to interview a plant ethnographically. It is, of course, provocative to transpose the idea of the interview from a human-to-human to a human-to-plant encounter. I've interviewed hundreds of people, but what can I take from that and apply to a plant? I usually start by informing the subject about the research project, obtaining the interviewee's consent, clarifying issues of anonymity, and engaging in a bit of small talk. Once we reach the point of feeling comfortable and being ready to see where the conversation might lead, I start with open questions on issues I've read up on and want to address.

A lot can be left unsaid in a conversation between two people – but where to start when the unsaid *is* the conversation? How would the situation even come about? When would you be ready? And for what? As always, I, like Hartigan, began by reading up on the field. I explored biologists' representations of plant morphology and habitats, and the questions critical plant studies pose about their sensitivity, consciousness and intelligence.

Citing the philosopher Michael Marder, Hartigan says that plants' vegetative states fly under our conceptual radar, such that "all we can hope for is to brush upon? the edges of their being, which is altogether outer and exposed, and in so doing to grow past the fictitious shells of our identity and our existential ontology".[9] The idea is that humans, like other creatures, are intimately entangled with the world around them, to a degree the modern Western self-image – of a strong subject rooted in the world as a first nature (an "I" *in* the world) – finds difficult to comprehend.

## plurality of species

The very name anthropology suggests that deviating from an anthropocentric viewpoint constitutes a bit of a shock for the discipline. Like the humanities and sociology, humankind and its communities have long been the its primary domain. It may well have been a feat in itself to isolate the human aspect from angels, gods, plants, animals and minerals in order to study our particularities and variations, but multiple studies suggest that such academic siloes are no longer the way to go. Every discipline has to figure out how it connects with all the others. The justification most frequently propounded for this in the humanities and social sciences is that humankind, as a collective mode of existence, now influences *all* life on Earth. Industrialisation, nuclear bombs and climate change have left their mark all over the globe. Humankind has become a geological force on a par with volcanoes and continental drift, hence the concept of the Anthropocene, meaning the "age of humankind", an umbrella term that refers to the fact human history is inextricably entangled with the history of the planet, encompassing everything from minerals to gods. In this world, we are more connected to all that surrounds us as third nature than we are accustomed to if we restrict our thinking to the concepts of first and second nature.

The old hypothesis that it's enough to study the human in isolation from other life forms is no longer productive. This upheaval in how we view the world is now widely accepted. It is equivalent to the Copernican turn, which put the Sun at the centre of our planetary system; the Darwinian turn, which positioned humankind as a step in the gradual evolution of the species; and the Freudian turn, which placed gods, angels and demons inside human beings. If, as the French anthropologist Bruno Latour puts it, we are to understand ourselves as "terrestrials amid terrestrials",[10] i.e. as a species entangled with other species to an extent we don't fully understand, then everything we make, eat and surround ourselves with is woven together with what we call surroundings in the second nature, but are preconditions in the third nature. Even if your computer is made by other humans, the materials in it haven't forgotten where they came from. They can still be traced *back* to the mountains from which they were extracted.

I had thought about interviewing a potato plant, a species I love, and supplementing it with studies of a product such as a bag of crisps to follow its backstory, milestones and tangents – to understand the history of breeding in South America and later on other continents, the technical details of manufacturing, agricultural practices, nitrogen-fixing potential, and so on. Another possibility was lawn grass because studies of its colonial history could have served as inspiration for the study of lawn products and related practices.[11] The latest "intentionally wild" practices, in which the lawn is peeled away and replaced with wildflowers, might show the way to an understanding of biodiversity on a small scale.

To cut a long story short, it occurred to me one day that my interview subject had to be a chicory – the variety with the blue-bluish head. The colour changes throughout the day, from bright violet to almost white, which isn't really a colour palette that appeals to me, but the chicories, with their morning-blue petals, strident, branching stems, toothed tops towards the flower heads – which bloom on dry soil for months – are both austere and easy to recognise for the untrained eye. Inspired by the guide on my botany course, I was considering the Arctic starflower because "it doesn't look like much, but is so nice".

I also considered other, more rare, exquisite and perhaps endangered species, like snow parsley, but chicory and I appear to have been circling each other for years. I know it's just my imagination, but I like the idea that it saw me first – which might be where my minimal plant sensitivity comes into play. But chicory also appealed for less personal and more cultural-historical reasons. The best known is probably that its taproot is used as a coffee substitute and as pig feed. A chicory field in full bloom must be an overwhelming sight.

Hartigan began his interview by observing the plant. First, he would focus, partly by drawing it, then extend his attention to other species nearby in order to free himself from his own preconceived assumptions about what plants are and can do, and to come closer to its specific sensory qualities. Later, he reflected on how plants are different from people (they're not as mobile, for example) and how they're similar (they share genes that predate the split into plant and animal kingdoms, for example, including the ones that control "circadian rhythms", i.e. our internal clock).[12] Moving from observation to description, Hartigan then began to appreciate the botanical knowledge built up about the morphology of plants, which gave him a language for the details of the leaves, stems and flowers; to smell and touch the plant in order to complement the sense of sight and make the sensation tactile, broad and tangible (as opposed to just looking at it); and to observe the plant's reproductive structures.

Finally – and here his experiment veers away from the botanically inspired parts of his interview, and towards a more sociological perspective – he decided to consider the social position his particular specimen occupied in relation to others. This involved seeking out other specimens in other botanical gardens, and studying the plants' surroundings, provenance, growth, care or even eradication, as some of them ended up categorised as weeds or invasive species.

Hartigan's method inspired several parts of my Anthropocene-inspired ethnographic plant interview. I had decided that I wanted to try and get closer to the chicory not by caging it like a bird, buying one, or digging up a nice specimen. The idea you could buy your way into a relationship like this with a domesticated plant encased in terracotta seemed dubious.

## training

At first, I was confused about the plant's mode of existence – specifically, whether I could have a relationship with a single plant or the species as such. I was unclear about the identity status of plants. Is each one a subject in their own right, or are they copies? Ancient oaks can achieve the status of individuals – with names, a history and a large community around them in the form of other plants, animals and people. Grasses and tulips gather in flocks, birch attracts multiple fungi, insects and birds – far more than spruce, for example. The chicory usually likes to bunch together, too. I eventually settled on a polyplantic relationship and bought several bags of chicory seeds to cultivate a relationship from scratch. After studying how the unassuming plant reproduces, I sowed the seeds in a bed of not-too-acidic soil, and waited.

While waiting, I learned as much as possible, expectantly studying the morphological features of the young plant and the social life of chicory. In the Netherlands, I found the product *Chikko: Not Coffee*. On the packaging it says the drink is "naturally caffeine free, slightly bitter and earthy with a nutty aftertaste". It's a chicory drink that tastes a bit like cocoa when mixed with milk, but I agree with the packaging that the taste stands on its own. Years ago, I had the misfortune to discover I can't drink coffee without severe stomach pains, so perhaps chicory and I were destined to become entangled.

Reference books mention that chicory has a high content of tannic acid, inulin, folic acid, tannins, escutelin and minerals, which together, in metabolic ways I don't fully understand, are said to have a beneficial effect on digestion for both people and animals. As I continued to peruse encyclopaedias and natural history books, I found out that people in the 17th century believed a dried or pickled chicory root served with sugar would improve their health because it "opens the entrails that digest food".[13] This put me on the trail of the plant's biochemistry. More potential connections with non-human species emerged, with new research suggesting chicory in animal feed makes pigs taste better!

Two years earlier, on my week-long botany course, Peter Wind, an experienced biologist, introduced me to what he called the "language of flowers", which he has been learning since he was given an illustrated book of flora as a child. He spent ten years studying biology and has been involved in classification work, such as revising species lists and red lists. At one point, he hung a magnifying glass on a string around his neck and doesn't seem to have ever taken it off again.

*Dansk flora* (Danish Flora) lists 1,381 species, and Peter's PowerPoint presentation showed that Asteraceae (also known as Compositae or composites) are the second most species-rich family in Denmark. Chicory has 131 relatives in this family: asters, daisies, dandelions, marigolds and sunflowers, but also perhaps less obviously, tansy, thistle and chamomile. All are defined by radiating leaves, a basal rosette, and flowers "in heads surrounded by a sweep of tall leaves", which are "either screw-like or sit in 1–3 usually distinct heads" (the chicory has two). Like other Asteraceae, the chicory is epigynous (that is, the lower cup is completely attached to the carpels). More specifically, the head is shaped like the dandelion – and blue.

I returned to my notes from the course, during which I had been introduced to hundreds of flowers and hundreds of flower words. Sometimes, the two worked well together – for example, we found ourselves in a rich fen surrounded by bog star, with its white, five-pointed flower, and admired it for a long time. Some of the people on the course had last seen the species six years ago, for others it was their first time. We took photos and kept saying things like, "How nice is that?" We hung around it for a while. As I wrote in my notebook later that day, "It was a special experience", because our presence and silence engendered a profoundly reflective atmosphere, the sort of feeling you might get looking at a newborn child or a work of art. Other times, word and plant came together slowly, thanks to a botanical key, magnifying glass, plucked specimens and long conversations between the people on the course, some of whom were seasoned veterans. Others were almost as green as me and our sight outpaced our language on the field trips. As touched on, a plant's being is way ahead of our ability to describe it. Early on, Peter had assured us that the language in *Dansk flora* is too complex for beginners, because "dark strings" or "usually" are relative descriptions, and may lead us down the wrong path. From that perspective, flower words often far surpassed our observations, despite the fine glossaries, drawings and comparative terms, which only experienced and diligent enthusiasts with a sense for schematics are able to produce. The schematics themselves seemed like a barrier rather than a bridge to understanding plants. How much time was I supposed to spend internalising this knowledge, which botanists have taken centuries to amass? And would doing so bring me closer to the plants or – at least at first – push me further away? Isn't that the curse of systematic knowledge? That it's based on generalisations[14] in which the individual lived experience of the elements disappears?

For biologists, the complications continue to stack up because classifications change all the time as new scientific findings are made, and because some plants are difficult to classify, so they have to make choices.[15] Linnaeus' system was based primarily on the number of stamens and carpels in the flower and endowed every organism with a two-part name consisting of genus and species. Modern biological classifications are based on Darwinian systematics. The daisy family, including chicory, are relatively simple, but in other families, the conditions are far more complex (paraphyletic or polyphyletic – try looking it up yourself!). During the shift from Linnaeus' system, in which the classification reflected only a morphological similarity, to the modern systems reflecting relationships of genera, animals and plants have switched places. To the fascination and annoyance of the plant community, familiar families, genera and species have been split into smaller units or merged into larger ones and assigned new names.

During the rest of my chicory studies, into which I inveigled my mother early on – she's a former librarian and plant friend and accompanied me on walks along the river where I live and other places we've wandered over the last couple of summers – I was disturbed to discover I've misunderstood chicory, and I'm not the only one. In a long list of links about chicory compiled by my mother, I found an article from the newspaper *Fyens Stiftstidende* in 2010.[16] Under the heading "A chicory isn't just a chicory" – which could also be the introduction to a philosophical treatise but in this case offers a useful overview for chicory beginners – the article quotes a reader, Laurits Larsen, who notes that "actually, there are as many as four *versions* of the plant":

1. The cultivated plant (*Radix cichorii*), a taproot plant that, when cut and dried, was used as a coffee substitute.
2. Endive (*Cichorium endivia*), a variety of common chicory produced using a special cultivation method and used in salads.
3. Wild chicory (*Cichorium intybus*), a fibrous root plant quite unsuitable for both of the purposes mentioned above.
4. Some chicory have white flowers.

It was seeds of the "wild chicory" – according to the seller's website, a *Cichorium intybus* – that I had bought and scattered in the garden, so it wasn't going to yield non-coffee or the salad I had intended to cultivate in a bucket by pulling out the roots the next autumn, covering it with sand and then waiting for light-yellow lettuce shoots to sprout. *Intybus*, I now know, was introduced from southern Europe – according to some sources, as a medicinal plant – so is not native. It was later *cultivated* as *Radix cichorii* and *Cichorium endivia*. According to the Danish Red List,[17] *intybus* is considered "not relevant". Nor was chicory one of the 112 plants about which I had diligently written notes during the course about Denmark's wild plants. Just as we passed hundreds of sorrels without anybody singling them out, and most of us didn't bother with the grasses at all, there are plant hierarchies everywhere, as a result of which some species are considered more visible and esteemed than others.

## wild expert

I decided to write to Rasmus Ejrnæs again and ask if he could help me out with the species question. Is there just one chicory, or several? He replied: "The cultural history of plants is not my area of expertise, but apothecary names have no scientific validity. As I understand it, chicory is used as a coffee substitute and to grow salad leaves. [...] However, I have some doubts whether it is the same species as our wild chicory or another species or subspecies."

I appreciated how open and generous Rasmus was and enthused by this lack of clarification about chicory and its cultural and classification history. What constitutes a species or subspecies remained an open question, even as the seeds in the soil were about to embark upon their secret metamorphosis.

During the opening debate at the Nature Meeting in Hirtshals in 2017, under the theme "Reason and feeling: Why is nature actually important?" Rasmus advocated buying up "genuine nature, the best nature", giving it to other species and letting nature decide, letting it manage itself. By mapping the diversity of Danish species, including in the Red List, he and his colleagues documented that many species – too many – were endangered.[18] "They have a right to be here, too, they're part of nature, just as nature is part of us – on a deep level," he added. After the debate,

I asked how this enthusiasm for "wild" nature started. He replied that it came from everyday family life. "The intense experience of birth, life and death," which he "extrapolated to other species". Just as we experience an intense alertness and sense of solidarity within the family in times of crisis, it is possible to have the same feeling with other species. As a biologist, Rasmus knew scientific work requires distance, but his long observations of plants, as mentioned in the previous chapter, had also given rise to a new sense of solidarity. That answer surprised me. I had intuitively associated "wild nature" with the first nature's separation of the human and the natural, but for Rasmus there was a connection – and mutual inspiration – between the human and the wild.

In the interview that followed, he elaborated on the connections. During his many years of observing plants, he has cultivated the ability to recognise hundreds of them, and over a thousand species of fungi. For example, he says, "last year an adders' tongue appeared in my garden. I'm pretty sure it was the first time, but it can live underground in a kind of fungal symbiosis for years. I think I know where it came from, because seven or eight years ago I did an experiment which involved taking some soil home, and I put it in the garden. All of a sudden, up it pops. It's interesting to live with nature, observe what it does, how it changes and how the species out there use each other."

Rasmus wants to find places in Denmark that retain "a little spontaneity", and actively seeks out "the pure and unadulterated". For example, one day, on his way to the local supermarket, he spotted a wrinkled peach mushroom in an old elm trunk on the forest floor. "The second wrinkled peach mushroom ever found in Denmark!" But he asserts that it needn't be such a rarity. If we abandoned the herding and gardening paradigm that characterises the way nature is managed in Denmark, we could have a flourishing diversity of species. In his book *Natur* (Nature), he writes about how, from a botanist's perspective, things are moving in the wrong direction, and reveals the flip side of the love of plants: "Once you open your senses and get to know species or good places in nature, you feel a sense of togetherness, and the extinction of species [...] inevitably feels like a sad loss."[19]

"What would it do to *us* if landscapes grew wild?" I asked. What if the "intentionally wild" movement, which Rasmus promotes in Danish gardens and public spaces, became the norm, and large swathes of our national parks were allowed to grow wild in a way that allowed large animals to create "variation in the ecosystems by grazing and trampling"?[20] Would the outer landscapes be the only thing that changed? What about our inner ones?

Rasmus pondered for a moment. "So we wouldn't be wandering in and out of the Garden of Eden, we'd be fully realising the wildness within all of us – and not just as a hobby or holiday project, but as a more permanent state? We'd be adopting the role of open, receptive witness in our daily lives, in research, and so on – as if we kind of discovered we were fully present, all the time, in the here and now?" he replied.

"Hmm," I said.

"The 'wild person' is slightly invisible. It's not something that's within reach. It's hard to picture," Rasmus added. He followed up with a proposal that echoed the sentiments of the beachgoers and birdwatchers: "We could be curious beings who seek out a nature that is nobody's and yet everyone's, i.e. we'd be allowed to go there. Just turn up and be curious about the animals, plants, senses and scents. A form of self-effacement that lets us be more at one with Creation. Discovering we're part of something bigger. Opening up to that possibility. It's something you can't force, it has to happen spontaneously. Once you let go, the door remains open. It's a form of surrendering to the fact you don't know what will happen. A process not confined to a single academic discipline but almost without limits. Less about identity and self-absorption, and more about what's going on around you."

Rasmus then went on to point out the ethical benefits this wild human would enjoy by indulging in curiosity and surrender: "I think it would be appropriate considering some of the challenges we face as human beings. Like sharing scarce resources with each other. It would be good to look out for others, not just ourselves. The wild person can engage with the other 40,000 species. That should keep us busy for a while."

I tried to picture it. What kind of policy would set aside land, money and time for human rewilding? What types of ethical practices would create space for other species? Having just embarked on my chicory journey, I wondered if there were other plant communities in which I could be re-created as a human being. Perhaps I could begin by finding like-minded people and inviting them to a chicory gathering, to chicory weekends, exploring the potential for other forms of curiosity and surrendering to wild studies, free from artificial limits set by academic disciplines.

Rasmus went on to describe how the world, as first nature, shouldn't just consist of "reserves that humans peer into". It should also be "nature reserves that allow us to understand the wild dimensions of human life". Other species could teach us to share, live and die – and understand that every single life is part of that process. "A lot of us would like our carcasses to be scavenged when we die," Rasmus said at another point, just in passing.

This image of dead people not rotting away six feet under or being reduced to ashes, but lying there waiting to be consumed (how, where and by whom?) – lodged itself in my head. We didn't dwell on the topic of death. But it kept rearing its head, as an unavoidable part of wild nature, an aspect far removed from the reductionist concept of nature as something pure and beautiful, something that makes us feel good. Rather, it is an image of a nutritious process of putrefaction, an inextricable part of the hunger, the endless cycle of consumption, which benefits plants and animals alike. It is an image that reflects the inbuilt fragility in the logic of the wild, third nature, the entanglements of which are both fascinating *and* frightening.

"If you let go of the urge to *do* something, it's like dying a little," said Rasmus. "It's a privilege, an egotistical thing, to exert mastery. It's scary if you don't *have* to do anything. It feels like dying a little while you're still alive. In that sense, I have a lot of respect for wild nature. We can't just be all spiritual about it. Take people who spend time alone in the wilderness. Sure, they might have spiritual moments, but mainly they're just really fucking hungry and lonely. Romanticising wild nature just isn't for me. I think we need to be realistic and say we will use the bulk of the landscape, because we need it to produce food and to transport us around the world." Since then, I've read on Facebook that Rasmus supports rewilding half of the planet.

Confronted with these concepts of the wild, my chicory experiment felt a bit threadbare. But then again, I thought, it would be a big ask for my first step to be to make the humble godsend from the roadside the subject of the wildest experiments. For the time being, there was no life to observe. Nonetheless, I felt eager to turn the nature reserve that was my garden into more than something I simply "peered into".

# the feeling, the movement

For a long time, the intybus I had sown, which I might have been able to make coffee with after all, seemed to have been a failure. Accustomed to disappointment in my horticultural improvisations, I instead felt glad, and thoughtful, about my rucola, poppies, cornflowers and borage. But then, one day in July, just after my holiday, I spotted a good-sized chicory with branches and six flowering heads. When the surprise abated, I began to think about how to proceed. I looked into whether the lower leaves, which range from feathery to roughly serrated, and the upper ones, which are unlobed and somewhat smaller, could be eaten, and whether the flowers could be used in salads, like those of borage. I read Inger Christensen's *Alphabet,* a catalogue of creation and annihilation – "the cicadas exist; chicory, chromium and lemon trees exist"[21] – and spent countless hours ruminating on how language and being reach out to each other. I hesitated for so long that my new approach might best be characterised as dwelling.

Every day, I would look at the chicory in different lights and through the magnifying glass. I saw that the anthers join together to form a tube, while the filaments are free of each other and attached to the corolla tube.[22] I ignored Hartigan's advice and didn't draw the plant, but took photos of all the details I could remember from the botany course: the stiff stems; the planed, coarsely notched leaves with coarse hairs; and the curves in the leaf axils, which are imprinted on the stem and visible at several stages, from small green bud to fully grown flower.

Like Hartigan, I didn't get the "feel for" the plant that I had hoped might become part of the relationship. Striking studies are being conducted on plants' intelligence and sensitivity, using complex arrays of sensors and tracers. Putting it in layman's terms, one scientist has described plants as akin to slow animals, able to hear, see, smell and react to whatever they perceive. But it's difficult to derive practical inspiration from these experiments, as I don't have the equipment. Daniel Chamovitz's popular book *What a Plant Knows* is a fascinating read, but it didn't lead me to a closer relationship either. Chamovitz says that plants see – not in pictures like humans (and some animals) – but leaves have a rudimentary vision and distinguish between red light (which has a long wavelength) and blue light (which is shortwave). They know whether light is coming from the right or left, *and* send messages to the stalk (which is blind), telling it to lean toward the light it needs.[23] In other words, my chicory can't tell me apart from other people but knows (as I do) when somebody casts a shadow over it and blocks the sun. The plant's photoreceptors detect that we are taking its food and it responds (albeit slowly) by emerging from the shade.

I reached out to other teachers. On one of my visits to Liv Tvermoes' little house by the sea, she passed a vase of red tulips, cradled the head of a flower in her hand and said, "You can talk to them." On a later visit, I asked what she had meant. She hesitated, seemed a bit impatient with me, as if I should know the answer. After a slightly awkward silence, which Liv seemed to accept as part of our collaboration, she said, "It just gives you something. When you see a tulip, it's red and then there's black bits and it's as if there's something that can move *and* be moved. *As if* we can talk to it. We can't, of course, but I can't help feeling we can, you know? We won't get a word out of it. Just that... unavoidable... sense that it's beautiful." Liv was searching for the right words but hadn't found anything better than to compare figurative language with spoken language. I was on the verge of asking her to elaborate, but she looked at me with an impatience that made me keep my mouth shut.[24] Since then, I have read anthropologist Nurit Bird-David's description of a hunter-gatherer people, the Nayaka of South India, which made me think of Liv. For the Nayaka, "talking with trees" means "to perceive what it does as one acts towards it, being aware concurrently of changes in oneself and the tree". According to Bird-David, talking to a tree means "expecting response and responding, growing into mutual responsiveness and [...] possibly into mutual responsibility". I will return to that later.

The inevitability to which Liv refers – that the tulip is beautiful and that something moves and is moved – is in itself a beautiful thought, perhaps even a theory of how exchanges take place between living beings. Rasmus would no doubt agree with her and support the aesthetic theory that "the beautiful" or "the lovely" is moving. According to Rasmus, paying attention to what is beautiful shouldn't be limited to special areas out in the wild, but should follow us indoors. "There is a beauty to good ingredients and good food properly prepared," he said. That plants can be "beautiful" was one of Liv's understatements, given that she found them anything from hysterically elegant to almost sublime. The chestnut tree outside her front door was a friend she talked to every day. If a guest plucked a dandelion from her lawn, she would be downright – albeit silently – aggrieved.

After getting to know Liv, her lingering by the window and the patient attention she paid to the everyday differences in the sea, I noted Chamovitz's insistence that plants and humans resemble each other on certain levels and realised that it is what is plant-like within us that the tulip and chicory move. The figurative language of flowers moves our vegetable existence – or, we might say: the vegetating mind. According to the American philosopher Jane Bennett, we can understand this vegetable kinship as "cross-body filiation."[25] I have no doubt that Liv felt a close connection with her tulips, dwelled on them, admired their creaking and colour, and sniffed at their distinct (if not particularly striking) scent.[26] It occurs to me now that on that particular day, she even looked like a tulip – with the shape of her face and red lips, and her light green clothes wrapped around her frail body. She absolutely embodied Kohn's ideas of figurative language and the basic sign processes shared by plants and humans, more so than botanical and floral language.

To vegetate is, paraphrased from the *Dictionary of the Danish Language*, "to live like a plant, especially eating, drinking, sleeping and nurturing one's bodily well-being without working, without being engaged in (great) physical or spiritual activity. To vegetate is to indulge in quiet enjoyment of life; to lead a vegetative existence; also used derogatorily as to be lazy and loaf about, as well as: to lead a life of leisure." The definition reflects the derogatory plant-identity politics to which Liv objected in her reserved manner. She told me how she sometimes met people who wanted to know what she did and what plans she had, and how she usually chose to hide the fact that she took their enquiries as an insult. She didn't *do* anything. She wasn't *busy* with anything. She had no *plans* at all. To dwell was captivating in itself.

For centuries, plants have been described as languid and lazy – traits strongly contested by the latest research, which has received considerable public attention in recent years. In fact, plants have a rich biochemical language (which forms the basis for myriad medicines), engage in multisensory communication and interact with their surroundings in ways that will undoubtedly end up surprising us in the future.[27] Some of them are even slow-moving predators, which lure and deceive their prey.

We don't always recognise these attributes, and it can take finely tuned instruments to detect some of the most advanced plant languages and perceive these vegetalising activities that green the world. There is a long way to go until, as the writer Ursula Le Guin has cunningly suggested, we are able to understand the sunflower – let alone speak fluent chicory or tulip. Nonetheless, she encourages us to keep trying.[28] With their many biochemical talents, multi-sensory impressions and highly generous contributions to the world, in the form of fibres, nutrients, poisons, symbiotic relationships with insects, each other and us – not to mention their mountains of carbohydrates – the history of plants is still young. Can we, their kin, approach them with humility and ingenuity, and learn more about them?

## the next year

Since the chicory is a perennial, I hoped that our relationship would endure. I drew up a list of ways to deepen my ecologising plant relationship over the following summer:

- I would see if I recognised the rosette if and when the chicory hopefully bloomed again. The seeds from the summer's single plant had spread across a large area. Perhaps more plants were on the way that hadn't flowered the first year.
- I would observe whether the flowers turn with the sun, like sunflowers.
- I would study which insects swarm around it, and whether some settle on the flower – a social relationship I had previously overlooked. A sub-task was to learn to tell the difference between bees and wasps.
- I would read up on photosynthesis and soil microbiology, going further than the pedagogical models that make it so difficult to understand the genesis and life processes of specific flowers.

- I would study the plant's taste, scent and biochemical qualities more systematically, and find out how best to harvest its seeds to ensure that it survives and grows again in the years to come.
- I would study in greater detail what it means to vegetate in a plant-like manner, and use other people's relationships with plants as a source of inspiration for questions regarding life span, intensity and community.
- I would experiment with new relationships to other plants and what they entail in terms of responsibilities. Plants have different needs for fertilisation, watering and pruning, and some require more space than others to thrive. Which plants displace other plants? And how could I create space?

Throughout the following spring, while pursuing my literary and practical studies, I checked the flower beds every day, waiting for my chicories. At first, I found it difficult to tell, given all the other plants here, but as the stems shot up with astonishing speed over the next few weeks, I was left in no doubt. Three chicories were on their way. They seemed to be thriving, and the buds started to grow as expected. In the days just before they flowered, I tried to guess which bud would bloom first. One day, during my regular observations, I spotted six other plants that I had flatly ruled out as chicory. The leaves were less jagged and not as bristly. They grew faster and didn't stop until they were taller than me.. This is unheard of – at least, according to the literature – which doesn't account for people running around sowing chicory in nutrient-rich garden soil.

I kept an eye on the buds, and almost convinced myself that the rampantly branching stems were chicory. I even tried to sneak a peek inside a bud, curious to know whether I'd see any hints of blue. I didn't. It was still early summer, but in recent weeks, the warm and sunny weather had spurred on the roses, berry bushes and herbs.

When I turned to look at the Love-in-the-Mist and borage in another bed, I suddenly saw a chicory popping out of the green. I felt like a birdwatcher finally spotting an osprey or a penduline tit. But then – what? Something new. A half-toppled plant *without* pinnatifid or rough leaves, "only" unlobed and somewhat smaller, had failed to attract my attention all spring. An ordinary foxglove (another plant with recognised medical talents) had sprung up next to it, one pink bell after another. Could this lanky newcomer be a *radix* that had snuck in between the *intybuses*? Had it literally popped up while my back was turned? By noon, it was bright blue, its head facing up towards the sun. It spent the whole day zigzagging in and out in search of light. As the sun set, the first flower heads, all white, unfurled, and then closed again as one. When the sun rose again, seven dark blue heads appeared. Another 270 buds were on their way, on this one plant alone. And I identified nine others. It was a chicory summer. Half wild, half dragged in, half shepherded.

I write like wind
that writes in water
with stylised monotony

or roll with the heavy
alphabet of waves
their threads of foam

write in air
as plants write
stalks and leaves

or loopingly as with flowers
in plumed circles
filaments dots

I write like the water's edge
writes a tideline
of seaweed and shells

*Alphabet*
Inger Christensen

helene

One April day in 2017, Bo Bang Petersen donned an old blue boiler suit, went out onto his stretch of coastline, on the hillside east of Tisvildeleje, and took a saw to the overgrown beach roses and sea buckthorn. As chair of the local coastal protection guild responsible for an 800-metre stretch from Tisvildeleje towards Helenekilde (Helene's Spring), he knows the history of this area and the dynamics of the beach and the water. All his life, he has observed how the sea has constantly transformed the coast, as have rainwater, spring water and the groundwater that seeps through the hill from the land behind.

Bo explained how he has spent years protecting sections of the hillside against plants like giant hogweed and Japanese knotweed. He pointed to a concrete wall at the bottom, built in 1929 and reinforced about 40 years ago, and at the scattered, decaying remains of old pilework. He explained how groynes are perpendicular to the coast, breakwaters parallel, and how the boulders in them are continuously replenished. Gesticulating and laughing, he made repeated references to past controversies between landowners and changes to the landscape since the Ice Age.

Organisations such as the Danish Society for Nature Conservation (DN) try to keep coasts "free" and "wild" under legislation from the 1930s,[1] as seen west of Tisvildeleje, on the stretch that leads past Melby Overdrev to Liseleje. However, countless types of coastal protection have emerged from a tangled web of partnerships involving landowners, local councils and government agencies, not to mention landowners' own DIY experiments.

Kneeling down, Bo drew lines in the sand, gesticulated and explained in a rapid-fire manner how to work with the hillside, and how official agencies and neighbours don't necessarily understand the dynamics. He told me that while we might think that the biggest threat comes from the sea, given the power of the crashing waves, you actually have to look the other way. He shot me a determined look: "These days, activities on land are the main threat to the hills." Reefs, waves, sand, rainwater runoff, currents, wave energy, conditions on the seabed, weather and the character of the cliffs change in ways not always predictable. The Danish Coastal Authority (DCA), the local council, other land-owners and the Danish Nature Agency (DNA) all do their best to understand the coast. Bo summarised their points of view one by one, alternately supporting and refuting their observations, assumptions and investments in fascines, wells, pilework and the many other technologies deployed to buttress the coast, pre-serve good sandy beaches and protect seafront properties owned by members of his guild.

We met again a few weeks later. I wanted to follow up on our chance meeting on the beach and hear how he was getting on with the article he told me he was writing on the history of the coast.[2] He agreed to show me the area around Helene's Spring and demonstrate the forces at work. As we walked along the beach towards the spring, Bo held forth on various episodes in the history of this spot, including the storm on New Year's Eve in 1921, which led to the founding of the guild; the effects of icy winters on the old pilework; and storm Bodil in 2013, which led to the collapse of most of the brand-new construction work at Helene's Spring.

Incidents like those teach us to be careful with language, and never take cause and effect lightly. According to Bo, the windy and wet conditions brought on by the storm had made visible what landowners, cloudbursts and the council had been preparing for – a hillside saturated with rainwater, its muddy open subsoil filled to the brim and starting to move. It's one thing for the sea to swell up in areas of (more or less) adequate coastal protection; it's quite another for a hillside to withstand the torrential downpours that come with storms. Without correctly laid, cleaned and maintained drainage, or if the reinforced areas are too big, the hillside becomes sodden, increasing the likelihood of landslides.

"I love my hillsides," Bo said, looking at me insistently again. Halfway along a path from the beach up towards Helenekilde Badehotel, we came across two granite basins, each approximately one-metre square, into which Helene's Spring ought to flow. At the bottom was a mushy, algae-filled liquid. A Danish Nature Agency poster proclaimed *Helene Helligkilde* (Helene's Holy Spring) the best-known of Denmark's approximately 700 holy springs. It stated that in the Middle Ages this was the site of "a big holy-spring market that attracted traders and guests from near and far", that the spring "may have been in use since ancient times" and that "the spring enjoyed royal protection under Christian IV [and] thousands came here seeking cures". The poster even encouraged people to drink the water: "Try it yourself [...] the water may still be enriched with special powers." The latter instruction may well have been somewhat tongue-in-cheek, and was definitely written before Storm Bodil, when leakage from the waterworks was added to the spring. Part of the plateau made of small boulders had slipped, revealing a jumble of protruding pipes, half-covered and half-uncovered stakes, patches of slimy clay, churned-up turf and bigger boulders temporarily frozen in mid-descent.

Two years later, I found myself back at Helene's Spring with the archaeologist Liv Appel to inspect the damage. Some residents think the devastation is bad for the town's brand. Liv introduced me to the convoluted bureaucracy surrounding the authorities' efforts to "preserve and present the ancient monument". For me, this spring had become what is known in Celtic mythology as "a thin place", somewhere you peek into another world – in Ireland, the world of the little people. Here, it is into the many worlds of Helene, as the hillside is sliced open, its guts brutally exposed – a stratigraphy of drainpipes and layers of soil. Why have so many stories spilt forth from this site? A little further inland, among the holiday homes, is *Helene Grav* (Helene's Tomb). References to Helene are found all over Tisvildeleje. The name is used for roads, holiday centres and the local school. Painters, journalists and writers have all helped to keep the story of Helene alive.

As we stood there, holding shards of red pottery from the reign of Christian IV', which Liv washed on the beach and took back to the museum to supplement its other finds – coins, potsherds and bits of crucifixes and crutches – I realised I felt like the amber-hunters down on the beach. As the Danish saying goes, "First the man takes the amber, then the amber takes the man." Helene had become a story I was now chasing and she had her claws in me. I followed her around in interviews, documents and books. For centuries, maybe even millennia, people have flocked to this place, attracted by the site and its history. Many of the historical traces have been wiped out, discarded or blown away, but there are a remarkable number of written sources describing miraculous healings and the midsummer markets. The church, kings and scholars have all been there and written their part of the story, too.

When Bo and I were looking at the basins, I asked him for his thoughts on the Helene legend. He pointed out a rock about 90 metres out in the water, west of the groyne. Legend has it that after Helene, a Swedish woman, was killed and thrown into the Sound, this rockrose up out of the waters to carry her body to Zealand. After the stone brought her ashore and laid her on the ground, the hillside opened up and a spring burst forth. At least that's one of the multiple versions of the legend.[3] Sometimes Helene is a young woman (a Scanian princess, to be exact); sometimes a widow with three children; or even one of those three siblings. She is killed in various different ways (except in at least one version she survives), and is often referred to as a saint. The spring always gushes from the hillside after she has come ashore. In the versions in which she dies, she sinks into the ground on the way to the cemetery at Tisvilde Church, often because the men carrying her (monks, farmers or fishermen) curse their burden. Bo's response was instant, "It's just a tall tale. Lots of places have them. But if the rock wasn't out there, we wouldn't be here."

As we stood there looking out over the water, I didn't realise I was about to embark on a prolonged magical history tour. But I knew from the work of other anthropologists that there is good reason to take the underground and its mythology seriously.[4] It tells stories from a time before the world was divided into nature and culture, a time when human beings weren't yet nature's stewards, hadn't positioned themselves at the centre of everything; back when everything was entangled – just as we now again see that they (and many other new things) are again.

## the helenes

It is true that Helene legends are found in many different places. In Sweden, England and many other European countries, stories of Helenes and springs flow together throughout history and have crystallised into a wealth of different types of texts. It is difficult to determine the exact order in which all of this happened. Stories of other women and springs have emerged all over the world. Humans and landscapes have been intertwined for millennia. As Bo said, "The Helene story and this rock are why we're standing here, in this spot." The power of tall tales is that they grab our attention with adventurous, counter-intuitive, improbable storylines, full of exaggeration. But we can also see them from different perspectives, via the people who tell them – and, as we'll see, via the people who would prefer they weren't told.

Bit by bit, I collected about a hundred texts about Helene and the spring. Some stories arguably predate the written word and have their origins in ancient animistic beliefs; others are modern, associated with the planned restoration of the site. The story spans thousands of years, and it all became a bit of a muddle, as I was doing other things at the time, too. I made it a habit to ask people in the area about Helene. At first, their responses were brief, even reticent. The stories didn't really mean much to Liv, for example.

"Do you know what the Helene story is about?" I asked, during one of our conversations.

"Nah," she said, "I don't. The legend just belongs here. You're told it's not true. But it sticks in your mind."

It sticks in the mind – but perhaps only just. Was the legend in danger of going round in circles, shrinking until it became an empty symbol, devoid of meaning?

The chair of a local association put it like this in *Tisvilde Nyt* in 2017: "We no longer believe in the healing power of the spring. But the Helene legend means her name and story still resonate, which is why so much is named after her and relates to her and her story. So how come we accept the rapidly decaying state of the Helene Spring?"[5] He suggested that, in the past, the spring and Helene were intertwined, but now they are drifting apart. It seems to me that Helene's meaning has changed. She has become a symbol of Tisvilde itself, almost disconnected from the imagery of the spring, the broken shards from which the water pours, while the sea crashes, crashes, crashes against the shore.[6]

The story, which some call a legend, myth or fable, is occasionally dusted off for marketing purposes. It is used to attract tourists to the town and was used recently as branding for the pilgrimage route *Tisvildevejen* – which, like many other such pilgrimage routes, is a new invention. By 2019, the site of the spring was a ruin and the tomb falling apart, crammed between holiday homes, identified only by a smudged DNA poster, but I started to find more signs of life from Helene. So keep an eye on how you think about myths, because stories can sink their claws into you. Good stories and myths are sometimes compared to viruses, and I dare say this one infected me.

## the myth, the water

From an anthropological point of view, ever since ancient people began to distance themselves from their old gods, there have been three main approaches to understanding the nature of myths and their function in various societies:[7]

- Myths have a historical basis and echo what remarkable people once did, or how imposing places affect people.
- Myths are a type of poem about the nature of human life and the forces, values and conditions that permeate it, such as love and death, and each generation retells the myth as it sees fit.
- Myths are stories that establish a cosmological order in which social hierarchies are defined and access to the sacred is restricted.

My own approach to Helene spans all three. However, this in itself raises a question – how can myths embody three such different meanings at one and the same time? There are many theories about that. One of the more promising ones, stressed by anthropologist Alfred Gell, is that myths are a kind of advertising, which in itself taps into an ancestral form of magical thinking we have never lost. It just takes new forms. Basically, adverts do the same as myths: portray an ideal scenario. On the Trobriand Islands in the Pacific Ocean, garden magic consists of long rhymes about the ideal garden.[8] Adverts present idealised forms of products, the implication being that "this beautiful car will transform you and your life".

Fresh spring water often comes with a story attached. Myths, legends and tall tales work together with the real world in this way. Magical stories heap one fantastic, ideal event on top of another, like a smart, "costless" technology, as Gell put it. A nature guide told me one day that he sometimes retells myths when he takes groups out into the countryside. For example, "If we have climbed Troll Hill and are looking down at the gnarled trees, the valley floor and the many plants, the path *through* the trolls is sometimes the quickest." The implication being that the trolls help generate the impression of a landscape that is alive, full of stories and strange creatures.

The beauty of myths is that multiple layers of meaning can be at work simultaneously. The myth can be perceived as a real story that refers to the past, as a good story living its own life here and now, and as a questionable account. For storytellers, listeners and interpreters, these three approaches to myths are like stage lights that sometimes shine together or in quick sequences, sometimes one at a time. But when we carefully observe our own way of thinking, e.g. when we hear a good joke, which is itself a kind of magic, we can feel each of the meanings constantly flickering on and off, in the blink of an eye. We know we're being seduced, absorbed into a picture, a meaning that seems natural and fixed one moment, completely imaginary the next.[9] Or vice versa. At first, a story may sound exaggerated or overly fantastical – and yet, despite our better judgement, it gradually worms its way under our skin. It's like sitting in the theatre watching stilted delivery and awkward gestures for the first few minutes, only to be swept away later on.

When I now look at all my many documents and how they link to other texts, Helene has turned out to be a cornucopia of myths, a concentrate of meanings that seep deep into Danish history, into time-honoured ideas about life and – as we will see – especially about women.

Archaeological excavations have shown that Helene's Spring has been on the verge of falling into the water before, but has been repeatedly rebuilt, fenced off and reshaped. Bo tells me, with detours tangents along the way, that an average of 1–2 metres of hillside have been lost every century. Perhaps the rest of the story will soon slide into the water, too. Perhaps the best view isn't the best asset of the hillside at Helene's Spring.

## on the name trail

Karl Erik Frederiksen is a journalist, a storyteller and the person who fed me the most clues about Helene along the way. He has spent his life collecting local myths and legends. They've fascinated him ever since his mum told him about her mother, who – when they slept in the same bed – would keep telling her stories about the headless person running around in the field, and how the two of them were equally scared. His dad was a driver who worked the area around Tisvilde, collecting dead animals. Karl Erik would sometimes accompany him to places like Ellemosen and Helene's Spring, and listen to his dad's stories.

One afternoon, we were at Karl Erik's place, close to the house where Ove Kunert painted the Helene story in 14 murals.[10]

Karl Erik has been collecting Helene stories for more than two decades. He's fascinated by Helene (and by many other Danish folk tales, like Slattenlangpat, King Valdemar's Ride, the Sea Bull, the Røde Ran treasure), and by the thought that these stories have been told, retold and changed constantly as people have made them their own. "Think of all those who have stood at Helene's Spring, looked at the source, tasted the water and swum out to the big rock. Their first thought wasn't that this feature of the landscape is the work of the Ice Age, or that the rock is a boulder from Sweden. That would be a bit thin," he says. "But if you use your imagination, you can see a woman has been lying on the rock. I've seen it myself."

Hunting for more versions of Helene story – and other good local tales – we met a couple of times at the Royal Library's reading room in Copenhagen. We were given a small trolley with piles of white cardboard folders, full of handwritten accounts, newspaper articles, transcripts from books and other material from the folklore archive. One of the things we found was a quote from the mid-20th-century professor and painter William Scharff: "Since ancient times, Tisvilde has been known beyond Denmark's borders for the great miracles that took place at St. Helene's tomb and at the spring with its healing waters [...] Even when my grandmother was young, many sick and crippled people came from far and wide to drink from the spring and rest on the grave on Midsummer night. She told me that many crutches and canes were left on the grave in the morning, as were wooden boards daubed with expressions of gratitude for miracle cures."[11] In other words, less than 200 years ago, Helene's Spring was both hospital and church, not to mention a marketplace – and, as we'll see, of great royal interest. All of this occurred in a pre-modern, pre-secular era, and it was all entangled with St Helene.

The first trail Karl Erik laid for me was the name. He had studied the question a few years earlier. He thought there had to be a Helene in the story somewhere, someone who inspired a story that has persisted ever since. There are many other Helene myths, ranging from the ancient Greek Helen, daughter of Zeus, to Helen of Constantinople (Emperor Constantine's mother, who destroyed the Temple of Venus erected over Jesus' tomb and was said to have acquired the cross itself), and many other versions of Helene around Europe. Karl Erik lists 13 other Helene springs in Denmark, as well as several in Italy, and he has visited one in Cyprus. Over the centuries, Helenes around the world, including in England and Scania, have made other springs burst open and miracles happen.[12]

However, there is some local history behind the myth. Liv Appel and two colleagues have been working with a hypothesis based on medieval archaeology,[13] in which the Helene story is part of a wider circle of legends based around the Sound between Denmark and Sweden, and inspired by shipwrecks and beach-combers known to people in the local fishing villages. They write that there are many parallels with Swedish legends, including stories of springs where bodies have washed ashore, and in which Helene is one of three siblings. Appel's assumption, therefore, is that the Helene legend is rooted in the local fishing communi-ties' medieval storytelling tradition, as well as a "pagan belief in the power of springs on the longest day of the year" dating back to ancient times. This tradition was perpetuated by the Catho-lic Church, which built a chapel (probably in the 15th century) where a relic may have been kept. In this way, it can also be assumed that Helene of Tisvilde was "originally identical" with Saint Helena of Skövde, who, according to a Swedish legend (the oldest known documentation of which dates from 1288), was attacked and killed by her son-in-law's relatives.[14]

All the names are enough to make you dizzy and want to study other historical sources, which indeed I have. As early as 1650, Erich Hansen wrote about this Swedish saint in *Fontinalia Sacra*. However, in 1919, Bering Liisberg, in *Domina Helena*, and later Michael Pers, in *Tro og kildevand* (Faith and Spring Water, 1999), rejected the theory, suggesting by way of multiple assumptions, that the Helene in question is completely different, and it would be better to follow a more local trail, one leading to the third wife of the famous and influential chief, Chancellor and crusader, Esbern Snare. After his death, and her illegitimate relationship with Valdemar II (Valdemar the Victorious), this Helene is believed to have fled and spent years "alone in St Karen's forest", which is thought to have been close to Helene's Tomb, and was "sought out as a holy woman", according to a local version of the legend. Acknowledging that he is venturing into the realm of pure make-believe, Bering Liisberg nonetheless entertains the idea that Helene, after giving birth to King Valdemar's son, fled in despair over her sins and sought penance in an ascetic life as a hermit in the forest. There, "loving hands" built a chapel with a "Mother of God" image, in which subsequent generations worshipped after drinking from the spring.[15]

So who was Helene – Swedish saint, Danish king's mistress, or someone else entirely? The truth is far from clear. But what counts, as Bo said, is how we look at it. What do we see if we look at it as a storyteller and feel the effect the story has on us? What if we perch on the slope and then swim out to the rock? Whether or not there was ever a real live Helene, she's unlikely to be the sole reason for the story. The name Helene has become entangled in the streets of Tisvildeleje, in seaside hotels and in the expectations of holidaymakers and people visiting the beach. The attempts to attach the name to a specific person turn into various nameless drowned women, historical figures about whom little is known but plenty of stories have been concocted, or any number of saints and ancient goddesses. We are the hillside on which the waves of history wash up – and flow through.

There's nothing wrong per se with all these fantastic ambiguities. Perhaps quite the contrary, as Karl Erik said. Definitions of reality tend to be less fixed under the stage lights. Humans have never been content to stick to "reality". We are able to imagine both the "impossible" and the "possible", and in doing so posit hypotheses about the uncertain, the potentially crucial. According to psychologists of religion, this cognitive mechanism developed during human evolution, and is useful for things other than religion – such as being able to assume that danger is near without being able to see, hear or otherwise sense its source (e.g. a lion lurking behind a bush). Although there have been many missteps along the way, in the long run, this capacity has ensured human survival.[16] In this way, people – some more than others[17] – seamlessly merge an imaginary "if" with the real "is", and weave the two so closely into the narrative that they appear to have never been separate or stood on their own. Today, we tend to think children are more naïve and impressionable than adults, but maybe we're wrong.[18]

## creation

During the fieldwork, I met Kim Huus, who has studied the history of religion, and I mentioned my research, including the Helene story. He told me he has been visiting Tisvilde all his life and has a deep and close relationship with the place. He loves Tisvildeleje, has spent all of his summer holidays there with his parents, in a holiday home on Sankt Helene Vej (St. Helene Road), and later bought his own holiday home in Holløse. And all that time he has been going to the forest and the beach. He especially loves the way it used to be – a small fishing village, with a long winding road down to the beach. When I ask him about the Helene story, he says he has always had "a veneration for the legend" and doesn't see it as "an old wives' tale". He has passed it on to his own children and grandchildren. When he first heard the story as a child, he was "all ears, it was fascinating, and as serious as Tirs væld", which is the name of another spring nearby

He notes that similar myths are found all over the world. "A young woman is born of the sea – for example, the fertility goddesses Aphrodite and Venus, but also many others. There are numerous myths about emerging from shapelessness. It's a form of Creation – one echoed, incidentally, in the ritual of baptism." Kim is referring to a research tradition that has discovered myths from every era and all over the world about the connections between women, water and the earth.

It is a tradition with strong critics among historians of religion and sociologists – not to mention anthropologists, many of whom even developed a whole theoretical phobia with regard to such studies in the early 20th century. However, I can't help but find broad comparisons that transcend cultural traditions utterly fascinating. Expanding on this idea, Kim refers to the historian of religion Mircea Eliade.[19] According to Eliade, creation myths are about how something "comes into being", and therefore how something "is" – whether the whole world or part of it – as a result of some kind of first act, usually involving beings (gods, heroes, holy women and men, etc.) who create "the first things" (worlds, crops, creatures, etc.). In these myths, great creative forces cause the world to exist in a "strong time". The myth is then restarted – like the engine it is – when it is re-enacted (celebrated, retold). In this way, myth links modern humankind to "the first time" or "all times", and the individual place to "the biggest place" (the cosmos, the world) at the creative centre of which stands the myth.

According to Kim, the story of Helene has clearly "bound the landscape together: the big rock, the source of the spring, the shrine and the chapel where Helene's Tomb now stands, and Tibirke Church, which itself is located by Tirs væld (another spring) and is the place to which the entourage heads". As a child, Kim cycled around all of the Helene roads. He ran up and down the hillside and walked the beach endlessly. The topography has become part of him and endowed him with an identity. Similarly, we might say that Helene, as a creation myth, has endowed this place – the hillside, the town, the whole area – with an identity. Albeit one hard to pin down.

The pier at the end of the winding road is very important, so much so that the locals raised a small fortune to rebuild it after it was almost washed out to sea. It speaks of other stories about other strong times in Tisvilde's history – about the harsh life of the fishermen and their boats, about waves, drownings and cold winters. Will Helene, the basins and her story be restored, too?

The anthropologist Keith Basso, citing Bakhtin, suggests calling such phenomena *chronotopes* – i.e. where specific times and places come together in linguistic expressions such as place names, but also accommodate specific times. In these time-place names, like Helene's Spring, stories become visible as objects of reflection that help shape people's images of themselves and the moral character they attempt to embody. In this way, they are taken as sources of wisdom.[20] Just as the myth creates the first time – in this case, when the rock rises from the sea, when the spring water gushes for the first time, when the source opens and the tomb is established – it also creates a link to these places for those who embrace the myth. They stand together in a world in the process of being created and continue to form themselves in new images.

Through the many visits to the spring over the centuries, perhaps most notably in the 1600s, but also before and after, Helene's Spring has persisted as a chronotope, where the story of the spring water has been retold, and the water has been drunk as the best and strongest of water – *water's water*, as it were, its pure essence. The tomb has, therefore, been visited because it is the source of Helene's creative power. In many versions of the story, told over the centuries, the spring water, the soil and the stone on the tomb are magical and life-giving. But eventually they lose their enchantment, leaving the basins and the tomb as relics, monuments to the power of the past. Several sources describe Tisvilde as "an *older* Lourdes" (my emphasis).[21] Echoes pop up in the repeated retelling, for example in Kim's account of his fascination. But in collective history, the power of the spring and the tomb have almost ebbed away, trickling into the ruins. The stage lights still flash, just, on and off – sometimes a lighthouse by which we can still navigate, at other times, a tragic but life-giving ghost that haunts the area. How come spring magic was so prevalent in the 17th century? And how did the lighthouse lose its power and become a vague flicker?

## protestant water

Most of the written sources about the history of Helene's Spring date from the 17th century onwards. There seems to be no doubt that the spring and tomb became a cultural institution during this period.[22] As Bo said, the hillside, the spring, the rock and the tomb have been elements in many "collaborations". Thousands of people visited Tisvilde in the 17th and 18th centuries, especially at Midsummer.[23] In those days, a ritualised practice of drinking from the spring and then visiting the tomb – or perhaps, in some cases, even sleeping there – seems to have arisen. For this ritual to have an effect, the visitors might even have to perform it three times, and perhaps take some of the water and soil home with them.

What the visitors experienced, who they were, and to whom they directed their hopes and thanks for their miraculous cures is open to question. We know very little about the specifics, and many people have tried to work out how the pilgrimage site survived the Reformation. As it turns out, Helene's Spring was the object of a tricky ecclesiastical balancing act.

In 1570, Frederick II issued the first decree forbidding superstitious reliance on the power of the springs.[24] Pilgrims were allowed to drink the water, but not to credit Helene with any beneficial effects. She was a Catholic saint after all, and at the time of the Reformation, saints were considered needless and idolatrous intercessory figures between man and God. The ban doesn't seem to have had the desired effect. In 1617, the bishop of Roskilde forbade "worship of Helle Lene [...]at said spring, including the raising of crosses bedecked in hair or fabrics in her honour""[25]. This Protestant scepticism about Catholic images of saints also resulted in the demolition of the 15th-century Catholic chapel at Helene's Tomb.[26] However, the Church didn't lose all interest in the spring water.

Later that year, the Bishop of Roskilde ordered that "the power found in the water be attributed to God".[27] The historian Jens Christian Johansen describes how visits to springs were permitted as long as there were no pagan rituals, such as those that took place at Midsummer, and as long as saints were not credited with any intervention. This acceptance was down to a recognition that spring water could have "natural" healing properties, e.g. for treating eye disease. As Arvidsson emphasises,

17th-century theology strongly prioritised Creation. God was seen to work through the healing powers he had bestowed upon the water.[28]

According to the Swedish theologian Bengt Arvidsson, who studies 17th-century theological history, there was a specifically Protestant water theology at the time, according to which the positive power of water derived from the Almighty himself. Water was thought to heal both body and soul, as it was part of Creation and the natural order of the world, created on the third day. As God's gift, the good spring water was, they said, an image of the soul and eternal life, the spiritual, living fountain of grace and salvation that is Christ.[29] Or, as one theologian saw it at the time: God, in his wisdom, made sure that every country had whatever remedies for illness they happened to need. As such, it was recommended that people refrained from expensive spa holidays abroad. Hansen, with typical national fervour, concluded that Helene's Spring reflected God's special love for Denmark.[30]

In an account written in 1647, Ole Worm – who was, among other things, Christian IV's physician – describes how there seemed to be more visitors to Tisvilde's spring than in previous years. Chronicling his visit to Tisvilde, Worm reports spending the night in the King's House and visiting the fenced-in King's Spring as His Majesty had developed a fondness for the waters – so much so that he had the road to Tisvilde extended so local farmers could bring water to him when he was unable to be there and bathe in it.[31] Worm goes on to say there were three springs (where there are now two), and he marks on a map several make-shift springs that had been dug on the hillside in an attempt to find their source. He also retells the story of St Helene, as told to him locally. According to Appel, Worm describes "how he saw at the springs crosses adorned with rags, ribbons and hair, as well as crutches, sticks and wheelbarrows left behind by the cured".[32] To this day, it is common to find rags, ribbons and hair at sacred trees and springs, symbolising that visitors have transferred what ailed them to the spring. The crutches, sticks and wheelbarrows serve as triumphant evidence of miraculous cures. Those who came here channelled their thoughts, suffering and hope into these objects.[33] It might be said that these objects collaborated with the visitors. The tangible was closely interwoven with the intangible. That is still the case today but, as a rule, the focus has shifted to new dominant narratives that fit in with the tale of how material riches are connected with spirit and power.

Worm says nothing about the King's opinion of the qualities of the spring, or whether they derived from the water itself, Helene or God. However, at the King's request, Worm studied the water and concluded it was of no better quality than other springs, but nor was it harmful. He never met anybody the spring had cured. Nevertheless, Christian IV bolstered popular belief in Helene's Spring by regularly visiting and taking the waters.[34]

While all sorts of different interests seemed to be converging on Helene's Spring in the 17th century, they started to diverge in the 18th. In 1769, Bishop Erik Pontoppidan wrote in the *Den Danske Atlas* (The Danish Atlas) that Helene's Spring, like others in the country, was still worshipped by simple souls with a "superstition descending from the Papacy". Pontoppidan doesn't deny the "cures still said to be taking place". However, it is worth noting that the reason for this is no longer attributed to the water being imbued with divine power. Instead, Pontoppidan emphasises that the journey, imagination, hope and trust may have added "a little or a lot" to the "mineral spring water". Referring to Dr Lange's *Lære om de naturlige vande* (About the Natural Waters) from 1756, Pontoppidan asserts that "good water", "pure and fresh air", "exercise" and "a calm mind" can "improve and cure" long-term weaknesses and physical defects.[35] The spring water was now pure in more than one sense. It was free not only of contamination (as eventually verified with the advent of the microscope), but also of idols and superstition – and even of the Almighty.

After this, the Helene tradition seems to have gone downhill, as illustratively described by Søren Kierkegaard upon visiting Tisvilde in 1835.[36] In *Journals and Papers*, he begins by describing how the sufferers may have sought out the mysticism of Helene's tomb. He finds it "altogether beautiful" that people deem it necessary to sleep on the grave. He then wonders why a tent had been set up opposite the site, "where there is revelling and carousing and where a few people have stationed themselves to mock those who come to inspect it". Here, he paints a scene in which the locals seem to have a sense of awe for the healing they say they have witnessed, and laud the place as somewhere worth visiting. At the same time, however, Kierkegaard thinks that because they are talking to him – and that he, by virtue of his appearance, may be assumed to have a different point of view – they also mock the idea of the spring, and assert that they do not have faith in it. Kierkegaard then notes that in order to maintain both views at once, the people insisted that any cure was at least in part due to divine intervention.

Unable to explain the cures, Kierkegaard says that "they push it away onto something more remote, just to be rid of it". In doing so, he says, they "make the matter curious" in order to attach "God's assistance" to it.[37] It had, nevertheless, long been official Church policy.

According to Kierkegaard's theology, God has, however, moved further away from the tangible nature of earth and water. In doing so, he elevates the idea of transcendence, making God what might be called hypertranscendent[38] – a God about whom we now claim to know nothing, a God we can only believe in as an assertion.

Not much of Helene remained, either. The water had no special power anymore and God was disappearing from history. The myth, like the place, had been slowly dismantled. In 1843, the painter Johan Lundbye wrote, with a mixture of empathy and indulgence, "there is something delightful about seeing sick people come from afar for the sake of a drink of water".[39] Hans Christian Jarløv[40] wrote that the crutches and crosses had been cleared from Helene's Tomb at Denmark's most famous sacred spring and hidden away in the attic of Tibirke Church in 1864. Henrik Cavling wrote in *Politiken* in 1886 that he saw two sick women at Helene's tomb on Midsummer's Eve, wrapped in blankets they had brought with them.[41]

The wooden building above one of the springs, as featured in a drawing by Jarløv,[42] was destroyed and removed after the Christmas storm of 1902. The three springs described by Worm were reduced to two, and several smaller springs on the bank, near the source, became overgrown and disappeared. Holiday homes shot up everywhere, and ever since the arrival of the first summer residents, and right up to today, the main attractions have been the beach, sea, forest and cafés on the main street. An undated brochure from the tourist association, which Liv Tvermoes had lying around, describes the Tisvildeleje seaside resort as a "world of beauty". It states that it is easy to get to Tisvildeleje on the Gribskov railway (which was extended to Tisvilde in 1924): "There were times," it says, with enough vagueness to add an air of the legendary, "when Tisvilde – just as it is now – was a place of pilgrimage and a destination for the many who needed to rebuild their faltering health." A tourist map I found at Liv's house refers to the faded past of "St Helene's Spring", describing it as "a kind of Danish Lourdes".

The spring is essentially dead – or almost completely dry. The dominant Protestant theology removed God from the water, just as he was removed from all other springs, trees, marshes, fens and heaths, and took up residence in a hypertranscendent "absolute other". Read both hypertranscendently and in theological terms, all of the birds and flowers in the hymn book, as well as the sea and the sky, are just images that lead to Our Lord on high. In this Lutheran theology, God is so transcendent that nothing of Him can be recognised or sensed. Religious experiences became unfashionable, the magical became romantic and self-absorbed, and credibility shifted to the Gospel story of Jesus emerging victorious, with baptismal water as the redeeming sacrament – at least, seen from the perspective of ecclesiastical history.

In one 17th-century version, Helene herself was on her way to the Church. In Swedish history, she was a saint. In local history, she was a beaten and repentant woman, due to her unholy dalliance with Valdemar the Victorious. In all of these tellings, Helene's Spring is also a Christian story, but it ends with both Helene and the spring being marginalised.

## the original femicide, universal ambivalence

Most texts don't overly emphasise Helene's womanhood. She is a person who transforms and sets free qualities of the landscape, who personifies the rock, spring water and earth. We can also look at this from the opposite perspective, in which the landscape has personal characteristics. Leaning into the words of the anthropologist Kirsten Hastrup, Helene's Spring has been "an ongoing conversation with an animated landscape".[43]

This animistic approach, according to which landscapes have the same inner qualities as people, is far removed from the perspective of the indoor person.[44] Few people give any thought to the inner lives of foxes, trees and cliffs, or their relationships to each other. The naturalistic worldview dominates.[45] We usually insist the human mind is unique and we don't share subjectivity with natural phenomena. However, we do differentiate by making the usual (and not-so-logical) caveats about dogs, horses and other farm animals who are not produced to be eaten, who we give names, personalities and life stories. Elsewhere in the world, animism has a stronger hold and manifests itself in practices such as shamans visiting, learning from and living with other species; and in legal contexts, with rivers, mountains and forests being granted rights as legal entities – an acknowledgement that their existence deserves representation and must be respected.[46] Might we imagine Helene's Spring having legal rights one day? Or perhaps the Gudenå River, the Danish territorial waters, roadside trees, amphibians or forests? We have rules and regulations for Danish landscapes, but no courts or conservation boards in which the land, water or trees are represented. If we did, how would it change our assumptions about human stewardship of nature?

Perhaps animism is making a comeback in new and different forms. At least, that is the claim of the religious historian Jens-André Herbener, who asserts in *Naturen er hellig* (Nature is Sacred) that we are on the cusp of an era in which "nature-loving pagans will return in large numbers", in the form of nature worshippers, indigenous peoples and green Christians who will reprioritise nature.[47] Perhaps they'll seek out Helene's Spring for inspiration, reach out to Helene. Or perhaps, as I will show in the next chapter, they will visit other threatened areas where new religiosities are emerging.

However, what I really wanted to address was Helene *the woman*. It was Kim, the historian of religion, who made me aware of the countless vegetation myths worldwide, in which crops (or other crucial sources of nourishment and wealth) flourish after a human sacrifice[48] – specifically, the original murder of a woman. What if Helene isn't just a Swede, saint, mother, sister or princess but a woman – indeed, the archetypal woman? If so, why is she killed, what's behind it, and how can anything good come from it? How can spring water and healing flow from a murder? And isn't this a very ancient crime or attack we're talking about?

The anthropologist Sherry B. Ortner argues that, all over the world, women are secondary. Although there are societies in which women have had a great deal of influence, Ortner says it doesn't alter the fact that, pretty much everywhere, women have been seen as closer to nature, while men are its primary and most important processors. The work done by men has also been valued more highly than that of women, who are either relegated to a completely marginal role or take on a mediating role between nature and culture – for example as child-bearers, more connected to the domestic sphere than men. In this way, Ortner says, the story is caught in a loop, confirming itself again and again, a loop that will only be broken by recognising men and women as equals in creative cultural history.[49]

In cases in which women have been marginalised, Ortner adds, it is no great surprise they are symbolised in a fundamentally ambivalent way: as impure, as a harlot or witch, as a princess, mother goddess or saviour, often all at the same time. The male has been defended and elevated as the norm, the female as deviant. In all ways. According to the legend, Helene throws herself from the coast, fleeing from a man – or his family – because she did something wrong, transgressed, and must be punished. And Helene, who is too heavy to carry, is elevated to nothing short of holy status. The myth transforms her from being persecuted and pushed to the edge, to landing on the other side and being celebrated, remembered and sanctified.

The ambivalence described by Ortner is most clearly and intensely expressed in the 17th century. In 1617, the same year in which the Bishop of Roskilde issued a ban on worshipping *Helle Lene* (Holy Lene), Christian IV issued his sorcery decree. As medieval historian Louise N. Kallestrup shows, the decree criminalised "good" or "white" magic, including Catholic protection and healing rituals (such as making the sign of the cross), which had previously been permitted. Healing magic was seen as "the beginning of something much worse, namely harmful magic and the pact with the devil".[50] The following five years, in particular, saw brutal persecution and a sharp rise in the number of women who were accused of witchcraft being put to death. Kallestrup's theory is that, in addition to the surge in Doomsday thinking of the time, and the fact that the King saw himself as a Lutheran householder charged with ensuring the safety of his subjects, the persecution was also driven by a personal and lifelong fear of certain women.[51] Christian IV, who bestowed honour and dignity on Helene's Spring and regularly took the waters there, was also personally responsible for instigating the witch trials.

The marginality of women can be traced further back in history – but the question is, how far? While Ortner says women have always been secondary, other traditions question that supposition. There is a whole literature that refers to ancient sources and scattered archaeological evidence of pre-Christian nature worship of Mother Earth. The philosopher and historian of science Aksel Haaning shows how this deification of women returns relatively briefly in 12th- and 13th-century philosophy and theology, in which the woman is seen as an image of the Mother of God, or *anima mundi*, a world soul – "as a source of growth in the plant kingdom, sensory ability in animals and knowledge in humans".[52]

From the 4th century onwards, it was a dictum of Christian faith, writes Haaning, that "Christians worship the Creator, not the Creation". By implication, we should not seek God in nature. As monks reached heathen territory, they cut down both the "Great Mother's shameful cult" (as the theologian Augustine put it in the 300s) and their sacred groves. As such, nature was considered to have suffered the same fall as humankind, and the view of nature became divided in two. On the one hand, nature triggered fear because it was destructive, unpredictable and seductive; on the other, nature was a testament to its creator, and as such triggered admiration and rapture. "This split," writes Haaning, "allows for an aggressive rejection of nature, an unconscious hatred, and on the other hand, an excessive and equally unconscious idyllicisation."[53] In this sense, Haaning agrees with Ortner's theory of ambivalence, but not that it is a universal constant. There have been other versions of history, too.

I consulted theologians about whether church historians had specifically addressed the meaning of springs in the transition to Christianity; and with archaeologists, about whether any research sheds light on what they meant in Bronze and Iron Age Scandinavia. The answer was that no such literature exists and it is uncertain whether the spring cult can be traced back further than the 17th century – and if so, how far. Countless finds have been made of Iron Age gold and other treasures in marginal locations such as marshes and rivers, and theories abound as to whether these were deposited for later use or were offerings to the gods. It is more likely that animal and human sacrifices (women, men and children) were part of an exchange with the higher powers. However, the springs have left no special traces.[54]

Instead, I was repeatedly referred to the books by the theologian Mads Lidegaard, which are considered highly unorthodox. Inspired by, among other things, the Roman author Tacitus' *Germania*, from circa 100 CE, which describes how the Germanic peoples (which can be assumed to include the Zealanders, i.e. people from the island on which Tisvilde and Copenhagen are found) collectively worshipped the motherly earth, Lidegaard collects folk tales from all over Denmark. To these, he links assumptions about an ancient Nordic cult, linked to, among others, the Romans' Terra Mater and the Greeks' Demeter, as examples of a larger complex of prehistoric beliefs in goddesses, in which the Earth is sacred and endowed with spirit.

According to Lidegaard, "nowhere in nature" was the Great Mother closer than in the spring as the crystal-clear, health-giving waters were deemed to gush forth directly from her groin. Lidegaard contends that behind Danish folk legends and belief in sacred stones and springs (and much more) lies the idea that the "great goddess Mother Earth" was "the mother of all deities among farmers from grey prehistory".[55] He believes that over the centuries, the ancient agriculture-based myths about Mother Earth have been reshaped, made taboo and resisted by male-dominated religions, such as the Judaeo-Christian nomadic faith and the Norse Ásatrú culture, which demonised the ancient goddesses of the Vanir, casting them as evil women and witches.[56]

It is a bold theory. Is Helene part of an ancient cosmological plot to systematically marginalise women? In the Christian context, the Virgin Mary, the mother of the Son of God, was denied a place in the Holy Trinity. As feminist theology has long since shown, Protestantism pushed women even further down the hierarchy and elevated humankind, in the image of the man, to the status of steward of Creation.

It is no great surprise that Mother Earth is still seen as having a role to play by both neo-heathens and a science-inspired philosophy that attempts to conceptualise ecological crises in new ways. James Lovelock, the British scientist, taking inspiration from the author William Golding, named the Earth's biosphere "Gaia". He asserts that Gaia is a "physiological system [that] appears to have the unconscious goal of regulating the climate and the chemistry at a comfortable state for life".[57] In this way, Lovelock turns to an old myth, which he terms a "metaphor", to bring scientific knowledge to life and convert it into responsibility. Lovelock writes: "Metaphor is important because to deal with, understand, and even ameliorate the fix we are now in over global change requires us to know the true nature of the Earth and imagine it as the largest living thing in the solar system, not something inanimate [...] Unless we see the Earth as a planet that behaves as if it were alive [...] we will lack the will to change our way of life and to understand that we have made it our greatest enemy."[58]

Is Gaia, as Helene once was, a reminder of an ecology in which the water, the sea, the sky, the birds, the plants and all the other creatures, microscopic and gigantic, living and dead, are best understood as being just as alive as human beings – which we easily understand as a combination of tangible matter and that intangible thing called spirit, personality or soul? Is the water – which bears aloft the heavy rock, which drowns, which heals – a reflection of a female Earth? The water that flows around the body and the body that floats on the water[59] may, therefore, still be worthy of myth. Helene was once the rocks produced by the Earth's eruptions. Helene was once the water that pours out of women and cliffs. If the abandoned, almost ruined Helene's

Spring, with its algae-filled water and entrails spilling out, has anything to offer in the modern era, it perhaps speaks mainly of our sick planet, on which the power of water now manifests in more frequent floods, poisoned wells and parched soil.

If the story of Helene were told today, it wouldn't be about evil Swedes, beachcombers or cruel kings, and would only peripherally concern the Church, which lost interest in forms of nature other than the human and, in some versions, suspected women of dangerous sexuality. Nor would the new myth be about witches or queens. Instead, perhaps, it would be about how magical and animistic language is a way of talking about and sensing the fullness of life and the crushing power of the world around us. It would be about the landscapes, with their rocks, hillsides, springs and groves, which don't belong to us, but include us nevertheless. I think it would be about how we leave it to our children to have a glowing, magical faith in the world when they play with the water, the pebbles and all the other life on the beach. About how we don't want to see the darkness in the way they and we toy so violently with the planet's forces. About how Bo and all the other coastal people work tirelessly to look after their local hillsides, while sea levels continue to rise globally. About how Liv and other beach people look out at the awesome forces of the sea and sky and sense their own mortality. And about how Kim once found a dead woman on the shore; how people live and die in this way, eventually sinking into the living Earth, because a person can only be borne by water for so long. There are always people who are beached – sometimes in the light, sometimes in the dark.

Helene's Tomb, which used to overlook fields and woods, perhaps Karen's Forest, is now squeezed into a bend in the road on Sankt Helene Vej. A small circle of stones with a wooden door marks the unassuming entrance. A few larger stones here may have once served as the foundations of the old 15th-century chapel. Karl Erik told me one day that he had once seen women at the tomb on Midsummer, but didn't know what they were doing. Meditating perhaps. I could always ask around, he said. Several times, I have considered visiting Tisvilde at Midsummer, in search of further traces of Helene. I have also considered following the whole Midsummer trail more consistently through history, tracing ideas about this particularly powerful solstice, the bonfires, the witch burnings, and more. Despite the many remaining loose ends, I decided to curtail my Helene mania and dim the stage lights.

In most versions, the story of Helene, Helle Lene or St Lenis is a gruesome tale of death, violence and an indefatigable will to live, despite everything. As Karl Erik warned me, "Once you know a story, you can tell it in five minutes or 60." He has invited me to tell the story along with him one day. Perhaps, as Kim said when we talked about myths, it can be retold, re-enchanted, in a new way that speaks of Tisvildeleje's unique qualities. Perhaps it can show how there is not as much difference between the human and the non-human as modern narratives would have us believe.

Many legends are out there, slumbering in the landscape. Perhaps the path through them, the semi-magical path, is sometimes a shorter and more effective form of ecologising, in which water and earth are not just resources or part of the world around us, but flow through us, as they flowed through Helene.

So here is my story, Karl-Erik.

"Once upon a time, there was a woman who was furious and unhappy with how people treated her, which alternated between persecution and idolisation. Eventually, she couldn't spend even a moment alone without shadows pursuing her and every sound being terrifying. She ran about, zigzagging between her accusers, lungs burning and feet torn to shreds. When she reached the sea, she slipped into its dark green depths. At the bottom, a colossus let her rest on it, as if on a wing. Once she had calmed down, the two of them sailed on, entwined, through the waves. The water washed over the woman's weightless body and through her insides with rolling nausea, as she floated between life and death. The night was dark, the ships floated on the horizon, unapproachable, and a mist drifted across the surface, boiling and steaming, on the one night of the year when the warm western waters mixed with the cold eastern currents.

The next morning, a man who had been out fishing but caught nothing was packing up his gear. A winter swimmer from Copenhagen had just jettisoned her dressing gown. An estate agent was out walking with her demons. An outdoor kindergarten on a trip swarmed down the slope to the beach. They collected diamonds and sand-hoppers and played with the sugary sand. 'Look, a fairy,' they said. 'Do you want to play the cat and the old lady?' The adults make no attempt to shield them from the elements because the children had grown robust from being outside all winter, on the 'windy' (as they called the beach). They had seen all sorts of small animals, some of which they had put in their 'nature box', while others were squashed between cold fingers.

The fairy was so still that the children lost patience. When one of them found some diamonds in the washed-up seaweed, they flocked together. The man who had been fishing had seen beachcombers before, but nothing like this. As a boy, he had seen a woman on the shore, naked as a fish, while out for a morning walk. He had grabbed hold of her, realised how cold she was, and ran all the way home to call the police. Later, he read about the woman's sad life, and how her dreams had shown her that 'in the sea, you vanish if you go the wrong way'. He froze at this image, and at the next one, from a summer's day when a child of the same age drowned at the pier. Everyone stood there, huddled together. They didn't realise time was standing still until it hiccupped back into action.

'She's dead,' said the estate agent. It was an uncomfortable situation, but she didn't let it bother her. 'We need to get the poor woman on land and cover her up.' She waded out into the water. With the angler's help, she pulled the woman up above the seaweed line. It started to rain as they looked at the disturbing sight – her body with seaweed wrapped around her ears, sand in the corner of her mouth, and blood-dark hues on her skin. The man didn't think she looked totally dead. The Copenhagener no longer felt like a swim.

A retired engineer came running down the stairs. He'd seen the huddled group from the hillside and realised something was wrong. 'Have you called a doctor?' he asked. His shirt was already soaking wet. Water dripped down their faces. Nobody answered. They were watching water trickle from the woman's mouth, hands, feet and loins. Veins sprang from her body of water, extending onto the beach, mixing with the seawater and the water trickling down the hillside.

The engineer turned towards the hill. Then out to sea. He spun around in disbelief once more. Water was converging from everywhere. As the waves grew bigger, more water poured from the hillside. The distance between the grains of sand grew wider and wider under their feet. They were sinking in it, up to their ankles, as the land began to slide. Large, shapeless clumps of trees, grass and drainpipes. And the waves lapped them up. The estate agent took off her jacket and ordered the others to help move the woman and lay her out on it. Half-stumbling, half-sinking, arm and leg muscles on fire, they dragged the woman away from the shore, through sand, lumps of clay, old shards of pottery, rotten thanksgiving crosses and the boulders that had formed the old spring basin. Behind them, the hills, the sea and the rain formed a single, indiscernible mass.

When they were on solid ground, further up Slugtvejen, the vicar approached. He liked to walk in wild weather because it helped attune his mind. At the grocer's, he had bumped into an atheist writer with whom he liked to converse because clever ironies intertwined so beautifully beneath their umbrellas – even if they had to shout at each other through the wind. Both tried to avoid staring at the woman lying in front of them. They were struck dumb by the nakedness, the water running from her body and the uncertainty. Gusts of wind whipped up the sea even more violently, tossing around branches of trees and the contents of overturned rubbish bins, forming crazy shapes. The engineer understood that the rain was now forging wide rivers of water that not only snaked along the asphalt but permeated it, cascading down through the grey gravel. He converted the flow to cubic metres per second while his recurring nightmare – waves engulfing his family's holiday home – came true. The man from Copenhagen saw his car swim away before he became too cold to see anything.

A minute or so later, the estate agent, angler, engineer, vicar and writer ran as fast as they could up Solvej, towards Sankt Helene Vej. There, they met the outdoor kindergarten, sporting their rainwear and rubber boots, on their way to their minibus. They also met the journalist, who had been sent home from work with a broken foot. It was difficult to understand their disjointed story. Everyone was talking over each other and had their own version. But he knew right away that Helene had returned. Since then, the journalist has been trying to piece the story together. And this is how he told it to me.

Helene vanished in the landslide behind them, and there she still lies. The new views and the hillside have calmed down again. The rock lies below sea level. You haven't truly visited Tisvilde if you haven't stood on it. Every year, children place diamonds and sandhoppers on Helene's Tomb. Each time, they fill their water bottles with fresh magic water before running down the slope to play with the sugary sand. Every year, people in Tisvilde dream of the sea that gives and the sea that takes, of the bowels of the earth and all its dark stories. Because the water in their bodies remembers everything."[60]

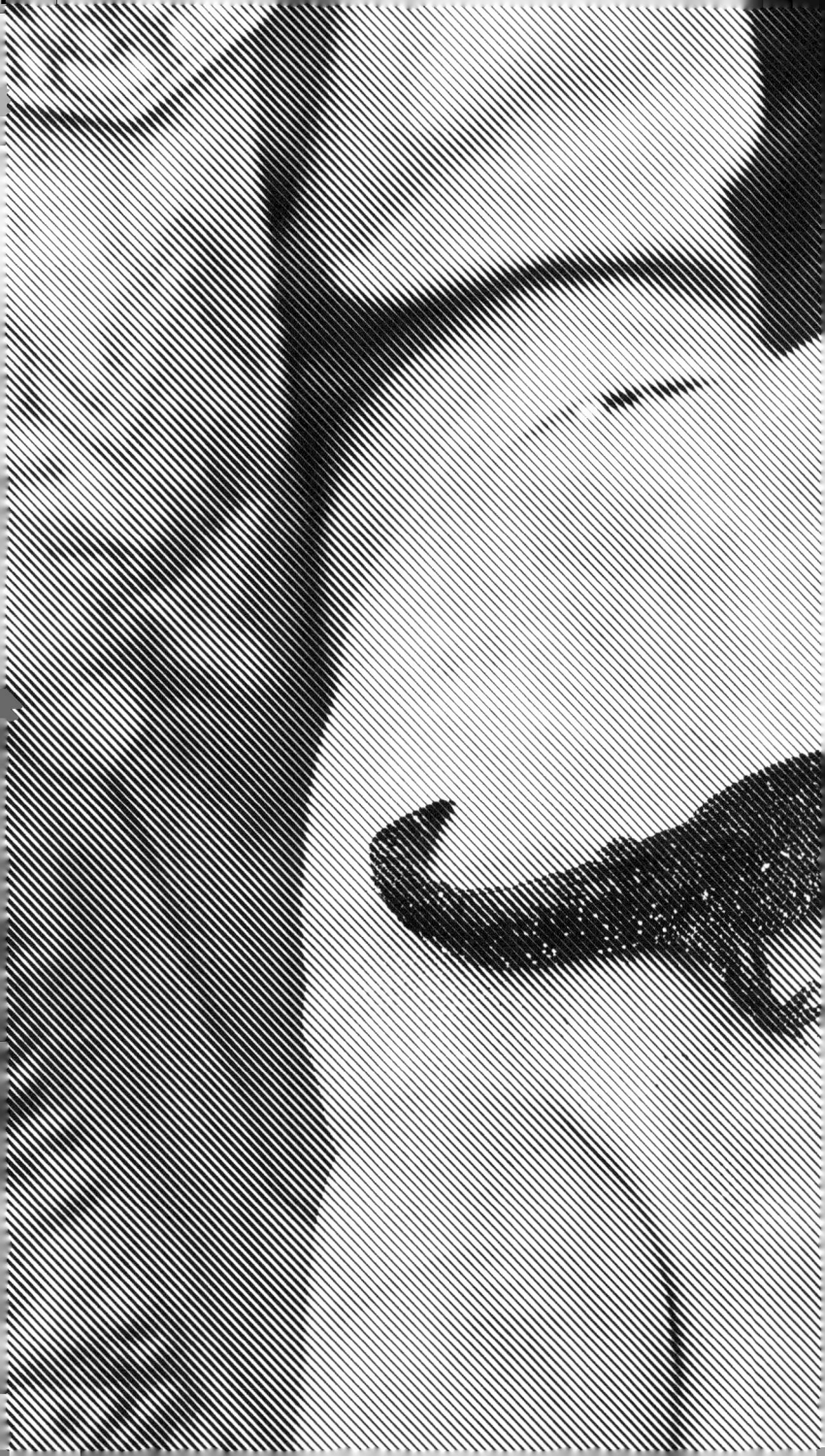

the common

As part of the fieldwork, I kept an eye out for examples of how different groups of people try to help remodel outdoor nature by changing the way their surroundings are managed or establishing new communities. As mentioned, I began by looking at the New Nordic Coast – a project at Gilleleje that never came to fruition – before I sought out the beach people, the bird people, the plant people, the myth people and many more. I followed the work of the Aarhus Biologists, my term for a group that includes Rasmus Ejrnæs and Morten D.D. Hansen,[1] who work on biodiversity and nature management and believe far more of Denmark's landmass should be given over to wild nature.

The Aarhus Biologists have made their presence felt in a range of restoration projects, especially the Mols Laboratory research station, where wild horses "have to live on plants, bushes and trees", in biodiversity research, in large-scale outreach projects aimed at promoting knowledge of the most common species, and in online debate forums, especially on Facebook. In the chapters "jizz" and "plant blind", I described how Rasmus not only associates wild nature with its own intrinsic richness and beauty, but also with places where people "can learn spiritually". As a researcher, he moves more freely than most scientists, transcending domains normally separated by the norms dictated by the History of Big Differences. For example, he finds it "highly problematic that we deprive production animals of so many of their essential life functions". They're not allowed to form herds, move about, mate, produce offspring – "nor are they allowed to die a natural death".

The reality is that the animals aren't allowed to do these things in the Mols Laboratory either, as current legislation sets limits on wildness: "As our animals are *domestic* under Danish law, we are obliged to put them down and send them to the knacker's. So we do. We'd prefer to leave them out for scavengers like foxes, ravens and carrion beetles – but that would be illegal."[2] According to the Aarhus Biologists, Denmark's landscapes are, with few exceptions, subject to a management paradigm that regulates everything and is based on human needs. Leaving dying and dead animals lying in the wild for the good of biodiversity violates the animal welfare principles that apply to animals behind fences and under human supervision. For Rasmus, these limitations prevent an understanding not only of the conditions for animal life, but also of "our own nature", because it fails to acknowledge how connected we are to "wild nature".

## we live here

In 2019, I began closely following the dispute over the Beach Meadow (Strandengen) on Amager Fælled (Amager Common), on the edge of a new neighbourhood on the island of Amager, south-east Copenhagen. It seemed to me that, like the Aarhus Biologists, Amager Fælleds Venner (Friends of Amager Common, or AFV) were at the centre of something new. They were shaking up the concept of nature in a way that resonated. Until 2020, when they became an actual organisation, AFV was just a loose group of locals protesting against development on the Common, construction projects and homes for humans rather than the creatures who already "lived there" – a term AFV has often used. The slogan "We live here" is usually seen and heard on their marches, demonstrations and other actions. But the "we" in question isn't human. The placards feature drawings of Morris's wainscot moth, the lark, the great crested newt and many other inhabitants of the Common, to which AFV has endeavoured to "give a voice", and presents them not just as natural history phenomena, as creatures that have their habitats on the common, but also as voices in "our" democracy.

Nature lovers, community groups and neighbours have often protested against plans to domesticate new tracts of land. The heaths, beaches, forests and marshes have long had their advocates – in fact, it could be argued that every square metre is being fought over, all over the country. The Danish Society for Nature Conservation was set up in 1911 to promote conservation and public access. Since 1937, when the right to pursue conservation cases was brought in, it has described itself as "the voice of nature" and encouraged others to play similar roles. Over the years, the Society has also had to address the question of which nature should have a voice, a topic that has sparked public controversy during elections for the top post in the organisation. Is the main purpose to preserve "good" first nature, or is it to manage second nature, for example, by promoting particular cultural landscapes or organic farming?[3]

According to the Society, approximately 15% of Denmark is currently "covered by nature", but "in reality, only about 0.5% of the landmass is protected by law and managed in ways that promote biodiversity and not used for commercial production".[4] "Real nature" accounts for less than 1% of the total landmass, which is widely regarded as a world record low, and Denmark is frequently compared to Bangladesh and the Netherlands in that regard. All of the other European countries have much larger proportions of "real nature".

The Society's desire to spread the voices of the "under-1%-nature" is in line with the work of the Aarhus Biologists and the Friends of Amager Common, who want to secure areas for what they often call "cool nature". For them, the "best nature" consists of areas with the potential to be rewilded and become "nature's own party venue" or "the real adventure". They ask whether we can afford it, though. Or should everything be part of one big budget and be streamlined and ultra-efficient?

The Society recommends that 30% of the national land-mass be allocated to nature, two-thirds of it as a "nature zone" for biodiversity purposes without any production considerations.[5] The idea is to fence in whole areas and introduce large grazing animals that will knock down certain trees, dig up the soil in specific ways, and otherwise create a diverse landscape with habitats for multiple species. Instead of humans herding, hunting and tending, the idea is to create an ecological system reminiscent of a time before humankind dominated the landscape – apart from the fact that virtually all of the large predators have disappeared. The Aarhus Biologists and Friends of Amager Common share the basic idea that humans need to make room for other species. In their experience, if you let outdoor nature take care of itself, it won't be long before even the most domesticated areas are rewilded.

## the wolf question

In recent years, the most heated discussions at the annual Nature Meeting in Hirtshals, at which nature managers, educators, foundations, associations, biologists and politicians meet to swap ideas and engage in lively debate, have concerned the issue of fencing in wild grazers like bison and horses. What are the benefits, and is it fair to restrict public access to only a few gates? Horse riders and dog owners predict that enclosures with wild horses will be dangerous. Numerous arguments against fencing have been made on aesthetic, biological and local-history grounds, including that it is a contradiction to enclose "wild nature" in reserves.[6]

A 2017 report published by the Danish Board of Technology showed that if you take all of the already adopted plans and targets and combine them with expectations for future initiatives, it would account for 130–140% of the Danish landmass.[7] Similarly, the Danish Nature Agency's map of state forests and the other areas it manages suggests that more space might well be on the wish list of the oak and beech, spruce and black woodpecker, otter and maples, larch and cormorants, beavers and mountain bikers, night jars and roe deer, pearl-bordered fritillary and European stonechat, ant lions and outdoor nurseries – not to mention thousands of other species and groups.

The wolf, which returned to Denmark around 2012 after an absence of a couple of centuries, is a whole debate on its own. Does it have a role to play in promoting a more diverse ecology in Denmark? Could its presence help change the way we think about our place in the world? Or is the wolf still an enemy? Wolves, wild boars and many other (re)introduced species attract attention and have been met with everything from calls to exterminate them again to pleas for humans to make room and expand our understanding of what ecological spaces might accommodate.

The wolf issue is a good way of posing difficult questions. Is the wolf part of first nature, but a species that we no longer classify as native, and therefore eligible to be eradicated again? Or should the wolf be deemed worthy of conservation and fenced in, as something with intrinsic, wild value? Is the wolf a part of our second nature, a species we can try to live with – albeit sometimes as difficult neighbours? Would the numbers need to be monitored and regulated? Would the state be prepared to compensate the owners of lambs and sheep eaten by wolves? Or is the wolf part of the third nature, where humans don't take precedence, a species with which we have to make room and share space? Does doing away with everything dangerous also do away with all that is glorious? If humans were prey, might it

172

spur greater respect for other species, as we find our place in a wider ecological community?

It is hard to get to grips with the third nature. As a concept, like the wolf, it poses questions about familiar boundaries between the human and the natural. The idea assumes that ecological crises, climate change and dramatic declines in biodiversity will force people to rethink their place in the world. It heralds difficult transitions and reorientations. But all around the world, ideas are also emerging about how this new world might take shape. At global summits, in major economic foundations and in the world of science, there are visible signs of a shift in priorities, and of longer-term plans for new infrastructure that will reverse climate change and promote new energy sources. Big technocratic systems are being introduced, and calls for innovation and redistribution are getting louder. The wolf *has* arrived.

## the battle for the beach meadow and the lark plain

I spent a couple of years following the Friends of Amager Common in the media and on Facebook. In 2019, I took part in *Arternes Optog* (the Species Procession) and attended some of the many public hearings about the common. Along with some of my anthropology students, I also followed the setting up of the NGO Embassy of Species. Frej Schmedes, one of the people behind AFV, launched the initiative in Copenhagen in autumn 2019. At the time, *Arternes Ambassade* (the Embassy of Species) already had branches in Aarhus (in collaboration with the Natural History Museum) and in several other towns and cities. The Aarhus Embassy describes its purpose as follows: "The ambassador's role is to give the species a voice in the day-to-day debate. We attend public meetings, engage with the media and organise our own events. The idea is to make nature part of democracy."[8]

I found it interesting that the participants envisaged plants and animals becoming more active voices in democracy, part of a democratically oriented ecology, as seen elsewhere in the world and achieved by various different means. For example, rivers have been made legal entities, which gives them a voice.[9] This new organisation, too, claimed to represent the "voices of nature", and found innovative ways to listen to and manifest those voices. Inspired by this, I asked several groups of students if we should investigate the potential for new ways of ecologising.

We collected material about the start of the Embassy of Species and the "*Kampen om Strandengen*" (Battle for the Beach Meadow). Some of the students focused on technological solutions to climate change, regenerative agriculture or alternative outdoor experiences, such as forest kindergartens, and the philosophical bird, mushroom and moss tours organised by a student chaplain at the University of Copenhagen. Others turned their attention to recycling cafes, climate activism and vegetarianism. I focused on the Beach Meadow on Amager Common, which a diverse group of people and associations had been vigorously defending for years.

In September 2017, a majority on the City of Copenhagen Council voted to abandon the plan to build 2,400 homes on 18 hectares of the Beach Meadow. In March 2016, AFV had reformed after a few dormant years. By the turning point in 2017, its Facebook group had almost 9,000 active users.[10] It had coordinated a series of meetings and actions, including waste collection, petitions, demonstrations, a human chain, participated in public consultations by nature conservancy boards, and organised bioblitzes (a more or less systematic identification of species in a specific area by experts and amateurs). Some of the events were organised along with the Danish Ornithological Society and the Danish Society for Nature Conservation, and after 2017, with organisations like Noah[11] and the brand-new Embassy of Species. From 2019 onwards, Extinction Rebellion was also involved. A broad coalition formed and its activities attracted enough people to spark media interest.

In autumn 2020, the AFV Facebook group reached 14,000 members. It had been turned into an actual association and took part in the protest against the construction of the "Camping Ground". Even though a new conservation order was issued for the Beach Meadow and construction work cancelled, they didn't celebrate it as a victory because they knew round two would start any day, according to Frej, one of the key figures in the AFV coordination group. The area close to the Beach Meadow had been earmarked for a new neighbourhood with approximately 2,000 homes. The project was part of the City of Copenhagen's efforts to pay off a DKK 1.9 billion debt incurred building its new Metro system.[12]

The local plan had specified that the spot would be the location of a campsite as well as the existing youth hostel. It included a reclaimed area previously used by the armed forces and for landfill – several metres of urban soil had been dumped there in 1974. The City of Copenhagen assessed it as having a "poor to moderate natural state".[13] According to the panel making the decision, the site was "barely even a landscape". These statements were read out at a meeting in the hostel in autumn 2019. At the same event, the chair of the committee described the area as "a bare field" where architects could "run amok". However, AFV called it Lærkesletten (the Lark Plain) and described it as a fantastic habitat with red-listed species, as well as a beautiful and distinctive part of Amager Common: "Here, you can meet birds that are rare in the city such as the skylark, lapwing and common snipe, as well as songbirds that fly in from tropical Africa, such as the whitethroat, chiffchaff and nightingale."

The Battle of Lark Plain had commenced. One side considered the area virtually worthless. The other considered it invaluably rich in species, despite its somewhat mixed history – as a forgotten landfill site into which plants and animals had moved. AFV set out to document the extent to which "nature" had returned, but also how the Lark Plain had taken root in the lives of Copenhageners, EU circulars and dreams of new species-rich communities.

The architects who won the competition named the site *Fælledby* (Common Town). In autumn 2019, they presented it as "a sustainable building project, close to nature, with a modern pond", a neighbourhood built in wood full of natural habitats, which will improve conditions for plants and animals. The committee was unanimous, describing the development as "convincing" and "visionary",[14] and the developers By & Havn (Town & Port) called it "exciting" and "innovative".[15] AFV condemned these statements as greenwashing and the project as "an extreme violation of nature on Amager Common".[16] Every time plans have been made for housing on the Common, AFV's response has been (quoting from various Facebook posts) that it would destroy "a unique oasis", leading to the loss of "a small piece of the miracle of life", "a pearl in the middle of the capital", "an orchestra of life", "a small pocket of our natural history", "natural heritage" and "our children's green lung".

In the run-up to the 2017 local elections, AFV adopted the slogan "We are the voice of nature" and plastered it on digital platforms, placards, banners and more. The military orchid, the moor frog, Morris's wainscot, the common twayblade, snow parsley, the lark and the great crested newt were all drawn into the democratic process by their human allies, who acted as the voice of these species. "Nature needs *your voice*. We must tell our politicians that they cannot solve the challenges facing

Copenhagen by building nature away." Votes were mobilised for Amager Common.

## feral common

Environmental studies has a long-standing tradition of taking an interest in commons and how they are managed. All over the world, people have banded together to manage communal resources, working together in innumerable ways, with results ranging from tragic overexploitation[17] to dynamic systems that work well and have firm roots in the social and cosmological order.[18] The concept of "the common" has changed over the centuries. It was originally a place where villagers kept animals, a kind of shared grazing area. As the History of Big Differences progressed, livestock moved to the countryside, and the common became a place associated primarily with people's use, much like "society" in general.

A major shift is currently underway in the cultural and social sciences. Under headings like "interspecies studies", "the-more-than-human" and "lively ethnographies", an avalanche of studies are broadening their scope to include plants, places and animals in order to arrive at new conceptualisations of how phenomena previously considered separate in modern thinking – as individuals, species and objects – are connected to each other in living, dynamic networks and interwoven communities. The focus is on plants as social actors that engage in exchanges and form societies with other plants, minerals, animals and humans. The precious mushroom matsutake, for example, can't be cultivated by industrial monoculture, but it thrives in interspecies collaborations in pine forests.[19] Other studies focus on how humans forge communities with mountains and the underground,[20] animals[21] and plants.[22]

Feral patches like Amager Common have attracted particular attention in recent years. Just as biologists know that abandoned gravel pits, polluted industrial sites and even sites contaminated by uranium can turn into astonishingly species-rich places in a matter of mere decades, cultural studies have paid greater attention to how abandoned areas, in particular the scars left behind by industrialisation and capitalism, can tell new stories.[23] Grim tales of abandoned mines, pollution, overexploited landscapes, epidemics that nearly annihilated indigenous populations and invasive species that have ravaged entire ecologies. However, they are also stories of life defiantly reinventing itself, living on in new "monstrous forms", haunted by the "ghosts" of both the past and the future.[24] And they are stories of regenerative practices, of new forms of agriculture, of farmers who insist it's possible to develop new practices that sustainably rebuild depleted soil by cultivating more-than-human communities.[25]

The third nature's view is that, despite the ecological crises, we need to be curious, and get used to the fact that the terrible *and* frightening also accommodates the weird and wonderful. In the book *Arts of Living on a Damaged Planet*, the ghosts of our time are the disruptive and destructive forces seen again and again in damaged ecologies. The plough's traces on the landscape are like a ghost haunting the upturned, levelled and depleted earth. Plants that can no longer proliferate are haunted, as the animals that spread their seeds no longer exist. Their ecology is disrupted. Proponents of the third concept of nature ask us to look around the landscapes and notice the ghosts: failed reclamation attempts, straightened rivers stripped of life, industrial complexes ripping chalk, sand, soil, stone, limestone, granite and peat from the ground, and factories that buried the toxins that continue to haunt the landscapes. Abandoned landfill and military sites, too. In some parts of Amager Common, a whole stratigraphy of ghosts is hidden beneath the grasses, sea buck-thorn and hawthorn.

The third concept of nature also asks us to be aware of the modern world's monsters, i.e. the symbiotic entanglements between humans and the world. Some have become ferocious, like invasive jellyfish and diseases caused by pollution, conta-gion and accelerated mutations. Symbiotic entanglements have always been a part of species' interconnected lives. Some sustain life, like intestinal bacteria that allow us to build an immune system, and the co-operation between certain flowers and ants, or between particular fungi and trees. However, many of them destroy life. The message of the third nature's crisis awareness is that human survival depends on learning how best to live and die with these entanglements.[26]

Ever since life began, there have always been monsters. But modernity tried to banish them by thinking in terms of individ-uals, isolated species and siloed production systems. The story of monstrousness focuses not on industrial agriculture's revo-lutions, in the form of crop yields, but on how the cultivation of monocrops and the interbreeding of farm animals enables the flourishing of parasites, antibiotic-resistant bacteria and harmful diseases. The message is that crises force us to observe our sur-roundings carefully and tell the monstrous, "non-secular" sto-ries.[27] Ghosts and monsters are part of the new metaphysics of the third nature that is emerging from the shadows of modernity.

Gone are the big stories about how we can meet nature and become one with it in unique moments of sublime tranquillity. Gone are the stories that suggest it's in untouched, protected recreational areas that we find real nature and our true selves. In literary contexts, this was the modern world's most romantic story about itself – the individual and the great unspoilt nature mirroring each other in stories of greatness and conquest. But now, according to the third nature, we need to look the other way. Just like with Helene: Don't look at the sea, when everything is happening on the hillside. Look at the undermining of nature's foundations by inappropriate car parks, inadequate coastal protection and landfill sites that can only retain vegetation in a fragile topsoil in "good" weather, not in "bad" weather – as the monstrous storms are called. But the storms, too, are just doing their job – as a result of the Sun and the greenhouse effect doing theirs – otherwise they wouldn't happen. Storms stir things up and transport huge amounts of sediment, which both breaks down and builds up coastlines. Storms blow down trees that provide shelter for other forms of life.

Look at Amager Common. Most of it is a relatively recent addition to the map, framed by motorways, the Metro, the airport, residential neighbourhoods, petrol stations, incinerators and water treatment plants. The Common was created by isostatic uplift, storms, land-reclamation projects and mountains of rubbish, in conjunction with the plants and animals that have taken up residence in this new nature, side by side with an old salt marsh. First, second and third nature are closely intertwined.

## orchid perspective

Nikolaj Kirk is a member of AFV's coordinating group, a TV chef and, according to the daily newspaper *Politiken*, in the "premier league of public debate".[28] In spring and summer 2017, he posted a nature serial on Facebook called "Frank Jensen and Amager Common", referring to the then Mayor of Copenhagen. In one of the videos, he walks around the Salt Meadow, attempting to interview some of the creatures about their views of the plans for new homes. They are conspicuously silent and don't want to talk. Earlier in the year, on 19 February, Kirk wrote: "Nature doesn't speak for itself. We speak for it. Preserve Amager Common. It's up to us."

In the videos, Kirk says he is "on the Beach Meadow". He doesn't expect Frank Jensen to watch every episode, but the personal and direct nature of the messaging and the silent testimony of the Common's residents is quite compelling. On 15 June, he says: "It's Wednesday evening, and I'm here on the Beach Meadow on Amager Common again. [Kirk then talks about where the Beach Meadow is – in case Frank Jensen doesn't know – while the camera pans.] It [here] is a central spot on the Beach Meadow [The camera is now down at grass level, with a purple flower in focus, and Kirk crouching just behind it.] This is the Southern marsh orchid, one of the orchid species protected in Denmark, and it actually grows here on the Beach Meadow. And, dear Mayor, dear Frank, this is proof that the Beach Meadow is full of biodiversity, full of important forms of nature, not just for Copenhagen, but for the whole of Denmark. This heath, this meadow, is very special to our city. It's our green lung. It's our life. That's why we're all in this together. Over 42,000 people have now signed a petition to preserve this tiny *little amazing flower, man* [said with extra emphasis] among other things. You can still be the mayor who said: 'I'll take up the gauntlet, find the courage, the will. I will move this building project.'"

Over the next few months, Kirk addresses the mayor in many more videos – in one, he places a photograph of Jensen among the thistles and willow-leaved fleabane. Kirk appeals to local people who feel connected to the 5,000-year-old story of the Salt Meadow, to its scents, colours and lovely, exotic orchids, the red-listed snow parsley, the utterly beautiful burnet moth, reed warblers, strawberry clover, nightingales, falcons and owls. One day in August, he finds frogs that have been run over by caterpillar-tracked vehicles during By & Havn's surveys. As usual, he turns to the mayor, asking for help to stop "the slaughter of one of our country's finest species".

In March 2017, Kirk speaks from the perspective of a plant: "Hi, I'm a snow parsley. I look a bit like a wild carrot or something. But I'm not. I don't live many places in Denmark. I actually only live on Amager, exactly where Jakob Hougaard, spokesman on nature for the Social Democrats, wants to build. By & Havn say they want to move me. But they can't. I'm pretty sad about it, because, I mean, where am I supposed to go? DO I JUST DIE?" And on 29 March, referring to the Bella Sky Hotel visible from the Beach Meadow: "Dear Frank Jensen. Should the hare move to a hotel when you've replaced its natural habitat with concrete buildings...?"

The voice of nature also directly addressed two other Social Democrats, Jakob Hougaard, the party's spokesperson for the environment on the Copenhagen City Council, and Mette Frederiksen, the Prime Minister. Hougaard responded on Facebook by calling Kirk's videos "ridiculous puppet theatre" and that he had no wish to debate with "a massive wall of one-sidedness". He asserted that Kirk wants to preserve what Hougaard calls "some totally unimportant mushrooms and beetles on an overgrown part of the Common nobody uses".[29] Instead, the money should be spent on infrastructure and public services for local people, which are "far more important".

But the puppet theatre prevailed in the first skirmish of the Battle of Amager Common.

## other materialities

One summer day in 2019, I was out on the Common a couple of times to meet Terese Verbena. On her Facebook page *Året rundt på Amager Fælled* (All Year Round on Amager Common), she regularly posted about ash, cormorants, buzzards, teasel, wood ear fungus, the wood mouse, blackbirds, the Wych elm, fieldfare, eranthis, water shrews, mute swans, the willow tree, common ivy, winter gnats, long-tailed tits, toads, great diving beetles, sweet violet, the common cowslip, the greater bee-fly and hundreds of other species. She says it all began as a daily Christmas advent calendar on AFV's Facebook page one December, and then became her form of activism, sharing knowledge about the wildlife we might bump into out on the Common.

Soon after Terese developed an interest in plants, she twigged that they're slower than us, so she had to slow down, too. "I came at it from the same place as everybody else. It was all just green, and I only knew the most common plants." Despite trying hard, she had found it impossible to learn about plants from books alone. Only when she started to wander the Common slowly, with books as aids, examining one plant after another, did the landscape open up and come alive. "It was alive already, of course, but now it came alive in a way I could understand." In her experience, if you want to know more about plants, start in your garden or a park, and take your time. Start by walking slowly, stopping – and maybe sitting down for a while. It has taken her a few years to get there. It takes patience, but it is rewarded. You also need to dare to use your intuition when it comes to the plants – taking an interest in the ones you keep seeing, for example, spending time with them and trying to see whether the plants (and animals) around you aren't just as exciting as lions and elephants.

I followed Terese down one of the narrow paths to the Common, just opposite the DR Byen Metro station. St John's wort was out, waybread lay flat on the paths, willows bent over the water, tall aspens shimmered silver and green in the breeze. Vetch – one of the first plants I learned to recognise on the botany course – were entangled in the dry, waving grasses. Terese went from plant to plant and seemed to greet them silently, sometimes touching them lightly. As if they were friends. Which they were. Traipsing after her, I was completely amazed at the effect her example had on my experience, as I attempted to strike up my own friendship with the plants. I wandered around as if watching a film. I wasn't, of course, but I felt as if my senses were strangely heightened. It was an exceptionally beautiful day – dry, the light shimmering, the colours sharp. Everything was lush. I thought back to that wet November day when I had cycled here – when it was all wet, yellow, foggy and muddy – and found it difficult to see the Common as a green lung. The busy roads, shooting range, airport and traffic were deafening, the views of the residential neighbourhoods and Bella Sky were at odds with the cold, muddy common.

I didn't see everything Terese saw, of course, but it was fascinating just strolling slowly instead of walking briskly, just the idea the Common was teeming with plants, from white clover to red clover, each with a life of its own, a habitat of its own, living beings we can approach with respect and with a vulnerable desire to be welcomed. "It really was as if everything was transformed," I wrote in my notebook. I could recall the feeling long afterwards. I walked around like Hans Christian Andersen, wandering from one magical story to another. The year before, it had been the birds and the sea. After being trained by Susanne and the others, I became hugely excited if greylag geese came cawing across the garden, or if I caught a brief glimpse of the kingfisher by the river. Similarly, after spending hours with Liv, it made me breathless just looking out over the sea and closely observing the waves and how the light constantly changes, moment by moment, on the many refracted surfaces. All of this happened without it necessarily being the same stories that are told, without it being exactly the same magic.

"I'm part of the Friends of Amager Common coordination group," Terese told me on our way back to the Metro, "but I don't have political contacts, and I worry whether anybody is going to turn up for the meetings we arrange. So I don't think I have much to offer, other than talking about some of the plants." I asked if it would be wrong to say we can fall in love with plants. I recalled a botanist once telling me he had an "erotic relationship with nature", and that he felt attracted to the plants, the colours, the scents and the astonishing variation in even the most frugal of plants. "It depends who you speak to," Terese replied. "I suspect I'd be sectioned if I talked about it to the wrong people at the wrong time. My relationship with plants isn't just decorative."

On *All Year Round on Amager Common*, Terese doesn't just present natural history facts associated with each plant. To convey her feelings for these living beings, she refers to fiction, folklore, 17th-century flora catalogues and medical traditions that have been verified and perpetuated to varying degrees by the pharmaceutical industry. She describes the elder tree as incredibly generous: "In early summer, she nourishes insects with her beautiful white umbels, and we get to taste a little, too." She goes on to say that the elder germinates easily and "grows in the strangest places, like gutters and hollows in other trees. If you're ever lucky enough to stumble across one of those small elders that have never had roots in the ground, ask it for a branch because a branch of a flying elder contains great magic."

These images come easily to Terese. We try to compare imaginations. Mine is only nurtured by prolonged training, compelling films, long novels, or through people like Terese, Liv, Karl Erik, Kim and Susanne leading the way. Terese is quick to come up with a good short story about plants. She pictures it and acknowledges that stories have the power to make the world as alive as it actually is, in ways that defy the tendency to naturalise and objectify the world she sees around her. That's why she carefully selects the stories she tells and urges great caution. Many plants, even on the common, are poisonous. That's precisely why, in some cases, they can have medicinal effects in small doses, and have been biochemically replicated. They're so alive they can kill, naturally.

### friends of the great crested newt

you dragon in hiding
clear water, visible
standing still in it
between prehistory and democracy
[...]
you old dragon in my spine
you, Nordic
of the earth
and water
mini-
giant,
big,
newt
fire under water.

In November 2019, Frej Schmedes recited the poem "*Ild under vandet*" (Fire under Water) at the opening of the Embassy of the Species in Copenhagen. Dressed in a white shirt and dark-green blazer, the 40-year-old cameraman read his verse out loud, visibly moved and nervous. He had just been appointed ambassador for his "beloved great crested newt".[30] The audience clapped and cheered. Frej has known the great crested newt since he was a boy, and always really liked them. He knows exactly where to find them on Amager Common, the conditions on which they depend, what they eat, how they reproduce, and how they develop from aquatic creatures with gills to walking on land and growing lungs. He has filmed the newt's whole life cycle, and follows their year on the Common. The great crested newt reminds him of dragons and dinosaurs, of adventure and life, of primeval times and the great tree of evolution, which we can feel in our spine. With its hands, feet and fingers, it resembles us, too. He is also familiar with the political and legal life of the great crested newt, as a protected Annex IV species in the EU Habitats Directive. The great crested newt lives in the waterholes on the Beach Meadow and Lark Plain. It's found in the centre of the water column, hiding in the growth among the plants and hunting insects – at least when it isn't hibernating in an old tree or under a randomly abandoned rag.

At the same event, several other ambassadors were announced for their favourite species – swift, goat moth, common lizard, rat, sea buckthorn, wasp spider, common twayblade, snowdrop, fox. In attendance were friends of the ambassadors, AFV activists and a small group of anthropological fieldworkers. The latter were attracted by the Embassy's political vision of "breaking the species-ecocentric worldview", as well as the ambassadors' direct declarations of love for species that many might otherwise consider insignificant. They use forms of communication that are both poetic and political and known from other Anthropocene-era representations of human relationships with the world around us.

The ambassadors wore ribbons with an emblem illustrating their species, all elaborately homemade and painted by Frej and the fox ambassador. Natural wine and snacks were served.

Birdsong and chirping played on the sound system. A camera crew from the free state Christiania's[31] TV team filmed the proceedings. People dressed up for the occasion, with several of the ambassadors decked out as their species. The three ambassadors from Aarhus represented green climbing ivy, glittering dragonfly and the bright lime tree.

Some of the ambassadors' speeches were anecdotes about their political convictions. Frej was one of two ambassadors to devote a poem to their species. The swift ambassador, Grete Sonne, rewrote a Steen Steensen Blicher poem from the early 19th century. The new version portrayed how a swift senses the city. The increasing trend of building houses with smooth glass-concrete façades makes it difficult for the swift to build nests. The species ambassadors' job is to raise awareness of practical issues like that, things that arise from interaction between humans and other species.

## the people of the species-rich community

According to Frej, the great crested newt is a "dragon from primeval times" and people are "young monkeys" screwing up the world. His relationship with the newt is the basis for his critique of humanity and its futile efforts to "tame the wild". In subsequent interviews with Frej, we repeatedly circle around what kind of people he thinks should form part of "species-rich communities" like those on Amager Common and in life in general. He prefers to talk about "species-rich" communities rather than biodiversity, which he thinks signals a colder, more scientific, taxonomical approach. While he sympathises with the sober cataloguing of species – for example, a 2014 survey on Amager Common found 290 plant species and 159 insect species in 49 sub-areas[32] – and recognises such inventories are important political tools, his passion lies elsewhere. He is more concerned with questions about living in a species-rich community and exploring how human beings, as "nature", are completely interwoven with the lives of the other species.

"We *are* nature," says Frej. "We're landscapes, too, and harbour many other species – bacteria, fungal spores, all sorts. The screaming naked ape is so busy positioning himself as *above* and *apart from* the world and has such a hard time letting go of that narrative that we keep concocting stories about how we are so much better than the other species and have eternal life." As you might imagine, Frej has a strained relationship with Christianity, not least because he finds it overly anthropocentric. People have used it to "elevate themselves above other species" and end up "alienated". He reiterates, "We are nature. We get eaten. We are no *more* than other species, even though there is a hierarchy."

I asked Frej what it means to live in "symbiosis with nature", his preferred term for the relationship to which he aspires. Putting the answers together, I arrive at this list, a kind of "wild ethics". Living in "symbiosis with nature" consists of the following:

– Using our senses, something every child can do, but most forget because urban culture is so appealing and direct we have to filter our impressions. "In nature, you have to open up your senses, wait and see." This teaches us patience and provides a necessary calm, a "rootedness". Whenever I've joined Frej on the Common to look for newts, it hasn't been the kind of outdoor experience people enjoy while hiking a trail. We've gone around in circles trying to pinpoint where newts might be living now, in which ponds and thickets, and what they might be doing. Are they still hibernating? Have the adults

woken up and headed to the watering holes? How far
have they gone?

- Getting to know the species, attending their "school" and
  understanding how brilliant they are, the complexity of
  their life cycles and chain reactions, as well as how much
  we need the other species. Evolution has churned out
  many creatures as complex as humans, albeit without us
  necessarily realising it. Going to other species' schools is
  humbling because there are so many things they can do
  that we can't
- Recognising ourselves in them because there is a sense of
  kinship that means we feel our shared family tree and like
  and care for our community, which a sense of belonging
  makes us want to protect.
- Having respect for other species and understanding that
  when we leave the city, we are leaving our homes and
  visiting theirs.
- Replacing hunting and farming techniques that are far too
  exploitative with mutually beneficial relationships, like
  those that exist between all kinds of fungi, trees, animals
  and plants.
- Working to ensure that other species, even seemingly
  insignificant ones, have habitats of their own and are allowed to live in them, which involves acknowledging that
  death and decay are necessities in parks and forests, that
  without them all of the life cycles will grind to a halt.

The points above are Frej's and not necessarily shared by everybody in AFV or other champions of biodiversity. The same goes
for his suggestions for change: More and more people should
move to the countryside and acknowledge that humankind cannot live alone. Farming techniques should enhance the soil and

support life cycles, while providing benefits for human beings. The school system should undergo a revolution with the introduction of holistic subjects, as part of which children learn about and take responsibility for other species, and – if they're on our menu – learn how to kill them. Like all political movements, the fight for Amager Common involves an assortment of voices.

Nikolaj Kirk's "Voices from the Beach Meadow" usually revolved around the other creatures as wonderful per se, and as delightful companions for the city's children. Kirk saw it as a democratic fight, and made a direct man-to-man appeal to Frank Jensen, suggesting he could be more of a hero than Kirk among the friends of the Common. Terese combined her botanical skills with a historically inspired animistic love story, while the metamorphoses of the newt connected Frej to a primeval time, full of potential for new forms of coexistence.

"The great crested newt is the past, from before we became Christians, and it's still here. Alive and kicking. It's like us, so we can connect to a primordial time, and to a nature we need and crave but have lost touch with. It lets us mirror ourselves in the wild, which we have a mythological relationship with because it's a dragon. Dragons fly and breathe fire. It is our primeval nature. It connects us to poetry, fairytales and to a mythology of nature that's true. It's no lie. It's the real shit. The real fairy story is here. It is. The real fairy tale with the dragon. It lives out here."

## dark- green enchantments

According to the American scholar of religion Bron Taylor, who conducts research into the spiritual traditions and philosophical foundations of green activist movements, a "dark green religion" has emerged since the 1960s, transcending what I have previously called naturalistic and animistic ways of worlding. He characterises it as a movement based on a "sense of belonging and connection with nature" and the belief that the Earth and its living systems are sacred, which *also* means they have value independent of humans. However, from Taylor's perspective, the idea that humans must, therefore, make space for nature, withdraw and respectfully consider it for its own sake makes this religion "dark", because it puts human welfare and rights second.[33]

"Religion" is his umbrella term for ideas and practices that connect people to what they value, depend on and hold sacred.[34] To his way of thinking, religion is about values – and includes not only traditional religions, but also spiritual practices and scientifically inspired representations. When established faith communities issue declarations in favour of a greener planet and respect for Mother Earth and Creation, or when activist groups fight for nature's own rights, they fall within a spectrum of (to use Taylor's terminology) more or less dark- green religiosity.

He argues that much of the dark-green creativity has emerged from a value system based on a kinship felt with the rest of life, often stemming from a Darwinian understanding that all life has a common origin. With this sense of family come feelings of humility and a critique of ideas about the moral superiority of humans, often inspired or reinforced by a scientific understanding of how incredibly little space humanity takes up in the history of the universe. The interconnectedness of everything on Earth is a metaphysical idea based on scientific knowledge of the subtle feedback mechanisms of ecological systems and the interdependence of different species.[35]

Taylor argues that the concept of religion isn't crucial to him, because people understand it in so many different ways, but he deploys it to compare phenomena that would otherwise be on opposing sides in the History of Big Differences. Gaia theory, for example (the creator of which, James Lovelock, is an avowed agnostic), is dark-green because Gaia's needs must always come before those of humankind. But while Lovelock himself sees no reason why this ethic needs a theistic basis, he does like to use religious metaphors, such as the Earth being our "home", "that we are all part of Gaia's family", and that our lost "love and empathy for nature must be renewed". He also asserts that our children should have an "instinctive belief in Gaia". Although religious metaphors and fables have their limitations, they inspire an intuitive understanding of God, and so Lovelock welcomes attempts to reconcile Gaian thinking with traditional religion. Areas of commonality such as these lead Taylor to say that the dark-green values are expressions of religion, regardless of whether the religious concepts are metaphorical or not.[36]

What other concepts might we apply here instead of religion? Enchantment is one possibility.[37] Frej suggested "mythological thinking", Rasmus favoured "the spiritual", and Terese's story revolved around "the magical". A dark-green thread runs through all of these concepts, and through ideas about how we can gain insights into valuing nature, the Earth and other species not only highly, but higher than humans. The nature enthusiasts, environmentalists and climate activists I've met have different ideas regarding exactly how it would all play out. In the next chapter, I will talk about how the shades of green vary greatly, and how values and care are seen mainly as matters of personal ethics, or are expressed as political convictions and activism.

## the diversity of (bio)diversity

In the preamble to the Convention on Biological Diversity (CBD) signed in Rio de Janeiro in 1993, the contracting parties acknowledge that they are "conscious of the intrinsic value of biological diversity and of the ecological, genetic, social, economic, scientific, educational, cultural, recreational and aesthetic values of biological diversity and its components". Secondly, that they are "conscious also of the importance of biological diversity for evolution and for maintaining life sustaining systems of the biosphere" and that "the conservation of biological diversity is a common concern of humankind".[38]

How to justify these acknowledgements and translate them into action has been the subject of controversy ever since. Are the values equal or prioritised? How can they be justified, legislated for and documented? What does biodiversity mean for the biosphere and for human living conditions? What goals should be set for biodiversity and what means used to protect it?

In the course of my fieldwork, I've come across multiple conflicting answers. Some argue that much larger areas in Denmark and elsewhere should be "given back to nature", on the grounds that minimal human intervention is good for diversity. Some, like Frej, argue that diversity is a necessity and that biological systems will collapse if more and more species are wiped out. Others, like Rasmus, maintain there is no scientific evidence that humans need all that many species to sustain life. Scientists and activists often argue that ecosystems are so sensitive that diversity is necessary, while field researchers argue that we should preserve species for reasons other than human survival or the economy.[39]

With many different forms of commitment and often heated debate at meetings and demonstrations, as well as in writing, people's concepts of nature are clearly shifting – as are their concepts of humanity. All of which leaves the indoor person with a great deal to ponder. How do we and other species interact with each other? On how many species do humans depend? Given that livestock and domesticated plants make up such a large part of life on this planet, who is dependent on humankind?[40] The indoor person has no hope of answering. How could we possibly know? The whole point of the modern world is not to bother with questions like those.

The word "ecology" stems from the Greek *oikos* (house) and *logi* (knowledge) and serves as a framework term for questions about places where humans don't live on their own. As mentioned earlier, I see different ecologies as different ways of expressing and combining the three natures. Emphasising the qualities of the first nature, the focus is on the separation between the human and the untouched, i.e. full things. On the one hand, this separation is criticised as an illusion, the argument being that first nature is dead. There is no great outdoors anymore.[41] On the other hand, the difference between humans and nature is thought to be essential because – as I showed in the chapter "to beach" – the difference creates space for transcendence and reminds humans they are "small". This kind of fascination and wonder can generate respect, awe and humility. In that sense, we might say that the separation between nature and culture is practised in different ways, and can result in both indifference and esteem.

The qualities of the second nature train our focus on humankind's stewardship of its surroundings. Human history has become more and more all-encompassing and can be described in terms of both great victories and huge mistakes. From the perspective of the third nature, the anthropocentrism inherent in humanity's long historical endeavour to be both gardener and shepherd (which leaves little room for anything other than a select few species) has been sharply criticised in recent years. It is vital that we cultivate the qualities of our entanglements, affinities and kinships, the collaborations between half-things. On the one hand, there is an understanding that ecological crises have given humans a chance to understand themselves in a new way by visualising how we are embedded, via our bodies and all the things with which we surround ourselves, in a world that is coming into being. On the other hand, while there is creativity in these endeavours, there is also widespread uncertainty about how the nature-culture person should find new terrain. The wild human, the earthling, the sustainable life, green solutions, symbiosis with other creatures – all of these are symbols and blueprints for experiments, battle cries, manifestos, pastoral letters and artistic projects.

The indoor person is challenged in their understanding of nature. They are unsure of the correct terms, of where nature is and what kind of individual they could become. Perhaps my field studies should have culminated in me signing up as a species ambassador for chicory and continuing my fieldwork as an activist, making a beautiful headdress of morning-blue petals and wrapping myself in its bristly stalk. Moulding my mind in the jagged leaves, trying to figure out how to best advocate for the chicory and its likes. I considered doing that, but hesitated for so long that the motivation faded and the moment passed. As a researcher in this project, my remit, I reasoned, was to be neither a natural historian nor an activist. I am halfway between, shuttling between field and desk, studying how the three natures converse about a greener world.

## new ecologies

In August 2018, the Species Procession set off from Amager Common and ended in front of the Danish parliament. Children dressed up in animal costumes, including a giant fabric tiger with room for 60 kids, demonstrators waved placards featuring animals and plants from the Common, and the author Josefine Klougart gave a speech that was later published in the daily newspaper *Politiken*. It was remarkable, albeit perhaps too long for some of the audience, who seemed to have trouble focusing, and less catchy than the other speakers. Klougart described how "we are selling out our shared nature", that species are disappearing, and how we have stepped "into a bell of silence". She went on: "We collectively repress the basic fact that we are not separate from nature, that it is not possible to maintain the distinction between man here and nature out there. We are not just part of the same cycle, we are nature itself."

After opening with a familiar critique of first nature, Klougart went on to connect this loss with the devaluing of "sensitive and aesthetic" experiences. "We have marginalised thinking that expands the world and lets us experience how we are filled with a creative force, the thinking that lets us experience ourselves as nature creating nature, rather than culture using, eradicating or subjugating nature." She concluded that in order to open ourselves up to art and nature, we need a new language capable of connecting us to nature, as well as new communities, new myths and new life forms that nurture our connection to the world.

Klougart was heavily pregnant, and referred to her as-yet-unborn child, saying that next spring she will pick "this baby up, go to Amager Common and listen to the nightingale". The tone of the speech connected the mistakes of the modern world with the struggle for Amager Common. Klougart herself sought to manifest the birth of the new world by including her own child in the natural order of the Common: "Later in the spring I will take the children under an apple tree, and there I will listen to what nature has to say."

During my fieldwork, I have met many people who have the feeling that something new has been happening in recent years. Many young people are looking for new platforms and networks where they can find new ways *to world*, which also involve new ways *to nature*. I've also met many older people who recognise similar shifts since their younger days. But there's also uncertainty about what this might involve in relation to the individual. The question of what constitutes "my nature" doesn't just pertain to the outdoors, but also to the new natures of the indoor people and how they come about.

The performativity of the puppet theatre, the child of the future, next year's Common, placards featuring Morris's wainscot, snow parsley and the political newt –about which we know know nothing yet. By finding new ways to connect with the moth, newt, parsley and other species on the Common, and by getting to know their habits and the requirements for their habitats, the activists try to break down the ingrained boundaries between humans and other forms of life. Through identification and imitation, transformations occur that have the potential to be politically potent. The democracy at play in the Embassy of Species is not part of Copenhagen City Council, but still exerts real political influence – just as the *Borgertinget* (Citizens' Assembly) has the opportunity to have "their voice heard in the drawing up of climate policy".[42]

Rumours of the death of the first nature are, I think, exaggerated. While modernity's narratives remain dominant, something is stirring. The protests are expressed not only directly, via resistance but also via proposals for new ways of being, ways based on feelings of kinship between humans and other species and involving both commitments to responsible management and the freedom to experience and learn from the weirdness of diversity.

It's hardly in honour of me,
that eleven sky-blue thrifts
every day face the strong wind
and keep nodding in welcome,
Welcome to the beach path. But I
nod politely back anyway,
and start my walk along the shore.

*The Spider*
Eske K. Mathiesen

ecologisation

On 25 May 2019, around 130 people kitted out in green vests with reflective flashes gathered, checklists at the ready, in front of the old Stock Exchange building on Slotholmen in central Copenhagen. They were the traffic and safety team, who then spread out across ten zones on Christiansborg Palace Square, in front of the parliament. *Tro På Os* (Believe in Us – TPO), a feminist grassroots group with seven members aged 22–30, was involved in planning, recruitment and safety for this group of volunteers for the People's Climate March. Everyone was eager to see how many people would turn up. About 15,000 people had joined the previous Climate March in autumn 2018. TPO hoped for a bigger turnout this time, especially as the daily newspaper *Politiken* had arranged for the Swedish climate activist Greta Thunberg to speak.[1]

"You feel really responsible," said Ida Nielsen Langendorf. "I mean, what if somebody gets hurt?" TPO had been involved in the planning for months, and the women were really looking forward to the march. Each volunteer was given a checklist with details of the route and what to do in an emergency.

Ida had written to me three months earlier, saying that she was teaching in "an ecological laboratory" at Krogerup Folk High School [2] and wanted to talk to me about it. The summer before, as a sociology student, Ida had taken a course in nature ethics, on which I was one of the teachers.[3] Shortly after she had enrolled on that course, she got in touch to say that she had trained in the Norweigian outdoor life tradition and would be happy to help if, for example, we wanted to "plan something in a shelter or the likes", as she was familiar with the countryside around Copenhagen. The course ended in the Pinseskoven forest on Kalvebod Common, at the far end of the island of Amager in Copenhagen. Underneath a flight path, with planes passing overhead every minute, we gathered in a small birch grove for the last lecture.

When I met Ida again, we agreed I could observe her more close-ly in the months leading up to the People's Climate March, two weeks before the general election on 5 June.

On the day of the march, sandwiches and muesli bars were handed out to the volunteers after a quick briefing from TPO. An hour and a half before the demo started, the media were set-ting up, and a TV journalist walked around memorising lines. Greenpeace members turned up with three-metre-high placards depicting the ruling right-wing politicians, photoshopped to look 20 years older and saying "sorry". Young people from the So-cialist People's Party struggled to manoeuvre a bulky, blow-up globe. As the square filled up, everyone ended up partially ob-scuring the view of everyone else – much to the frustration of the TV crews.

I talked to the Greenpeace campaign manager about where best to put signs and where to find the nearest bin. When asked, I showed my checklist with the route on it, which consisted of 11 right turns around the National Bank, National Museum and Parliament. People on foot and on bikes swarmed around these symbols of economic, cultural and political capital. The Bank and Parliament were empty. It was Saturday, and politicians were out campaigning for the European and Danish elections. The keynote speakers included Maria Reumert Gjerding, former MP and now President of the Danish Society for Nature Con-servation, who coordinated the day from the stage; and Connie Hedegaard, former MP and EU Commissioner for Climate, now chair of the green think-tank Concito, both of whom rhetorically addressed "the politicians" as if talking about others, not them-selves. As the day went on, it became increasingly unclear who the political actors were. Half of the party leaders were out on the streets. I was pretty sure that TPO saw this ambiguity as a sign that we were *all* political actors – not just the MPs, NGOs and activists, but everybody who turned up, no matter their level of involvement.

Banners hung from the city's bridges: "Fight for everything you hold dear", "Stop the airport expansion". Placards proclaiming "We have no planet B", "We want the birds and insects back NOW" and "Take care of the Earth" were borne aloft and swayed gently along the route. Somebody dressed as a polar bear rode a cargo bike, wearing a sign on their back saying "Help!!! I'm sweating!" The rest of us weren't. It was cold. Everything went to plan though, as we passed through traffic lights, and wove in and out between bikes and prams. A woman asked who the people wearing the vests were. I told her we were volunteers recruited through Facebook and personal networks. We were nobody special. She replied that she had come to "soak up the atmosphere" and that "this is important".

TPO explicitly wanted the event to be organised in a way that would enable parents and their kids to take part, especially those who had never been to a demo before. It was to be a welcoming, positive experience, with no clashes with the police, without the established parties, associations and organisations competing for space. Lots of friends bumped into each other along the way, and the volunteers worked hard to generate a party atmosphere. Before and after the march, speakers encouraged the marchers to "look around and love each other" and chant: "Cli-mate-march, cli-mate-march – *louder!* – cli-mate-march!!!" The large number of groups on the square meant the chants were a bit out of sync, but it was still a huge, well-coordinated and epoch-making event. A week later, the Social Democrats and the rest of the "red bloc" emerged victorious from the general election,[4] and parliament went on to agree to a 70% cut in greenhouse gas emissions by 2030.

"It goes to show that politicians listened to the massive demos during the campaign," said Gjerding, in an interview with the Ritzau news agency. She highlighted the People's Climate March, "when around 30,000 turned out – a clear signal from the voters".[5] On 6 December 2019, almost every MP (167 out of 179) endorsed an agreement on the Climate Act to "work actively for the Paris Agreement's goal of keeping the global temperature increase below 1.5°".

## studies of climate activists

Indoor people rarely take to the streets to demand change. When they do, it's a sure sign something is badly wrong. Helping to plan a demo is a way of channelling compressed energy productively. I had been going on demos all my life, but never organised one or been at the front, so working with Ida was highly instructive. In our conversations, and at meetings about the demo in other networks, I kept finding myself confused *and* fascinated by Ida's determination. No matter how patient she was with me, I was never in doubt for a second that she was involved because she wanted change. Both big changes and small. She's always been like that. Other people speak highly of her personal courage and enormous drive.

Even as a child, Ida was political. That's the impression I picked up from stories of her schooldays, about how she took responsibility – indeed, she was often given too much responsibility – for example, for classmates who weren't getting on as well as her. And that's what I thought when she talked about her time in youth politics, as a teacher in a folk high school, as a member of TPO, a sociology student, an outdoor guide and activist in the Green Student Movement. For Ida, responsibility was a mixed blessing. Yes, she sought out political responsibility, but she also felt that the more involved she became, the more she had to delegate. She's not responsible for generations of $CO_2$ emissions or intrusions into habitats on which other species depend. And no, she wasn't interested in the positive attention mustered by her peers, and especially by older generations, which seemed to add to her responsibility and that of other activists while detracting from their own. We don't need heroes, she says. We need collective effort, on multiple levels, with many different goals and by all sorts of means. And we're not all going to agree on everything because, as I learned, the climate crisis is entangled in every aspect of life – in all our choices, personal and political, which makes it a dauntingly big task but also the most meaningful one of all.

Researchers are paying more and more attention to what attracts young people to climate activism. In Denmark, a key turning point was COP15, when around 100,000 took to the streets of Copenhagen.[6] Some studies explore how desperation, fear, hope, anger and blame are central to climate activism, and how it reflects a distrust in the ability of established political and economic institutions to lead a sustainable green transition. Others focus on ecological grief and the shape and spread of *solastalgia* – one of the newer words in the Anthropocene dictionary, referring to the distress caused by tangible environmental destruction. It is a sense of loss, a bad feeling of homesickness, experienced by someone who no longer has a home to which they can return.[7] No single realisation or event tipped the scales for Ida, but on top of her political engagement and focus on global inequality, she also attaches great importance to her desire to cope for herself in the great outdoors.

I ended up following Ida for several years and recorded several long conversations in my office by the lakes, on trains and in cars on the way to and from workshops. Once, as part of a retreat called "Into the Wild", we spent a week doing "nature training" in a partially rewilded gravel pit, in our bare feet, with no sugar or phones. We improvised new multi-species communities in "Kastanjeforsamlingen" (the Chestnut Assembly),[8] and I took part in Ida's teaching at Krogerup Folk High School. I didn't always understand all of her references, e.g. to canoeing or feminist eco-criticism, but she made me feel welcome, as did her friends and fellow activists.

## assignment in cultivating (ecological) ethical practices

Ida welcomed us to a workshop at Krogerup attended by 15 students, all in their 20s and on a 24-week stay at the school. Along with Sarah Hellebek, Ida has developed a course called *Jorden kalder* (Earth is Calling), an ecological laboratory focusing on "horticulture, permaculture and organic production, knowledge of climate change and biodiversity, entrepreneurship and project management, political understanding and outdoor life".[9] This combination of subjects is unique in the world of Danish folk high schools and reflects the teachers' beliefs in political engagement and participatory education. Both were active in the Green Student Movement founded in May 2018, as well as in all sorts of other political and activist contexts. In 2019 and 2020, Ida combined teaching with the final year of her sociology degree. After that, she continued to be involved with Earth is Calling.

What is special about the course is that it addresses the qualities of the first nature (especially in the Norwegian outdoor tradition), the second nature (in the form of sustainable forms of cultivation) and the third nature (finding strategies for living and acting in a world in ecological crisis). The Krogerup website states: "The course is for all those who want to get closer to nature, get their hands dirty, turn climate frustration into hope, action and new initiatives along with other young people."[10] Activities like building bonfires, carving a spoon, walking off-trail, winter swimming, hiking in the mountains and sleeping in a shelter are interwoven with lessons on carbon footprint, social manipulation techniques and various forms of activism, as well as practical organic gardening on a bit of land right beside the school. The first time Ida taught on the course, she wrote to me that she had "met students who were uncomfortable in the rain", who searched long and hard for words for "the outside of the trees (bark)", and that she found it "touching to take them into the woods and teach them to stray from the paths".

The fact that young people who liked the idea of climate activism didn't necessarily feel at home in the outdoors reflected what I had learned from interviews and research collaborations with anthropology students. While some young city-dwellers as-sociate the qualities of the first and second nature with jogging around the lakes and parks, or vegetable gardens with relaxation, liberation, respite, tranquillity and beauty, there was also a clear tendency toward the opposite, i.e. some didn't make any great effort to immerse themselves in the forest or the sea. As one stu-dent put it, "I feel in touch with nature, right up until I see what lives in it." Bugs and birds sometimes look disgusting, dark lakes threatening, and wide-open seascapes overwhelming. Surpris-ingly often, these young people acknowledged they had minimal knowledge of other species and didn't connect their interest in climate activism with either first or second nature. Nor did they associate their interest with Danish nature more generally. They tended to identify rising temperatures, more frequent extreme rainfall, rising sea levels and other forms of climate change with the global South and the Arctic. In other words, their activism was more about global social injustice and distant landscapes and their involvement ranged from international collaborations such as climate strikes to democratic elections and personal actions, e.g. recycling, less $CO_2$-intensive consumer habits and using fewer animal products.

Ida invited me to Earth is Calling to talk about my research project. During the group's conversations, it became clear that all of the students were interested in changing the way they *world* in relation to the landscapes of the first, second and third natures. Regardless of their previous experiences, they were all also keen to take part in an experiment, which we called: "Exercise in cultivating ecological ethical practices". The participants would spend almost a fortnight attempting to change their approach to nature and note their thoughts and observations as the experiment progressed. What would they most like to change? What did the change involve in terms of training, working and collaborating with others? What did they hope to achieve by changing their practice? And how would they evaluate the change, i.e. what criteria would they use to determine whether they had achieved their goals?

This way of articulating the assignment was inspired by philosopher Michel Foucault's understanding of ethical practice,[11] and was intended to illustrate that changing personal practice isn't just a matter of inner motivation or a simple change of behaviour through more or less mechanically changing your habits. Testing and implementing new and different practices requires working with the world around us. It is inadequate to assume we will just change overnight, which often causes a lot of friction when we do try to make changes.

Talking to students and other young people from Copenhagen had provided me with some insight into the long conversations they had with themselves and others about everyday shopping, travel plans and eating habits. Avocados, a trip to Uganda to visit an old classmate and an internship in Strasbourg were all discussed in relation to $CO_2$ emissions. After much deliberation, they decided which of these were legitimate and why. They also weighed up a canoe trip to the wilds of Canada, daily bike rides and the role of meat. The outcomes for each factor were different, of course, but it was striking that they were all using $CO_2$ as a scale to assess their personal interactions with the world around them. Some of them calculated their carbon footprint in whole and half tonnes, but most did it more haphazardly.

Another source of inspiration for the exercise of cultivating an eco-ethical practice was the American philosopher Charles Taylor,[12] who distinguishes between "weak evaluations" and "strong evaluations". However, as I intend to stress the ethical dimension of practice, I have opted to use the terms "semi-ethical" and "fully ethical" when drawing on Taylor's concepts. Semi-ethical evaluation is about using your gut feeling to make a judgement about whether something is good or bad, whether you like it or not – e.g. two cakes in the baker's window. Fully ethical evaluations, on the other hand, are concerned with the quality of the motivation for choosing one over the other, in that the decision refers to a value or utility – in other words, whether a particular action is more worthy, good, bad or superficial. As such, there is a difference between semi-ethical preferences, such as "I love to go for a walk in the woods" because it feels good; and fully ethical ones, which are conscious, reflective *and* motivated, and so, according to Taylor, cultivate *responsibility*. In fully ethical evaluations, responsibility emerges not from the ability to choose between two things, but from clarity about your motivation. What really matters to you? If you're unclear about your motivation, you might still be said to have a degree of personal responsibility (e.g. you don't leave litter on the beach or violate social norms), but you may not be fully aware of your responsibility.

The students who took part in Earth is Calling generated a number of ideas for assuming greater responsibility by adopting practical, ecologised ethics. Some wanted to spend more time in the outdoors, actively connecting with nature, for example by winter bathing, sleeping outdoors or drawing trees. Their goal was to "sense nature", to get closer to it, partly to get to know it better and partly to enjoy a deeper sense of tranquillity. Others wanted to go vegetarian or vegan, cut down on palm oil, buy more second-hand clothes, learn to knit and crochet, eat locally produced food, learn to repair their clothes, air their clothes more often instead of washing them, use less water when cleaning, learn to make their own deodorant, research companies' climate profiles and explore sustainable travel options – all areas in which they saw potential for more sustainable practices. Others focused on approaches to activism, on shedding the fear of encountering opposition and entering into dialogue with others about the ecological crisis and what to do about it at individual and collective levels. In pursuing these goals, they addressed questions about how to maintain their integrity and values. Some of the students were already involved in political work, had changed their daily practices (e.g. by reducing their carbon footprint) or were taking other environmental issues into account and adopting new ways of acting outdoors. For others, these were new ideas and experiments. It was clear the group spanned many different types of inspiration, which paved the way for a range of opportunities to work together, but also that each of them had to find their own way to balance motivations, goals and ways of implementing and evaluating changes.

Ida rounded off her discussion with the students by saying she would spend the next fortnight learning not to let herself be led astray as she navigates the supermarket. Far too often, she doesn't want to shop in them, because she knows she'll succumb to temptation at some point. For one thing, it's difficult to work out where goods come from, and she knows that she often ends up putting things in her basket that she doesn't need. Her focus on how supermarket shopping led her to deviate from her principles resonated with the others. The consensus, I learned, was that you shouldn't stop trying to change, even if you encounter obstacles and take detours along the way.

One practical suggestion was to start small, with everyday actions, like making responsible choices in the supermarket – from the moment you walk through the door until the moment you walk out again. Everything comes from somewhere and is more or less sustainably entangled with its surroundings – which are also other creatures' surroundings. Just as a sense of responsibility can pop up and be forgotten in the supermarket, it can pop up and be forgotten everywhere else. "I am going to *insist* that sustainable shopping is possible," said Ida, committing herself to a fully ethical evaluation of every potential impulse purchase.

## multi-species healing

One of Ida's favourite texts is *Staying with the Trouble* by the American feminist and philosopher of science Donna Haraway. One of the great theorists of the third nature, Haraway is known for her surprising concepts, such as the idea that we should "make kin" with the other creatures of the world, multi-species "partial healing" and "collaborations and combinations in hot compost piles".[13] The task, Haraway says, is to embrace the difficulties of the entangled world, and find ways to live responsibly on Earth – not necessarily by hopefully or desperately imagining new futures, nor by focusing solely on the conditions and possibilities in the human sphere. We share the Earth with other creatures – right here and now. Ida is fascinated by Haraway's imaginative approach and linguistic innovations. This feminist approach to scientific work, which employs imagery such as balls of yarn, threads, knots and playing with string figures, imaginative narratives and surprising concepts, appeals to Ida's thinking about the scale of ecological crises and ways to engage in the struggle.

"Playing games of string figures is about giving and receiving patterns, dropping threads and failing but sometimes finding something that works, something consequential and maybe even beautiful, that wasn't there before, of relaying connections that matter, of telling stories in hand upon hand, digit upon digit, attachment site upon attachment site, to craft conditions for finite flourishing on terra, on earth."[14] When Ida tries to explain Haraway's brilliance to me, she stresses that her ideas allow us to think and imagine new ways of living *with* and *in* the world. Unlike the various traditions in critical sociology, which also have their place when it comes to offering an effective critique of capitalism and colonialism, Haraway's language encourages new encounters between humans and other species, and new possibilities for inhabiting the world right here, right now. While Haraway's critics see her work as airy newspeak, lacking consistent comparative analyses of the *state of the art* (a critique that Ida accepts on her more critical days), it is also capable of inspiring tangible projects that facilitate new ways *to world* – new ways of being outside, new ways of cultivating yourself and your surroundings, which are gentler than those fostered by the modern world.

It was on this basis that Ida organised the *Butterfly Meetings* in 2020, as part of her final sociology exam. In "The Camille

Stories: Children of Compost" Haraway recounts a writing experiment that brought Camille into the world – a child born to learn to care for endangered "earth others". In Camille's case, her charge was the monarch butterfly. She became a "symbiont", partially infused with certain of the butterfly's genes, microorganisms and physical characteristics.[15] Following an exploratory phase during which she read Haraway particularly slowly and thoroughly – partly due to a degree of dyslexia – Ida developed the methodological framework for three five-hour butterfly meetings, which were attended by six students from the folk high school. Could Camille's stories inspire new ways of meeting butterflies? Before the meetings with the students, she practised meeting butterflies, bought several books about them and asked experts for advice on where to encounter them. Regarding these preliminary studies, Ida writes in her thesis: "It took me by surprise how starting a long-term commitment and relationship with ?-butterflies turned me into an enthusiast. An enthusiast in the sense that I learned a lot about the behaviour of ?-butterflies, ?-butterfly species and habitats [...] I also became an enthusiast in the sense that my relationship with the ?-butterflies meant that I could also get annoyed with them and find them difficult. Once I had finally persuaded all of the ?-people to agree to a date for a Butterfly Meeting, the weather turned gloomy. I knew we would encounter significantly fewer ?-butterflies that day. The behaviour of the ?-butterflies was, therefore, incredibly poorly suited to the deadlines for a thesis. In the midst of all the hassle, I developed a form of gratitude whenever I was able to get close to the ?-butterflies."[16]

Throughout her thesis, Ida insists on prefixing both humans and butterflies with "?-". As she puts it, this allows for the possibility of "creating space to disrupt categories somewhat". What does it mean to be human or a butterfly (or other species)?

And how can meetings be organised to promote "planetary heal-ing processes" and "flourishings", in which "humans and animals intertwine in innovative new ways"? Conducting a Haraway-style yarn analysis of the material generated by the project, compris-ing the participants' notes, transcripts of focus group conver-sations and photographs, Ida hung clippings of the material on strings, to be sorted into three different themes.

In particular, she notes that, during the meetings, the students:

- became curious and noticed the butterflies and their physiology. They were fascinated by their colours, pat-terns and behaviour, marvelling that they looked like a "cross between a bird and an insect" and "that they have fur on their bodies".
- discovered that they lacked the language to describe what they were seeing and that the butterflies seemed secretive. Nevertheless, they tried to communicate with them in different ways: by singing to them, writing notes directly to them, and trying to get the butterflies to sit on their fingers. Sometimes they began to fantasise about the butterflies' secret lives, and what the world would be like if butterflies were big and humans small.
- enjoyed spending time with the butterflies – which came as a surprise
- even though getting to know a new species that flies so fast and is so easily frightened by humans proved to be difficult, fleeting and ambivalent, they sometimes achieved what Ida calls a "butterfly state". In the mo-ment, they became invisible, in their own world, forget-ting themselves, time and place, and "zapping directly into the reality", where "everything else was cut away".[17]

It was an original way of thinking about sociology, and shows that innovative theses are mushrooming on study programmes and posing experimental challenges to anthropocentric ways of worlding.

## ecologised ethics

When I met with the students from Earth is Calling after the Cultivating Ecological Ethical Practices assignment, we talked about what they had experienced. In particular, I wanted to learn about any opposition they had encountered.

One of the students who wanted to swim more often in the winter failed to set clear quantitative goals, e.g. swimming *every* day, but was fine with that. For her, it was mainly about following through on the urge to do something that she knew she really enjoyed. "It gives me a sense of wellbeing and calm." However, she also registered that in order to follow up on her thought "I want to go for a dip", she could perhaps learn to focus more on the "end feeling", i.e. the glorious sensation of emerging from the water, rather than – as she was inclined to – dithering about in a grey zone between not feeling like it or finding something cosier to do indoors instead.

The student who wanted to cut down on palm oil and eat vegan had also done ok, she said, but had identified a tendency to be compliant in certain social situations, e.g. if someone else had made a cake using eggs. If she was going to make changes, she would have to maintain "pretty strict discipline. It has to be all or nothing. Saying 'once in a while, on special occasions, I can cheat'... I find it hard to relate to that."

Others talked about:

- Feeling they needed to be spurred on by others to make changes. "I have so many ideas. But it becomes such a fog. I find it really hard to be that person myself. It's like, 'Should I do it?'" This group had succeeded in finding communities that follow up on initiatives.
- Discovering that it was important not to bite off more than they could chew at any one time: "It's okay that it takes time, and not to take the lead in everything." Even seemingly small actions help to nurture a sense of empowerment.
- How they work better in small groups of 2–4, because otherwise things become overwhelming: "If there are more than four or five or six of us, I back out. I feel a bit overlooked." They felt that various forms of organisation are needed, and the trust engendered in small groups was important for establishing a sense of connection and for the ability to muster the drive and determination needed.
- Identifying activities where there is strength in numbers, e.g. "collecting money and donating to a good cause, because all of us at the high school thought we flew a bit too often. Many of us were planning flights. It felt like a collective responsibility. We felt we had to do something." For generations, flying has been synonymous with freedom and expanding our worldview. Krogerup Folk High School in particular had a tradition of long trips to some of the world's hotspots. The team had plans for a hiking trip in Norway, but other journeys lurked on the horizon, too. These young people had to contend with an obvious clash of values between freedom of movement and cutting $CO_2$ emissions, a dichotomy that called for reflection as well as action.

- The difficulty of remembering your commitments, for example, not eating meat, because eating is a habitual action. "Seven hours later, I was handed a cheese and ham toastie and didn't even think about it. And I had a meltdown afterwards. I was so embarrassed I'd eaten it." In this case, the question of subjective consistency was a matter of forgetting yourself and your decisions in social situations. What level of consistency can you demand from yourself, when it comes to being a responsible person?
- Changes made in one place can be difficult to transfer to others. For example, eating vegetarian or vegan at the folk high school is easy, but can be difficult at home, where you might find yourself in need of a different argument than your sense of right and wrong. A new diet can also pile on the workload with extra shopping and cooking. In other words, unexpected ethical duties may crop up.
- That categorical language such as "vegetarian" can be inappropriate, and terms such as "plant-based" or more specifically descriptive language (e.g. "potato pizza") can circumvent the need to fit everything into a potentially problematic binary logic – i.e. vegetarian or not! Food is about much more than simply dietary preferences, and so identity-oriented classifications can be reductive and trigger conflict.

This short catalogue of reflections on practical ecological ethics from Earth is Calling presents just a few examples of how the relational understanding of ethics is applied in practice. This approach to ethics might be called *experiential* rather than *rules-based*. In other words, it is less about arriving at a specific formulation of what is right, more an exploration of how it is possible to move from a semi-ethical preference to a fully ethical act of meaningful engagement. For Earth is Calling, the fully ethical evaluation was conducted in the context of ecological relationality. The course offered an exploratory framework within which students and teachers were able to explore the potential for "staying with the trouble" in relation to the outdoors, the environment and the climate. The exploratory approach also meant they weren't taking out a mortgage on the future. The young people didn't promise each other – or us – anything. According to the anthropologist Stine Krøijer, the purpose of exemplary practice, as a form of activism, is to emphasise that which doesn't yet exist, but could manifest itself in an uncertain future.[18]

In his article "Living as if it mattered", the anthropologist Michael Lambek writes that "ethics is less an object to be proclaimed or to be dissected than a dimension or quality to be discerned and elucidated".[19] For Lambek, the following questions (among others) are crucial for everyday ethical practice when handed-down truths no longer provide guidance and ethics becomes an explicit phenomenon:

- How do we understand how we (and others) live?
- How do we restore meaning in a powerless situation?
- How can we live with compromise?
- How can insight into these issues be turned into action?

Ida's students were attracted to the Ecological Lab's experiments into how a world undergoing climate change and wracked by a biodiversity crisis might become a meaningful and safe place, rather than chaotic, random and horrifying. This led to practical exercises followed by reflective practice, in the form of "field notes", in which everyone kept a record of their experiences and thoughts, as well as shared conversations in various informal formats. The students also had the opportunity to participate in Fridays for Future or other activist events in Copenhagen.

Ida herself had been practising in the supermarket for a fortnight. In preparation, she had spent some time outside, getting ready. This process of disciplining herself continued for several weeks. She stayed away from Coke Zero and products like cheese and milk, which she attempted to avoid in her efforts to move towards a vegan diet. She still liked eating meat, but did so rarely. One day, at the buffet at Krogerup, she realised that she thinks a lot about her appetite, and the fact that she almost eats for two. This critical dialogue with the self and others was a recurring theme, in part because many ethical considerations can't be fully implemented overnight. Between half-ethics and full ethics lie countless reflections on the purpose of a new practice, how it is realised, and the difficulties and consequences associated with working towards this goal, including the potential ways in which it could be adapted. Since Earth is Calling navigated areas in which there were no government or other official recommendations, or they were too vague (for example, the new dietary guidelines),[20] this process of collective ethical training was necessarily experimental. It was more about setting goals, exploring ways to achieve them and assessing the strengths and shortcomings of the training, rather than achieving the goal itself.

## meaning and argumentation

One spring day, when we met in my office at the Department of Anthropology, Ida had a large medical bag with her. Birch pollen in the warmer months has taught her to appreciate winter, rain and cold. She regularly contracts itchy eyes, a swollen tongue and breathing difficulties, and has even been rushed to hospital a few times. For much of the year, this outdoorsy person just can't feel at home outside – a contradiction she finds funny. She is also amused by her recurring dream about whales wreaking revenge on humankind: "Whales are so intelligent. Despite declaring them a protected species, humans continue to destroy their habitats." It's a nightmare. Cracks are appearing in the world. The string figures are completely interwoven with each other.

Armed with medication and vigilance – specifically about black slugs, to which she is particularly averse – Ida completed an outdoor education programme, including certification as an instructor in Telemark skiing, first aid, canoeing, kayaking, climbing and more. Some of these skills are taught on other courses at Krogerup, whereas Earth is Calling concentrates on sensory activities rather than action, e.g. moving slowly, quietly and attentively in the forest, learning to light a fire and using a knife to carve a spoon out of wood, for example.

"The bonfire, in itself, is hugely liberating for the students," says Ida. "While they sit around it, carving a spoon or something, they don't give a hoot what I say. If I tell them to pack up their stuff, they don't. They just can't let go of that knife. It's hard to interrupt because it's an almost trancelike state. It's a bit like I'll snap them out of it if I say something. It's a bit awkward. It's difficult to do any teaching around a fire. Before they start carving, we discuss at length what they think is going to happen, or any doubts they have about the activity. They make all sorts of guesses. Then, once they start carving, they're no longer able to concentrate on talking. So they don't. And the non-language begins. And that's a difficult position for a teacher to be in. There's this idea that a learning space should be highly stimulating, and the students constantly bombarded with information. Insisting on silence isn't the done thing in an educational context. An activity like carving can produce a new language – but only if you accept the silence."

In addition to the butterfly state and the trance-like state induced by carving, Ida also repeatedly mentions what she calls the "canoeing-over-a-waterfall state", a kind of embodied thinking in which you "sweat adrenaline and are insanely scared" due to the imminent danger of being dashed on the rocks or drowned. Ida knows the feeling. She regularly takes to the water with a group of former classmates from her outdoor education programme called the Canoe Ladies. She loves canoeing. For many reasons. It's a low-cost technology that requires little equipment, a lot of people can be involved, and canoes can be used in a range of situations. It's great in calm waters but also when negotiating treacherous rapids. There are many types of embodied thinking. It can occur in situations of tranquillity and calm, or in the face of danger – be it knives, fire or rapids. That's why Ida seeks out all kinds of outdoor nature, including places with some kind of edge, which heighten our sense of presence. "I feel physically restricted and mentally shattered if I can't get out into the world around me and push myself to the limit, because I am in good shape. When you know you can cope with challenging terrain, it gives you confidence and freedom. It's hugely empowering. That's why I'm so interested in movement."

My impression of Ida's work at Krogerup, at the climate demonstration and in many other contexts, is that she is attempting not only to find paths that connect the qualities of the first, second and third natures, but also "to insist", as she puts it, that it should be possible to feel at home in all three. The kick she gets from canoeing on the rapids and the silence around the fire both provide space for the meaning behind the words, for the edges that are both dangerous and fascinating, and which must be approached with respect and skill. Resting, vegetating and outdoor exercise are prerequisites for long-term political engagement, but also a source of immediate pleasure and feelings of serenity, which we only partially make happen on our own. For the same reason, Ida sometimes drives to the far end of Kalvebod Common just to look out over the water. She insists it should be possible to feel at home in our physical surroundings, both indoors and outdoors, while understanding natural history, life cycles, forms of agriculture and production, and achieving a bonfire-trance state of self-effacing, qualified nothingness. It should be possible to make this earth connection by feeling at home in the world, to feel the kinships, healing processes and flourishings of which Haraway writes, and give them form in their immediate vicinity.

"If you focus exclusively on political activism in this society, you're heading for a fall. I've suffered burnout, and it was really bad," said Ida, reflecting on her years in youth politics. "There's a month or two I don't remember at all. Apparently, I ran all sorts of courses in Denmark, but my mind's a complete blank. Now, I find peace in being able to retreat into something else, and finding ways to get back up again."

During the first interview, Ida told me that she basically saw her existence as "meaningless" if she "wasn't doing something to make the world a better place". But it had been difficult to balance this aspiration with everyday life. Philosophers have debated the viability of a kind of hyper-ethics, which prioritises a single value, e.g. reducing $CO_2$ emissions, above all others. This functions as a kind of hyper-benefit, which not only helps the individual target their actions but also indicates whether other forms of good are *possible* or *impossible*.[21] For Ida, the concept has its dangers. "Political work is a huge burden. I ended up off work with stress for a reason. And I still don't think I've found the right balance. I place too many political demands on myself,

223

certainly when it comes to feeling good, but I also feel really bad if I'm not doing anything political. In that case, I don't see the point of life. I can't sit and just enjoy myself if I haven't done something meaningful. I often have arguments with other people about this, and keep letting others down. I've turned down all sorts of invitations to hang out and just have a good time."

The idea behind TPO was to combine the political and the personal, so that "you keep coming back to the group to understand what's happening and get ready to be active again". As an activist group, TPO "goes out, shakes up society and does something about it. But you almost always encounter obstacles. When that happens, you have to retreat and find peace in the group, and process it." Ida says that their climate actions have been met with resistance, particularly from older generations, who have found them provocative. She describes the group as a safe space in which to process these encounters, "where we take care of each other and push each other. It's not about being nice, necessarily. You also need to ask critical questions of each other and help each other move forward. The group doesn't stand still. The idea is to make action sustainable in the long term. It's about not burning out, physically or socially, so we can remain active for prolonged periods."

## ethical dissonances

On 24 May 2019, at the Fridays for Future demonstration in front of the Danish parliament building – while similar events took place elsewhere in Denmark and in 131 other countries all over the world – the appeal to young people was direct: "You have a special power because you have friends and family and parents who listen to you and care about you. You need to tell them: 'Isn't it time, mum and dad, to go completely vegetarian? Mum and dad might say 'Um' and 'Ahh'. So you say: 'Listen, this is really important, it's about our future.' Maybe for his 40th birthday – no, 60th – grandad will invite you to join him for a celebration in Thailand. And that's hard. Should you say no? You have to." Another speaker said: "I'm so pleased to see you all. To see that some people are speaking up [...] Every year, we outdo ourselves. Every year, we take a leap towards the abyss. We don't do it out of ignorance, but with our eyes wide open."

I meandered from the edge of the stage towards the more open spaces on the square, speaking to various people. Some found the tone too harsh or even downright irresponsible, given the many children and young people on the square, who were being encouraged to challenge their parents and other authority figures. After all, it's not the children who need to be the grown-ups. I spoke to Ida several times about the speeches. Her position seemed to be that if the campaign against ecological crises becomes the subject of what I have called the hyper-ethical approach, i.e. that this struggle is prioritised above all other values, then young people will run into far too many challenges and responsibilities that will weigh them down. As she put it on another occasion, "I don't think we're to blame, but we do bear a responsibility. It's not my fault Earth is the way it is now. But as someone who lives in the world, I believe I share responsibility for it. Everyone does. Unfortunately, I think we also bear responsibility for things that aren't our fault." At the same time, she was also wary about adults seeming to rely so much on younger generations that they excuse themselves for not doing anything.

Others jumped in enthusiastically, declaring that events like this help instil a sense of common purpose and community spirit. They enable the community to inspire each other, and other political actors, to turn their semi-ethical sympathies into fully ethical actions. The overall message of the demo is that there is room for change. We are invited to explore this potential and imagine something new – be it new forms of courage, goals or communities. As such, the messages are intended to be performative. We state that "we've had enough" and "we want to change the world", and share a frustration that change is not happening.

As I reached the edges of the crowd, I sat down on one of the stone steps next to the main entrance to the Parliament. Next to me sat a woman with short hair wearing a denim jacket, white cotton blouse, black jeans and trainers. She seemed to be alone, a bit tired, visibly wilting. I introduced myself and asked her if she would mind telling me how she felt about the demo. She (I never got her name) had retired from working in a kindergarten and wanted to take the pulse of the younger generation. She said, "It's an incredibly important movement, and I want to show my interest and support." She told me that she wanted to behave "properly towards our planet. We have to change our habits. And I think we're on our way." She turned and looked at me, then let out a sigh. Her shoulders sagged, and she looked down at the ground. "But I've been travelling all my life, and I'm still curious. So I'm one of the culprits on that front. It's probably one of the hardest things to change. I can't just hop on my bike if I want to go to Nepal [...] But I want to. I'll never stop eating meat either, although I will cut down. There are calls to put airfares up. I think that's good, but those of us who can afford it will just pay. I find it hard to look you in the eye and say all this."

I must have pricked her guilty conscience. Some indoor people don't have one. They'll say they haven't destroyed the climate single-handedly, that blaming yourself doesn't help or that it reflects a Christian sense of guilt – but, since they don't believe in a forgiving God, being aware of sin has little value for them. For some, feelings of guilt and shame leave them feeling apathetic and powerless. Other indoor types oscillate between a guilty conscience – a kind of low-level background ethics that sometimes inspires them to action – and a more positive and motivated sense of hope, constantly negotiating the contradictions between ideals and reality.

"I've travelled a lot," the woman told me. "I'm from the generation that associates travel with freedom, opportunity *and* broadening the mind. Plus we had the right to spend what we earned. We really need to change our mindset, prioritise our needs and find different values." She said her grandchildren were getting tired of her talking about the climate. But it bothers her. On overconsumption, she says, "I buy organic meat from a farmer close to where I live. I invite people over to use it up. But I feel sick to my stomach when I open my freezer and see it. Even if it's organic and good."

We spoke for 45 minutes. Before we parted, she told me that she catches garfish in the fjord. She and a friend go out in the evenings to set nets. They get up early the next morning, around 5 AM. She tells me it's wonderful when the sun comes up, and they pull up a few nice fish. "I call these 'magic moments'," she said. "It's so perfectly peaceful. Sometimes there'll be a seagull who wants some of the catch. It's like pulling silver out of the sea." She spoke, as before, through the sound of booming speakers. I imagined the scene. The fjord in the morning, the calm water, the flat light from the sun slowly warming the landscape. The blue-green surfaces and vivid patterns. The gentle gurgling sound of the inlets. The flat terrain that seems to magnify the space. The hazy light that shimmers as the earth accumulates warmth. I see the small boat in front of me, two women hauling up glistening garfish. I think of the joy of cleaning, seasoning and serving them, a few or an abundance. The flavour of the short journey from sea to table.

The woman looked up at me over her glasses. "But now there are SO many crabs. If you bring up a small flounder, there might be 20 crabs on it. And then you think: 'Oh no, it's been lying there unable to do anything.' There are just lots of crabs. Often, when you bring up a flounder, the crabs have eaten the head. They go deep. When we pull up the net, the crabs come with it and infest the boat. I kill them with a stone, to provide food for the flounders. I sit there and think I'm doing something good, but it's a drop in the ocean. What the hell is wrong with these crabs?"

They're tangled in the web. There are too many of them. They're foraging for food. These kinds of complexities are springing up everywhere. Danish waters are suffering from oxygen depletion. The fjords are dying. The crabs are some of the last survivors. The coasts will be flooded. New landscapes will emerge. New energy sources and housing will take up spaces that were once home to other species. How can we learn to navigate these ethical dissonances?

## the indoor nature

The fieldwork revealed that Ida's experiments in the supermarket were not an isolated example. In my interviews, young people in Copenhagen often brought up shopping. It's another arena in which the battle for nature is being fought. Some of the young people dumpster-dive regularly, others are in food co-ops or grow produce in their gardens. They are trying to figure out the most green and sustainable behaviour, and whether and how to practise it. They don't necessarily boast about it, and may not even consider reducing their $CO_2$ footprint their top priority. They prefer to focus on collective political work. "We barely talk about anything else," said one anthropology student.

"It's climate, climate, climate." For this group of students, the climate was the issue of greatest and broadest concern in the 2019 general election. It became the horizon for their lives and encompassed a whole range of priorities, from global justice to agricultural policy, and even bigger, existential questions. The climate crisis was everywhere, and so accessible anywhere. But what was the most effective strategy? Collective political action in the usual democratic forums or targeted activism to influence the democratic system, which itself might be said to be part of the problem? Could study programmes and research provide equally valid strategies for influencing the green transition? Does personal behaviour change anything – and if so, what?

I found their enthusiasm infectious and included their thoughts in my fieldwork. Just as I took inspiration from the ways in which Liv and Susanne *nature*, I followed in the footsteps of the young climate activists – including into the supermarket. We all end up there, if not every day, then often enough that it's a place we take for granted, even though its history and way of worlding deserve far more attention. I'm not just thinking about the economic aspects, about how goods cross borders, about sales logic, individual products' $CO_2$ emissions and their greater or lesser degrees of sustainability, but also the millions of micro-actions involved whenever we go shopping. In addition to being the most cultivated country in the world (alongside Bangladesh and the Netherlands), Denmark also has the record for the most square metres of supermarket per capita. The goods are presented in a specific order that has been perfected over a century. The system was introduced in the largest supermarkets in the US, and firmly embedded in Denmark during the rapid supermarket expansion of the 1970s. This perfect organisational system takes into account, to varying degrees, turnover, transport, shelf life, production conditions, customer behaviour and legislation.

The first thing that happens when we walk through the doors? *Shwoosh* – we are blasted with warm, dry air (at least in the winter months). After this, countless factors play a role in influencing what we put in our basket. In the few minutes it takes to buy stuff, a remarkable internal conversation takes place. Usually, it's silent and habitual. But it can also be an insistent, practical and ethical dialogue, with enough material for a novel or an eco-critical poetry collection.

Margrethe, a sociology student who described herself as 90% vegetarian, talked about a recent trip to the supermarket in one of the interviews. I asked her, "When you walk through the door, what do you see, and how do you prioritise?" "I go to the fruit and veg section first," said Margrethe, who was always wonderfully specific in her descriptions. "Yesterday I went shopping and bought broccoli because it was on sale. It wasn't Danish. Bananas were also on sale – delicious! Then we had to have apples. Yes! There were some Danish apples over here, right. So we bought them, which was good, too. But I've also bought other things, just because they were on sale. Then we bought organic milk and organic eggs from free-range hens. And full-fat double cream." Margrethe gesticulated to indicate her wandering attention and meandering path through the supermarket. Her priorities were vegetarian, organic and Danish – but not everything fell into these categories. There was also a degree of opacity, despite the labelling, product information, etc. "I don't know all of the factors in these equations. If I buy these carrots, how many have been thrown away before? Should I leave out the aubergines? Make something other than moussaka? Who knows the truth? The other day, as I was eating mackerel in tomato sauce, I thought: 'Where is this mackerel from, and is it OK that

I'm eating it? How did it end up here?' I could have cooked some chickpeas. But not as quickly. That's the great thing about mackerel in tomato sauce. I find it easier to eat fish than roast beef, but I can't say whether I just think this because roast beef has been shamed so much in the media. But then again I've heard that salmon farming isn't exactly kosher, either."

Does Margrethe's story sound familiar? How do each of us navigate the supermarket? Do we try to ignore our dialogue with the products? Margrethe and other students who reflected on their own and others' shopping have made me listen more carefully. It's a long way to the milk aisle. Along the way, there's much more information to be studied, and more objections to be debated. How many products on the shelves are actually sustainably produced? Should I, like Ida, insist that they are before I buy them? And if so, how should I go about it? My household's eating habits have changed several times. I've been surprised by how difficult it is to figure out exactly what shopping responsibly means. How can we incorporate our connections with the planet and its inhabitants into our shopping? And how can we apply this principle to larger scale markets – for housing, transport and government infrastructure?

Is it fair to say that indoor people are just as far removed from indoor nature as we are from outdoor nature, even though we are completely entangled in it? The intention of the supermarket – in fact, all of the supply lines and infrastructures that fall under the banner of "super", i.e. which cross multiple more or less compartmentalised spaces – has been to prioritise convenience. The fact that we have direct access to goods and are able to put them in a trolley– assuming we have the money to buy them – gives us a "super" sense of choice and control. However, this means we know very little about the products available. Half a century ago, this wasn't a problem. We didn't demand this kind of information back then. We do today. Rather, the supermarkets were a liberation, providing abundant quantities of anonymous and durable frozen food and other standardised industrial goods.

So what would an ecologised supermarket look like? How can each item we reach for tell us about its connections to the world, instead of the world disappearing into them? In every product, road and stream are the natures. The indoor people's nature doesn't stop at their windows, and an awareness of the outside world isn't limited to the outdoors. The indoor person has a lot of ethical work to do.

# new magic

The first colour photograph of earthrise, taken by one of the astronauts on Apollo 8's orbit around the Moon in 1968, offered a new perspective on the world and is often credited with leading to a shift in environmental awareness. No one had ever seen Earth from that distance before. As Commander Frank Borman put it, the globe was suspended in space, seeming like a beautiful, uninhabited blue marble. And yet, someone was home.[1]

How far has this shift in consciousness taken us? More to the point, has there been one at all – and if not, how do we kick-start one? In *Down to Earth*, Latour states that "the terrestrial" should be understood as a territory to which *we* belong. Not the other way around. The planet belongs to no one. When climate change mobilises the entire Earth system, the planet has started to play a role in the story. It interferes in our affairs and is itself a political actor. Only three astronauts – or extraterrestrials – had the opportunity to gaze through Apollo's windows. The rest of us, the Earthbound, have to work out how many *other beings* we depend on for our existence and find our place in a broader genealogy. In addition, we must attempt this even if political institutions equipped to deal with these relationships don't exist yet. We need to invent the right kind of institutions if we want to rediscover a habitable Earth. In the meantime, according to Latour, we must map our dwelling places by describing that on which we depend and asking "what other terrestrials also depend on it?"[2] In this way, climate issues become questions of multi-species social responsibility.

What was special about secularisation, which was part of the modernity project, was that our conceptual universe didn't have to be consistently connected through different social spaces. In the modern world, you could go to church on Sunday and be a pagan on Monday, or be religious in private while rejecting religion in public. The same moral logic extended to all spaces during modernity. It didn't necessarily strike a dissonant note if an environmentalist flew around the world for the sake of adventure or because of a personal relationship. It was a private matter, up to the individual. Similarly, in modern thinking, environmental and climate *awareness* can be separated from environmental and climate *action*, whereas it is intrinsic to an ecologised ethic that the world is *always* connected. In this way, climate change and biodiversity crises are not just environmental, technical or managerial problems – or political problems, for that matter. Rather, "climate", in a move towards ecologised action, refers to the relationship between people, the material conditions of life and the connections to all other living beings.

## weird, wonderful

The English writer Timothy Morton describes our relationship with the world around us as "weird", in the sense that there is no clear relationship between intention and effect.[3] None of us ever wishes for climate change when we get behind the wheel of a car, and our individual impact is statistically negligible. However, we can't say that we do *not* contribute to climate change when we drive. The same goes for the management of the land and its resources. This means that our connections are also "weird" in the sense of "wired", interwoven in a kind of Nornish way, into webs of fate, webs that connect us to the planet and to the human species, all living humans, all past and future generations. In this way, you could say that our weird connections are both planetary and cosmological, and move between the indoors and the outdoors. We're connected to things whose strange threads of fate and vibrant lives we don't fully – or only partially – understand. If we hold a tin of mackerel in tomato sauce, like Margrethe, what do we know about it? Where are its first-nature qualities, its impregnable qualities? How are our threads of fate interwoven with it? We used to be able to say that our relationship with most things was only about whether or not we could pay for them, and whether or not we wanted to buy them. The story is a little weirder now.

Nowadays, subjects like fish, coffee and mining are just as prominent in environmental anthropology as the hunting practices of indigenous peoples in the Amazon and the threats facing those communities. For first-year anthropology students, this comes as a bit of a surprise. And understandably so, as the study of fish, oil fields, apples, abandoned gravel pits and potatoes is quite new, the result of the new ecologisation of the social sciences. In these studies, the human is no longer the centre. Rather, the focus is on collaborations and entanglements that were downplayed or overlooked in the 20th century, but are unavoidable in the Anthropocene. We now study the domestication of salmon (a new species in agriculture),[4] the rearing and slaughter of cattle[5] and petroculture (the influence of oil on environments, economies, households and ways of life).[6] In this form of anthropology, nature is no longer just "out there". Rather, our concern is with the qualities of the third nature, and all of the entanglements that I found out there with "the nature people". Sociologists and political scientists study similar types of phenomena in the larger assemblies – of citizens, resources and states – which are intertwined with each other, and with life on the planet. They propose new approaches to political organisation[7] and offer recommendations for how a sustainable state can make society resilient in the face of ecological crises.[8]

If supermarket goods are always connected to the world – and we, like Margrethe and Ida, can ask where they and all the other items on sale come from – then the threads of fate and their connections to the world are everywhere. These are weird relationships, in which everything can potentially be entangled in everything else, and as such feels bound and constrained. So it is with threads of fate, Morton says, as spun by the Norns – inscrutable beings from Norse mythology, who remind us we live in a universe that is both finite and fragile, and about which we know only a little and nothing. As a consequence, the terms of these connections are always unclear. The jigsaw always has pieces missing.[9]

The qualities of the three natures are inexorably interwoven. But do we see traces of the new nature of the indoor person when we try to imagine these threads of fate and make their magic, their wonderful creation, tangible through chicories, myths, penduline tits, activism and supermarkets?

If Earth calls to the terrestrials, we need to do a lot of practical ethical work to describe all of our dependencies and rediscover a habitable planet. Recent decades have seen the emergence of thousands of ecological laboratories that conduct experiments in ways of living, shopping practices, eating habits, ways of travelling, farming, energy-saving, etc. New techniques, ethical practices and forms of political engagement are continuously emerging and being documented.[10]

Ecologisation thrives in networks that transcend modernity's binary differences. The hope is that, through the power of example, practice, inspiration, collective effort, political proclamations, structural changes, breathing space, cascades of trust and a vivid imagination, we can help shape the ecologised communities of the future.

I may have sallied forth in search of nature, but what I found was something else. I met people who spent years deepening their knowledge and love for landscapes, animals, plants and all things "more-than-human". I found views, birds, plants and mud holes teeming with life. I didn't find nature as such

– assuming it was ever there in the first place. Rather, I came across countless examples of ecologisations, moves towards losing yourself in and abandoning yourself to the world around you, ways of meeting nature halfway and finding kinships that make it perceptible – and which invite us to accept responsibility. It is an oft-repeated mantra in nature management that "what you love, you will take care of". I found this hope to be both weird and wonderful. It can't be taken-for-granted that the Norns' threads automatically weave love and responsibility together. It takes hard work, training, collaboration, experimentation and story-telling. A move towards ecologisation.

I also found the three natures indoors. It's not only on the most distant of coasts that the indoor people can discover nature, and even in remote places, humans have been roaming and working with the land for millennia, long before they started to call it nature or believe they could withdraw from it. No matter how much people have tried to keep nature out and ensure we are the only predators in the park, it has still moved indoors. It has been washed up on the shore, carried inside or propagated in our rubbish tips – and even in our bodies. Even indoor nature, I found, is weird and wonderful. Can we begin to decipher the history of objects, tune into them, and perhaps, subtly, find the natures that make up the Earth?

As I made my way out and into the three natures, I paid special attention to the magical moments, both intangible yet full of life. In the modern world, religions are institutionalised; but in the ecologised world, transcendences and communities are potentially ubiquitous. In this way, our connections to the Earth are rendered weird and wonderful, and the indoor person is able to become an earthling.

# acknowledgements

This book is the result of the work of two research groups. In *Relocation of Transcendence*, historians of religion David Thurfjell, Henrik Ohlsson and Atko Remmel looked at how nature connects with religious practices. David and Henrik, both from Sweden, did fieldwork in the forest around Stockholm, Atko in recreational environments in Estonia.

In *Enchanted Ecologies*, the anthropologists Stine Krøijer, Sofie Isager Ahl and Matti Weisdorf explored how enthusiasm for and connectedness to the living world relate to personal responsibility and political action. Ahl looked at regenerative agriculture based on a study at a Norwegian agricultural college. Weisdorf focused on a group of Danish biologists who, among other things, are trying to make enthusiasm for rewilded nature part of a biological *Bildung* to promote the biodiversity of the Danish landscape. Krøijer's interest in the political life of trees resulted in fieldwork among forest managers, farmers and climate activists.

The research groups spent four years working together to develop the methodological design and tested their analyses and arguments by visiting each other's fields, workshops and conferences. Thank you for your inspiration, commitment and generosity. Traces of the research groups' fieldwork and insights appear throughout the book. Thanks also to Bron Taylor, James Faubion, Nancy Ammerman, Linda Woodhead and the other anthropologists and historians of religion who have followed, inspired and commented on our work.

The first part of my fieldwork took place on the beach in North Zealand. I would like to express my gratitude to all the beach people, mountain bikers, birdwatchers and walkers, as well as the residents of Tisvildeleje and the surrounding area, the Danish Nature Agency in North Zealand and Tisvilde Hegns Sporlaug for your openness and patience. The second part of the fieldwork took place on Amager Common and in Copenhagen, among nature enthusiasts, environmentalists and climate activists. Along the way, I made detours to Aarhus, Ferring and Skagen, thanks in part to the help of Ingeborg Svennevig. Special thanks to Birte Andersen, Liv Appel, Susanne Borup, Andreas Egelund Christensen, Rasmus Ejrnæs, Karl Erik Frederiksen, Bo Thyge Johansen, Bente Lindegaard, Ida Nielsen Langendorf, Bo Bang Petersen, Frej Schmedes, Grete Sonne, Terese Verbena, Stig Toft Madsen and Liv Tvermoes for sharing some of your places and stories. Thank you also to those who wished to participate anonymously, and all those who contributed to the preparatory work and fieldwork. Thank you for checking the script for errors and omissions.

Thank you to the students on *Danmarks vilde planter* (Denmark's Wild Plants) 2017, at Silkeborg High School; the students on *Dyrk det* (Cultivate It), 2019; and *Jorden kalder* (Earth is Calling) 2019, 2020 and 2021 at Krogerup Folk High School; and the participants in the *Into the Wild* 2019 retreat for allowing me to share in your discoveries. Thanks also to the many students at the Department of Anthropology, University of Copenhagen, who have been involved in the *Enchanted Ecologies* research project: Thanks to the summer course *Naturetik* (*Nature Ethics*) 2018; students from Semester 1 in 2018 who participated in the extracurricular project *Klimaaktivisme* (Climate Activism) in spring 2019; students from Semester 1 in 2019 and 2020; students who participated in *Økologisk etik* (Ecological Ethics) 2021; and the courses *Naturetik* (Nature Ethics) 2019 and *Natur, miljø og klima* (Nature, Environment and Climate) 2021 for helping to collect and analyse material. The students expanded the field in directions I never expected or would have thought of on my own, to encompass moss enthusiasts, winter swimmers, scenery lovers and people with a love of second-hand clothes, hiking, outdoor nurseries, urban gardens, agriculture and other green spaces.

Thanks to anthropologist Adam Veng, who has organised workshops and fieldwork on environmental and climate activism for teaching assignments, for his many insights into political sensibilities. Thanks also to the thesis and PhD students who worked on related topics for their inspiration, and to Anne-Li Engström, who joined us in the field with her camera. Thank you to Charlotte Baarts, Helle Bundgaard, Jørgen Demant, Nette Hammershøj, Ingrid Brandt Jensen, Magnus Juhl, Stig Toft Madsen, Hanne Overgaard Mogensen, Henrik Brandt-Pedersen, Helle Rubow, Lene Rubow, Dorthe Gert Simonsen, Inger Sjørslev and the whole research group for your readings of previous versions.

Parts of the chapters, especially 'to beach' and 'ecologisation', have appeared in: "The Weird Magic of Becoming Ecologically Aware". *Journal for the Study of Religion, Nature, and Culture* 2025, 19 (3) 286–308. "The Indoor People's Enchanted Ecologies." *Environmental Humanities* (2022) 14,2: 475–493.

# notes

## natures

1   Ingold, *The Perception of the Environment*, 20.

2   Gribskov Municipality, New Nordic Coast, Gilleleje.

3   In fact, a lot of nature rooms have been built, especially in Sweden. They combine knowledge of natural and cultural history with an incentive to experience nature for yourself.

4   Haaning, *Den dobbelte arv* (The Dual Legacy); Stuckrad, *A Cultural History of the Soul*.

5   For other purposes, scientists have identified five, seven or more different meanings.

See, for example, Fink, "Et mangfoldigt naturbegreb" (A Diverse Concept of Nature) and Christensen, *Hvad er natur?* (What is Nature?).

6   In calling the third form "nature-culture", I derive my inspiration from the French philosopher and anthropologist Bruno Latour and the American biologist and philosopher Donna Haraway.

7   The Icelandic anthropologist Gísli Pálsson formulated the basis for the three concepts of nature used in this book. His

conceptualisations reflected the anthropological debates of the mid-1990s.

8   In Denmark, 57% of the land mass is under the plough, in Sweden 6%, in France 33%. Bangladesh, the Netherlands and Denmark are the most intensively farmed nations in the world. A total of 26% of the EU is farmland, cf. the Danish Society for Nature Conservation and the Danish Animal Welfare Society, *Sådan ligger landet* (The Lie of the Land, 6).

9   Tim Ingold extrapolates on this in *The Perception of the Environment*.

10  Massey, *For Space*, 140–141.

11  Haraway, *The Companion Species Manifesto*; Haraway, *When Species Meet*.

12  IPCC, Climate Change 2023.

13  Philippe Descola, in "Modes of being and forms of predication", 273 ff., uses "to world" [worlding] to explain how "ontological filters" create cultural variation. In the West, a naturalistic way of worlding is dominant, whereas in other parts of the world, an animistic form prevails. Marisol de la Cadena uses the term to emphasise that anthropologists need to be aware that people are not the only actors. As Inger Sjørslev writes in *Ting* (Thing), material objects, too, help create the world we inhabit. Inspired by all of them, I use the term ["to world"] to emphasise how we, our language, and the beings and things with which we interact help to give shape and content to the world.

14  The American physicist Karen Barad quotes Fulton's poem in *Meeting the Universe Halfway*, which is about quantum mechanics, the philosophy of science and ethics. Barad asks: "How can I be responsible for that which I love?" and argues that we are and should be responsible precisely because we are inextricably linked to the world – from the smallest particles to our bodies and beyond, into the cosmos.

15  In the literature, these major differences are referred to as dichotomies. A dichotomy is a whole that can be divided into two parts – and each part cannot contain anything from the other. There are no overlaps, only bifurcated differences.

16  This is largely inspired by the philosopher Bruno Latour's analysis in *We Have Never Been Modern* (although I don't agree with all of it). He critiques the big differences, the dichotomies, as the path to a different and better description of the composition of the world, one that transcends these differences. I prefer to describe how differences, including the big ones, are constantly *worlded*.

17  According to IPPC's latest re-
    port, published in 2023, "human
    activities, principally through
    emissions of greenhouse gases,
    have unequivocally caused global
    warming, with the global surface
    temperature reaching 1.1°C
    above 1850–1900 in 2011–2020."
18  In "Trajectories of the Earth
    System in the Anthropocene",
    Steffen et al. show how self-re-
    inforcing feedback loops and
    tipping points, e.g. triggered
    by thawing permafrost and
    deforestation, can destabilise the
    climate.
19  Latour, "To modernize or to
    ecologize?".

# to beach

1   Corballis, *The Wandering Mind*. A wandering body also seems to support a wandering mind.

2   Tvermoes et al., *Fiskerlejet i Tisvildeleje* (The Fishing Community in Tisvildeleje), 5.

3   Rosiek, *Danmark, Gurre, stranden*, (Denmark, Gurre, The Beach) 116.

4   In 2018, forests accounted for 14.5% of the Danish landmass. Ministry of Environment and Food, *Danmarks nationale skovprogram* (Danish National Forestry Programme), 13.

5   Löfgren, *On Holiday*; "Motion and Emotion".

6   Blicher, "Eneboeren på Bolbjerg" (The Bolbjerg Hermit).

7   Lundbye, in Svenningsen, *Seks år af et liv* (Six Years of a Life), 174.

8   Kierkegaard, *Journals and Papers*, 29th of July, 1835.

9   Ibid.

10  Garff, *Søren Kierkegaard – A Biography*, 59.

11  Bjørnvig, *Samlede digte* (Collected Poems), 475.

12  In *Livet ved Havet* (Life by the Sea), which is about the landscape and life in Tisvilde, Ole Hyltoft pays tribute to the "church of nature" and describes the evening sea as "a cosmic altar". However, as an "agnostic", he also corrects this religious language and states that his role as a poet is to make life bigger than it is (11, 13, 30, 41).

13  Wamberg, "Between Paradise and the Anthropocene Garden", 22.

14  Kelly et al.'s meta-study "Walking on sunshine", about the influence of walking on mental health, shows that the best-documented effects are in relation to depression and anxiety, and also that there are many variables to consider when evaluating these effects, such as age, socio-economic status, where you walk, how far you walk, etc.

15  Marc Vacher, "Consuming Leisure Time".

16  Foucault, "Of Other Spaces".

17  The position is referred to as panentheism, cf. Gregersen, *Tre slags panenteisme* (Three Kinds of Panentheism).

18  Sandbeck, *Den gudløse verden* (The Godless World).

19  Blicher, "Eneboeren på Bolbjerg" (The Bolbjerg Hermit).

20  Here I am inspired, among other things, by the sociologist Thomas Luckmann in *The Invisible Religion* and in "Shrinking Transcendence, Expanding Religion?". Luckmann's thesis is that in modern times we have become accustomed to religion having a monopoly on transcendence.

Inspired by the phenomenologist Alfred Schutz, Luckmann posits the idea that transcendence occurs everywhere in everyday life. See Thurfjell, Rubow, Remmel and Ohlsson, "The Relocation of Transcendence", and Rubow, *Bagom transcendens* (Behind Transcendence).

21  The philosopher Dorthe Jørgensen is one of the few modern Danish thinkers to assert the concept's relevance in a secularised context (see, e.g. "Menneskets modtagelighed for tro" (Humankind's Susceptibility to Belief) and "Etik og transendens" (Ethics and Transcendence)). See also the anthropologist Joel Robbins, who himself is inspired by Schutz and Luckmann (see previous note).

22  In *Den nye Gud* (The New God), the theologian Niels Grønkjær distinguishes between "classical metaphysics" as the idea "that some kind of unchangeable reality exists, extra-sensory in relation to the present one", and a "post-metaphysical" Christian idea of the deity, in which God is changeable and mutable (31, 38, 50). In *Fantasiens Gud* (The Goddess of the Imagination), the theologian Lars Sandbeck describes the dominant "aesthetic" conception of Christianity, the "narrative-poetic view of the Bible" and "existential theology"

as arising from a paradigm shift in theology around the middle of the 20th century (9–13). Sandbeck confirms my analysis in *Hverdagens teologi* (Everyday Theology), that theologians, generally speaking, have not succeeded in spreading an understanding of this paradigm shift.

23  Grønkjær, *Den nye Gud* (The New God), 22, 28, 44.

24  Wolf, "Transcendensen i følelserne" (Transcendence in the Emotions). Jakob Wolf himself is one exception. For him, it is a theological mistake to disregard the emotions, without which we cannot understand transcendence. According to Wolf, everyone must work out whether the transcendence they experience is of "unconditional seriousness" (God) or something "highly immanent" (an idol).

25  In *Global Religious and Secular Dynamics*, the historian of religion José Casanova provides a good overview of secularisation by distinguishing between three different social changes. The first is that the bond between church and state has loosened or been severed – a process that has been ongoing in Europe, albeit with national variations, for centuries. The second change is that people are less religious, e.g. fewer attend rituals such as baptisms and funerals. The third change is that

fewer people express belief in God. A fourth factor is, we might add, a weakening of religious transcendence.

26 Christianity's view of nature has been much-discussed. One of the fiercest debates was sparked by Lynn White's thesis that Christianity is behind the Western world's anthropocentrism and therefore ecological crises have a religious cause (see Rubow, *Three Ecologies in Danish Eco-Theology*. In the world of Danish theology, only a very few ecotheologians have attempted to overcome anthropocentrism. See, for example, Jensen, *På kant med klodens klima* (On the Edge with the Global Climate); Gregersen, "Deep Incarnation"; Ishøy, *Klimaklar kristendom* (Christianity for the Climate).

27 Parts of this analysis are also found in Rubow, "Bagom transcendens" (Behind Transcendence). In *Granskogsfolk* (People of the Pine Forest), David Thurfjell analyses the Swedes' "connection" to the forest (p. 39).

28 Schmitz, *New Phenomenology*.

29 Löfgren, "Motion and emotion", 33.

30 Schmitz, *Kroppen* (The Body), 13, 55.

31 Schmitz, *Kroppen* (The Body), 36; Wolf, *Krop og atmosfære* (Body and Atmosphere), 15–16.

32 I have previously quoted Massey, who described the landscape as an event. In *Correspondences*, Ingold advocates even more strongly for rendering landscapes as verbs. He says that we ought to replace many of our nouns with verbs – to stone, to tree, to mountain – in order to understand how all things are always in a process of becoming and how that happens. In this way, we can "correspond" with these things, by developing an awareness of the interactions and "in-betweens" in their openness, processes and dialogues. Ingold argues that this shift of attention from the world of fixed nouns to moving verbs has ethical implications because it suggests that things and beings are not compartmentalised into separate worlds. On the contrary, they are open and participate in an indivisible process of creation (7–8, 11).

33 Schmitz, *Kroppen* (The Body), 55–56.

# jizz

1   Jørgen Munck's user profile on netfugl.dk.

2   Liep, "Luftbåren kula" (Airborne *kula*: The appropriation of birds by Danish ornithologists).

3   The SMS exchange is also reproduced in Johansen, "Sortspættereden i Asserbo Plantage" (The Black Woodpecker Nest in Asserbo Plantation).

4   Hundeide, *Ornitologisk praksis*, (Ornithological Practice) 1.

5   The German sociologist Hartmut Rosa expresses the same criticism in *Resonance*. According to Rosa, if experiences of nature are detached from a practical, sympathetic understanding, the aesthetics of nature become a "simulacra of resonance" confined to oasis-like reservations that *legitimise* environmental degradation and climate change. The ideal, says Rosa, is that resonance is not restricted to special zones, but integrated into our everyday relationships with the world. Among the examples he cites are making parks edible and ordinary people taking energy and water supplies into their own hands.

6   In "Den taksonomiske taktstok" (The Taxonomic Baton), Stig Toft Madsen shows how, when it is difficult to identify rare species of birds, it is done by teamwork – and competition – between amateur enthusiasts, scientific taxonomic procedures and new technology. In Denmark, naming and classification is the result of "a communicative network of a few hundred very skilled and active individuals".

7   In "The Etymology of 'Jizz', revisited" David McDonald writes that the word, like "jism" and "jasm", initially expressed liveliness, exuberance and energy (as a bird might express), but has gradually shifted to its current meaning, which is the distinctive impression a plant or animal gives. *Netfugl* defines the term: "In birdwatching, the term is often used in phrases like '*it has a distinctive jizz*', meaning that a combination of the bird's shape and behaviour is typical of that particular species, as opposed to potentially confusing."

8   Morten D.D. Hansen, "Vi, som inhalerede" (We Who Inhaled) and the radio programme "Når naturen fortryller os" (When Nature Enchants Us).

9   In *For the Love of the Living,* Matti Weisdorf follows this biological "school" in the field and the laboratory. His impression is that this particular repertoire of enthusiasm only goes back about a decade, and that it would be a simplification to understand

it solely as an expression of personal preferences. Rather, it is deliberately cultivated and maintained to promote the collective enjoyment of nature in its rewilded versions, so we understand that we ourselves are nature and to allow us to participate in the same miracle, the miracle of life. The loud laughter is both an expression of a new professional ethos and new alliances between the disciplines of biology, activism and politics. In some respects, the enthusiasm of the new biological school is similar to the Romantics' enthusiasm for nature, but it differs in several ways. For example, it is far less national than Romanticism's fondness for the distinctively Danish landscape. It is completely devoid of classical metaphysics and emphasises, in a quasi-religious way, how miraculous it is that life exists at all, that it tends to reproduce, and that humans should realise their part in this process by "joining the party" and "making room".

10   Johansen, "Sortspættereden i Asserbo Plantage" (The Black Woodpecker Nest in Asserbo Plantation).

11   In *The Perception of the Environment*, Ingold is inspired by James J. Gibson's theory of ecological perception.

12   In *Correspondences*, Ingold describes this approach to things and to other beings as a process of becoming. Like Schmitz's concept of half-things, Ingold is concerned with how everyone participates in an indivisible world of becoming, 8.

13   Kohn, *How Forests Think*.

14   This section is based on Jesper Hoffmeyer's presentation in *7 ting vi plejer at tro på* (Seven Things in which We Tend to Believe).

15   Kohn's technical explanation of how iconic and indexical sign processes are always involved in symbolic ones is based on the neurobiologist Terence Deacon's work on human cognitive development as seen from an evolutionary perspective. Briefly, the point is that we as humans share much more language with the natural world than is allowed for by a focus on our uniquely human linguistic ability.

16   Sofie Isager Ahl translated one of the chapters in Kohn's book *How Forests Think* into Danish. She also interviewed Kohn, as published in "Skovrig tænkning" (Sylvan Thinking).

17   Ahl, "Skovrig tænkning" (Sylvan Thinking), 71.

18   Ejrnæs, *Den uendelige have* (The Never-ending Garden), 32.

19   Ejrnæs, *Natur* (Nature), 44.

20   Ejrnæs, "Natur for naturens sky-
     ld" (Nature for Nature's Sake).
21   Ejrnæs, "Det er er egoistisk kun
     at se ulven som en fjende" (It is
     selfish to see the wolf solely as
     an enemy).
22   Psychologically, experiences
     like these have been described
     by Mihaly Csikszentmihalyi as
     "flow states", in which attention
     is completely focused, the sense
     of time is transformed, and
     life becomes valuable in itself.
     *Finding Flow*.
23   See Bennett, *Vibrant Matter*.

# plant blind

1   Yinon et al., "The biomass distribution on Earth".

2   The American author Richard Powers uses the term "species loneliness" in an interview with Everett Hammer about his novel *The Overstory*. It was in this tale of people's kinship with trees that I first came across the concept of plant blindness. One of the main characters says to his father, "Kids in my class think a black walnut looks just like a white ash. Are they blind?" The father replies, "Plant-blind."

3   Ott, "Human Activity Patterns".

4   Thorsen, "Engang vrimlede det med hybenhjerter" (Once upon a time it was teeming with rose hips". *Zetland*.

5   Tybjerg, "Hver femte unge dansker tror en rødspætte er en fugl" (One in five young Danes thinks a plaice is a bird). *Zetland*.

6   Lovejoy, *The Great Chain of Being*.

7   Chamovitz, *What a Plant Knows*; Gagliano, *Thus Spoke the Plant*.

8   Hartigan, "How to Interview a Plant".

9   Ibid.

10  Latour, *Down to Earth*.

11  The inspiration for such studies could be Ries, "Potato Ontology" and Robbins, *Lawn People*.

12  Hartigan, "How to Interview a Plant", 265.

13  The physician Simon Paulli, in the first *Flora Danica*, 1648.

14  In *Friction*, anthropologist Anna Tsing describes botany's early classification systems as an attempt to find God's order in the universe. Just as God was supposed to be singular, Creation was assumed to be the expression of a single order. When botany later dispensed with God as the origin of a common order, the system started to express the order of nature. In terms of the concepts used in this book, botany helps establish nature as the great outdoors, with a logic and order of its own – a first nature that we can make the object of systematic study and knowledge.

15  Seberg and Frederiksen, "Hvorfor ændres klassifikationer?" (Why are classifications changed?).

16  Lund, "En cikorie er ikke blot en cikorie" (A chicory isn't just a chicory).

17  Moselund et al. *Den danske rødliste* (The Danish Red List).

18  Moselund et al. *Den danske rødliste* (The Danish Red List). Denmark is one of the most domesticated countries in the world. Many of its wild animals, plants and fungi are endangered. In total, 4,439 species, representing 41.6% of the total number, are red-listed, i.e. they can be assigned to one of the following categories: *regionally extinct,*

*critically endangered, endangered, vulnerable, near threatened* or *data deficient.* The overall picture is broadly similar to the previous Red List evaluation in 2010. The proportion of species that are *critically endangered, threatened* or *vulnerable* is 17.3%.

19  Ejrnæs, *Natur* (Nature), 44.

20  Ejrnæs, Bladt and Fløjgaard, "Rewilding som planmål i Antropocæn", 38 (Rewilding as a planning target in the Anthropocene).

21  Christensen, *Alphabet*, 3.

22  Frederiksen, Rasmussen and Seberg, *Dansk flora* (Danish Flora) 596.

23  Chamovitz, *What a Plant Knows*, 13–23.

24  Bird-David, "Animism Revisited", 77.

25  Bennett, *Vegetabilt liv og onto-Sympati*, 10 (Vegetable Life and Onto-Sympathy). The anthropologist Natasha Myers, in *How to Grow Livable Worlds*, suggests that we vegetalise our senses by taking an interest in the things to which plants pay attention, by following their rhythms and sensitivities.

26  We could also say – using a word connected with enchantment – that there was a special *resonance* in Liv's relationship with the plants, the sea and the light. The sociologist Hartmut Rosa writes in *The Uncontrollability of the World*, 32: "Resonating with another person, or even with a landscape, a melody, or an idea, means being 'inwardly' reached, touched, or moved by them. This circumstance of being affected can well be described as a 'call' or 'appeal.' Something suddenly calls to us, moves us from without, and becomes important to us for its own sake. The person or thing from whom or from which we experience such a call appears to us to be not just of instrumental value, but 'intrinsically' important."

27  Bennett, *Vegetabilt liv og onto-Sympati*, (Vegetable Life and Onto-Sympathy).

28  LeGuin, *Akaciefrøenes forfatter*. (The Acacia Seeds' Author).

# helene

1   "Kysterne er Danmarks vild- este natur" (The Coasts are Denmark's Wildest Nature), Danish Society for Nature Conservation, Frie kyster (Free Coasts), 3.

2   Pedersen, "Helene Klint og Kyst" (Helene's Cliff and Coast).

3   Thiele, *Prøver af Danske Folkesagn* (Extracts from Danish Folk Tales); Frederiksen, *Troldtøjets Sand* (The Sand in the Troll's Eye); Appel et al., "Sagnkredsen" (The Myth Circle); Pers, *Tro og kildevand* (Faith and Spring Water).

4   Rømer, *Tales in an Underground Landscape*; Cadena, *Earth Beings*; Hastrup, *A Place Apart*.

5   Friis, "Vejby-Tibirke selskabet. Manglende omsorg for vores område" (The Vejby-Tibirke Company. Lack of care for our area).

6   Cf. Kohn's concept of imagery in Chapter 4.

7   This threefold take on myth is inspired by Baal and Beek's *Symbols for Communication*, 14–15.

8   Gell, "Technology and Magic".

9   Barthes, *Mytologier* (Mythologies), 121–122.

10  The paintings are reproduced in Frederiksen *Troldtøjets Sand*, (The Sand in the Troll's Eye); 57–63.

11  Scharff, "Et gaardmandshjem" (A Farmer's Home) In the archive note, the quote is admitted- ly mistakenly attributed to a William Schwartz and the date is 100 years out.

12  Gad, *Helgener* (Saints), 128–131.

13  Appel et al., "Sagnkredsen" (The Myth Circle), 167–181.

14  Ibid., 170–1, 176.

15  Pers, *Tro og kildevand* (Faith and Spring Water), 326–329.

16  In *Religion Explained*, Boyer argues that religious beliefs trigger human mental sys- tems and that animistic and other imagery is both natural and irresistible. In "Religion's Evolutionary Landscape", Atran and Norenzyan argue that there is an evolutionary advantage in animating our surroundings because that makes it possible to form images of the unex- plained, such as whatever is making a noise in a bush: "Is it a predator? Should we be careful?" According to this theory, the ability to imagine and detect predators is an evolutionary advantage.

17  Luhrmann, who works both eth- nographically and with psycho- logical tests, shows in "The Art of Hearing God" that the ability to be absorbed in narratives varies from person to person, and that the degree to which so- cieties have historically practised the skills (e.g. meditation and

visualisation) that promote such an absorbed state has varied.

18   In *Tales in an Underground Landscape*, which is about Bornholm myths of "the underground", Rømer (who inspired my visit to the Folklore Collection archive) refers to the anthropological tradition, which claims that it is a specifically Western theory, often based on developmental psychology, that children are more prone to animistic thinking than adults. The argument is that, with secularisation, animistic thinking and myths have been relegated to children's bedrooms, and animistic thinking is universally considered to be part of childhood. However, in her studies from Manus in the Western Pacific, the anthropologist Margaret Mead found that the majority of animistic stories were for adults.

19   Eliade, *Myth and Reality*.

20   Basso, "Stalking with Stories", 44–45.

21   Gelsted, *Tibirke Bakker* (Tibirke Hills).

22   In "Holy Springs and Protestantism", 59, Jens Christian Johansen stresses that there are no written sources about Helene's Spring or other springs as pilgrimage sites in the 15th and 16th centuries.

23   In "En helig källas teologi" (The Theology of a Holy Spring), 92, Bengt Arvidsson quotes a letter from the Jesuit Henricus Lindanus dated 16 July 1658: "Seven miles away from here, according to tradition, lies a grave containing the body of the Swedish Saint Helene. Many miracles transpire at this tomb. Only three days ago, one such happened to a man who had been driven there in an absolutely pitiful condition, and who, by drinking the water that gushed out of a hill near the grave, recovered so well that he was able to return to Copenhagen on foot. Every Midsummer Day, thousands of Lutherans gather – there are no other denominations here – to worship."

24   Ibid., 61.

25   Arvidsson, "En helig källas teologi" (The Theology of a Holy Spring), 89.

26   Appel et al., "Sagnkredsen" (The Myth Circle), 177.

27   Arvidsson, "En helig källas teologi" (The Theology of a Holy Spring), 95.

28   Johansen, "Holy Springs and Protestantism", 63, 65.

29   Arvidsson, "En helig källas teologi" (The Theology of a Holy Spring), 97ff.

30   Johansen, "Holy Springs and Protestantism", 68.

31   Appel et.al. "Sagnkredsen" (The Myth Circle), 178.

32   Ibid., 174. Worm's map is reproduced in Liisberg, *Domina Helena*, 84.

33 Here, I am inspired by Henare, Holbraad and Wastell's *Thinking Through Things*, which helped formulate the material turn in anthropology, which also represents a way of approaching things as third nature.

34 Liisberg, *Domina Helena*, 13, 85–88.

35 Pontoppidan, *Den Danske Atlas* (The Danish Atlas).

36 Kierkegaard, *Journals and Papers*, 1835, Gilleleie. "The cure they use consists in sleeping at the grave every Midsummer night three years in a row, and taking some earth from the grave, for which a special spoon was provided. Also one must not forget the poor, for whom an alms box is set up in the town."

37 Ibid.

38 In *På kant med klodens klima* (At Odds with the Climate), the theologian Ole Jensen describes this transcendence as a legacy of rationalism, and also as an "exaggerated" transcendence. See Rubow, Three Ecologies in Danish Eco-Theology.

39 Quoted from Smidt, *Tisvildes trylleri*, (The Magic of Tisvilde), 7.

40 Jarløv, *Danmarks berømteste helligkilde* (Denmark's Most Famous Holy Spring), 10.

41 Cavling, "Sct. Hans nat ved Helene Kilde" (Midsummer Night at Helene's Spring).

42 Jarløv, *Danmarks berømteste helligkilde* (Denmark's Most Famous Holy Spring), 7.

43 Hastrup, "Icelandic Topography", 70.

44 Descola's definition of animism in "Modes of being and forms of predication".

45 Ibid. Descola's definition of naturalism.

46 In Bolivia, the Law of the Rights of Mother Earth recognises the ecosystem's right to live, and to clean water and air, and equates violation of those rights with treason. Biodiversity researcher Anders Barfod emphasises in Dalsgaard, "Naturlov – Ganges, Himalaya og Moder Jord" (Natural Law – Ganges, Himalaya and Mother Earth) that the law "sets a lower limit for private and public actors' exploitation" and "makes it possible to protest the greatest injustices against nature". On the other hand, the law does not distinguish between minor and major offenders, which, according to Stine Krøijer, has undermined indigenous communities' rights to territorial self-determination. This "reflects the danger that violations of nature's rights are primarily directed against poor and marginalised communities who are forced to draw on the ecosystem in order to survive" (ibid.).

47  Herbener, *Naturen er hellig* (Nature is Sacred), 95.

48  The story of Hainuwele, from an island in the Moluccas, is one of them. Hainuwele is a woman born from a coconut, who is killed and buried, but then dug up and dismembered. From her reburied body parts sprout previously unknown plants. According to religious historian Jonathan Smith's "A Pearl of Great Price", the myth has been the subject of countless interpretations by religious scholars.

49  Ortner, "Is Female to Male as Nature is to Culture?".

50  Kallestrup, *I pagt med djævelen* (In a Pact with the Devil), 85.

51  Ibid.

52  Haaning, *Den dobbelte arv* (The Dual Legacy), 147.

53  Haaning, *Naturens lys* (Nature's Light), 15.

54  Hedegaard, *Iron Age Myth and Materiality*, 122 ff., 160 ff.

55  Lidegaard, *Myte og sagn* (Myth and Legend), 12, 40–43.

56  Ibid., 99.

57  Lovelock, *Gaias hævn* (The Revenge of Gaia), 21–22.

58  Ibid., 30–31.

59  My inspiration here is Neimani's *Hydrofeminism*, in which she develops a metaphor of women as bodies of water.

60  The story is pieced together from accounts from Tisvildeleje about the dreams of beach people, memories of drowning accidents, suicides and unknown beachcombers, the terrible murder of a local woman in spring 2019, accounts of women's anxiety about being alone in holiday homes, and Liv's observations of the sea fog. To all of this are added elements from Niels Barfoed's book *Benedicte*, from which the quote originates, as well as notes from several students' fieldwork with outdoor kindergartens.

# the common

1 The group includes biologists at Aarhus University and the Natural History Museum, Aarhus.

2 Ibid.

3 Stoltze, *Danish Society for Nature Conservation.*

4 Danish Society for Nature Conservation, *Input til regeringens redningsplan for Danmarks biodiversitet* (Input to the Danish government's rescue plan for Denmark's biodiversity), 2020.

5 Danish Society for Nature Conservation, *Biodiversitetslov* (The Biodiversity Act). These targets are in line with the UN's Montreal Agreement, 2022. *The United Nations Association.*

6 In "The Trouble with Wilderness", the American environmental historian William Cronon argues that wild and pristine national parks crystallise an idealised notion of "pure nature", which undercuts the awareness that there are natural environments everywhere for which we need to care. The original inhabitants were even driven out from the US national parks.

7 Arler, Jørgensen and Sørensen, *Prioritering af Danmarks areal i fremtiden* (Prioritising Denmark's Landmass in the Future).

8 Arternes Aarhus' hjemmeside: Om Arternes Aarhus (Species Aarhus website: About Species Aarhus).

9 Clark et al., "Can You Hear the Rivers Sing?"

10 "Ethnographic Machines", Amager Fælledsagen on Facebook (the Amager Commons page on Facebook).

11 Noah's website <https://www.noah.dk/english/about-noah>

12 City of Copenhagen, "Ny løsning for Ørestad Fælled Kvarter" (New solution for the Ørestad Common District).

13 Orht, *Naturkortlægning* (Nature Mapping).

14 By & Havn, "Forslaget Fælledby vinder" (The Common Town Proposal Wins).

15 Duus, "Henning Larsen-team vinder" (The Henning Larsen Team Wins).

16 Schmedes and Friis, "Byggeri på Amager Fælled" (Building on Amager Common).

17 Harding, "The Tragedy of the Commons".

18 Rappaport, "Ritual Regulation of Environmental Relations".

19 Tsing, *The Mushroom.*

20 Hastrup, *A Place Apart*; De la Cadena, *Earth Beings*; Rømer, *Tales in an Underground Landscape.*

21 Lien, *Becoming Salmon.*

22 Kohn, *How Forests Think*; Coccia, *The Life of Plants.*

23 Ejrnæs, *Natur* (Nature). Tsing et al, *Field Guide to the Patchy Anthropocene.*

24 Gan et.al., *Arts of Living on a Damaged Planet: Ghosts and Monsters of the Anthropocene*.

25 Ahl, *Regeneration*.

26 Gan et al, *Arts of Living on a Damaged Planet*.

27 "Introduction", ibid.

28 Reiter, "Her er debattens superliga" (Here is the Premier League of the Debate).

29 Cf. Kirk's Facebook profile, 22 May, 2017.

30 This section appears in part in Veng, Juhl and Rubow, "Montage: Frej og den store vandsalamander" (Montage: Frej and the great crested newt).

31 <https://www.christiania.org/info-type/english-2/>

32 Michaelsen et al., *Vidensindsamling Natur 2013, Amager Fælled* (Knowledge Mapping, Nature on Amager Common 2013).

33 Taylor, *Dark Green Religion*, 12.

34 Ibid., 2.

35 Ibid., 13.

36 Ibid., 35–41.

37 In *The Enchantment*, Bennett attempts to breathe new life into *enchantment* in the modern era. The book was an important catalyst for the *Enchanted Ecologies* project (see Krøijer and Rubow, "Enchanted Ecologies and Ethics of Care" and Rubow, "The Indoor People". In *Naturens sprog. Historier fra virkeligheden om fortryllelse* (Nature's Language: Real-life stories of enchantment), Mickey Gjerris and I sought to stimulate new interest in forms of enchantment.

38 *Convention of 5 June 1992 on Biological Diversity* (CBD).

39 Lange, "Biologer frygter ukritisk forskning i biodiversitet" (Biologists fear uncritical research into biodiversity).

40 Measured in kilograms, livestock account for 60% of the world's mammals, humans 36% and wild animals 4%. Farmed chickens account for two out of every three kilos of bird life. Yinon et al, "The biomass distribution on Earth".

41 In "Waiting for Gaia", Latour formulates "the sublime" in such a way that there is no longer anything "outside", no untouched, nature, "except the Milky Way", that warrants this kind of awe. He argues that Earth's sublime potential has been exhausted, as it has been taken over by a power that we don't understand – namely that humans have managed to exert so much harmful influence without being able to attribute responsibility. Latour's position is that the sublime belongs to the modern understanding of nature and reflects an infatuated focus on the world as an expression of a *first* nature, but we are now realising that this idea is a delusion.

42 The Danish Ministry of Climate, Energy and Utilities. Borgerting på Klimaområdet (Citizens' Climate Assembly).

# ecologisation

1   Parts of this chapter are included in the article *The Indoor People's Enchanted Ecologies*.

2   The folk high school movement in Denmark emerged in the 19th century, based on the educational ideas of N.F.S. Grundtvig (see a short history here: <https://folkschoolalliance.org/a-brief-history-of-folk-schools>). Nowadays, they are a popular way to spend a form of gap year and concentrating on subjects like a sport, ecology, fashion, art, drama etc.. A comprehensive list of schools is available here: <https://www.danishfolkhighschools.com>

3   Sofie Isager Ahl, Matti Weisdorf (PhD students affiliated with *Enchanted Ecologies*) and I taught together.

4   Olsen et al, "Her er resultatet af folketingsvalget" (Here are the results of the 2019 general election).

5   Ritzau, "Grønne organisationer jubler" (Green organisations celebrate).

6   Moor, Vydt, Uba and Wahlström, "New kids on the block".

7   Kleres and Wettergren, "Fear, hope, anger and guilt in climate activism"; Cassegård and Thörn, "Toward a postapocalyptic environmentalism"; Nairn, "Learning from Young People Engaged in Climate Activism"; Comtesse, Ertl, Hengst, Rosner and Smid, "Ecological Grief".

8   The anthropologist Perle Møhl and the Chestnut Assembly met as part of a collaboration between Liselund Laboratorium Møn and Metropolis, Copenhagen International Theatre, in an attempt to have conversations in "treeish".

9   Jorden kalder (Earth is Calling).

10  Ibid.

11  Inspired by the anthropologist James Faubion's reading in *An Anthropology of Ethics*, 3 ff, 38 ff.

12  Charles Taylor, "What is Human Agency?", 16 ff.

13  Haraway, *Staying with the Trouble*, 1, 4, 70.

14  Ibid., 10.

15  A chapter (Camille Stories) in Haraway, *Staying with the Trouble*.

16  Langendorf, *Sommerfuglemøder* (Butterfly Meetings).

17  Ibid.

18  Krøijer, "Revolution is the way you eat".

19  Lambek, "Living as if it mattered".

20  The Danish Healthy Food Council, *De officielle Kostråd – godt for sundhed og klima* (The Official Dietary Guidelines – good for health and climate).

21  Taylor, *Sources of the Self*, 92 ff.

# new magic

1   Carlowicz, "All of You on the Good Earth".
2   Latour, *Down to Earth,* 59, 63.
3   Morton, *Being Ecological.*
4   Lien, *Becoming Salmon.*
5   McLoughlin, "Knowing Cows".
6   Rogers, "Oil and Anthropology".
7   Tønder, O*m magt i den antro-pocæne tidsalder* (On Power in the Anthropocene).
8   Willig and Blok, *Den bæredygtige stat* (The Sustainable State).
9   Morton, *Dark Ecology*, 6.
10  Gausset, Jensen and Hunt, *ViGør* (We do); Laage-Thomsen and Blok, "Civic Modes of Greening the City".

# bibliography

Ahl, Sofie Isager. "Skovrig tænkning – en samtale med Eduardo Kohn". In: Eduardo Kohn *Sjæleblindhed*. Copenhagen: Forlaget Virkelig, 2015.

Ahl, Sofie Isager. *Regeneration. Gensidigt helende praksisser i en ny jordbrugsbevægelse*. PhD thesis, Department of Anthropology, University of Copenhagen.

Appel, Liv, Søren Frandsen and Erik A. Jarrum. "Sagnkredsen om Helene, Arild og Thora i den nordlige Øresundsregion". *Alle tiders Nordsjælland. Museum Nordsjællands Årbog* 2015: 167–181.

Arler, Finn, Michael Søgaard Jørgensen and Esben Munk Sørensen. *Prioritering af Danmarks areal i fremtiden. Afsluttende rapport fra projektet Prioritering af fremtidens arealanvendelse i Danmark 2014–2017*. Fonden Teknologirådet, 2017.

Arternes Aarhus. *Om Arternes Aarhus*. rodnet.org/om-arternes-aarhus/ (Accessed May, 2021).

Arvidsson, Bengt. "En helig källas teologi före och efter reformationen. Helene Kilde i Tisvilde och Erich Hansens 'Fontinalia Sacra', 1650". *Kirkehistoriske Samlinger*, 1991.

Atran, Scott and Ara Norenzyan. "Religion's evolutionary landscape". *Behavioural and Brain Sciences* (2004), 27: 713–770.

Baal, J. van and W.E.A. van Beek. *Symbols for Communication: An introduction to the anthropological study of religion*. Assem: Van Gorcum, 1985: 14–15.

Barad, Karen. *Meeting the Universe Halfway*. Durham, NC: Duke University Press, 2007.

Barfoed, Niels. *Benedicte – en skæbne*. Copenhagen: Gyldendal. 2013

Barthes, Roland. *Mytologier (Mythologies)*. Copenhagen: Samlerens Bogklub, 1996.

Basso, Keith. "Stalking with Stories: Names, Places, and Moral Narratives among the Western Apache". In: Edward Bruner (ed.) *Text, Play and Story: The Construction and Reconstruction of Self and Society*. Washington: American Ethnological Society, 1984.

Bennett, Jane. *The Enchantment of Modern Life: Attachments, Crossings, and Ethics*. Princeton, NJ: Princeton University Press, 2001.

Bennett, Jane. *Vibrant Matter: A Political Ecology of Things*. Durham, NC: Duke University Press, 2010.

Bennett, Jane. *Vegetabilt liv og ontoSympati* (Vegetable Life and Onto-Sympathy). Copenhagen: Laboratory for Aesthetics and Ecology, 2018. [Translated from English]

Bird-David, Nurit. "Animism Revisited. Personhood, Environment, and Relational Epistemology". *Current Anthropology*, 1999: 40, Supplement S: 67–79.

Bjørnvig, Thorkild. *Samlede digte*. 1947–1987. Copenhagen: Gyldendal, 1998.

Blicher, Steen Steensen. *Eneboeren på Bolbjerg*. Copenhagen. Lindhardt and Ringhof, [1834] 2019.

Borman, Frank. "Earthrise: The Story of the Photo that Changed the World". *National Geographic*. <https://www.youtube.com/watch?v=BsShNeDvccc> (Accessed May 2021).

Boyer, Pascal. *Religion Explained*. New York: Basic Books. 2001.

By & Havn. *Forslaget Fælledby vinder arkitektkonkurrence om Vejlands kvarter*. <https://byoghavn.dk/forslaget-faelledby-vinder-arkitektkonkurrence-om-vejlands-kvarter> (Accessed March 2024).

Cadena, Marison de la. *Earth Beings: Ecologies of Practice Across Andean Worlds*. Durham NC: Duke University Press, 2015.

Carlowicz, Michael. "All of You on the Good Earth". *NASA Earth Observatory*. <https://earthobservatory.nasa.gov/images/144427/all-of-you-on-the-good-earth> (Accessed March 2024).

Casanova, José. *Global Religious and Secular Dynamics*. Leiden: Brill, 2019.

Cassegård, Carl and Håkan Thörn. "Toward a post-apocalyptic environmentalism: Responses to loss and visions of the future in

climate activism". *Environment and Planning E: Nature and Space* (2018)
1,4: 561-578.

Cavling, Henrik. "Sct. Hans nat ved Helene Kilde". *Politiken* 1886. Article
reproduced in *Vejby-Tibirke Selskabet 1967–1968*: 2–5.

Chamovitz, Daniel. *What a Plant Knows: A Field Guide to Your Garden – and
Beyond.* Oxford: Oneworld. 2012

Christensen, Inger. *Alfabet.* Copenhagen: Gyldendal, 1981.

Christensen, Inger. *Alphabet.* Hexham: Bloodaxe, 2018, translated by Susanna
Nied

Christensen, Jens. *Hvad er natur? Naturbegrebet på spørgsmål.* Department of
Sustainability and Planning. Aalborg: Aalborg University, 2007.

City of Copenhagen. *Ny løsning for Ørestad Fælled Kvarter* (New Solution fo the
Ørsted Fælled District).

Clark, Cristy, Nia Emmanouil, John Page and Alessandro Pelizzon. "Can You
Hear the Rivers Sing? Legal Personhood, Ontology, and the Nitty-Gritty
of Governance". *Ecology Law Quarterly* (2018) 45, 4: 787–844.

Coccia, Emanuele. *The Life of Plants: A Metaphysics of Mixture.* Cambridge:
Polity Press, 2019.

Comtesse, Hannah, Verena Ertl, Sophie M.C. Hengst, Rita Rosner and Geert
E. Smid. "Ecological Grief as a Response to Environmental Change: A
Mental Health Risk or Functional Response?" *International Journal of
Environmental Research and Public Health* (2021) 18: 734.

Convention of Biological Diversity <https://www.cbd.int/convention>
(accessed May 2024).

Corballis, Michael. *The Wandering Mind: What the Brain Does When You're Not
Looking.* Chicago: University of Chicago Press. 2015.

Cronon, William. "The Trouble with Wilderness or, Getting Back to the Wrong
Nature". In: William Cronon (ed.) *Uncommon Ground: Rethinking the
Human Place in Nature.* New York: W. W. Norton & Co., 1995: 69–90.

Csikszentmihalyi, Mihaly. Finding Flow : The Psychology of Engagement with
Everyday Life. BasicBooks, 1997.

Dalsgaard, Kathrine. "Naturlov – Ganges, Himalaya og Moder Jord har samme
rettigheder som dig". *360° – Verden i Udvikling* (2018) 1.

Danish Healthy Food Council, The. *De officielle Kostråd – godt for sundhed og
klima.* <https://raadetforsundmad.dk/viden/publikation/de-officielle-
kostraad> (Accessed March 2024).

Danmarks Naturfredningsforening. *Frie kyster. Danmarks Naturforenings
Kystpolitik,* 2012.

Danmarks Naturfredningsforening. *Input til regeringens redningsplan for
Danmarks biodiversitet,* 2020.

<https://www.dn.dk/media/54552/dns-input-til-regeringens-redningsplan-for-danmarks-biodiversitet.pdf> (Accessed January 2021).

Danmarks Naturfredningsforening. *Biodiversitetslov og 20 procent vild natur: Her er redningsplanen for naturen.* Press release 6.1.2020.

Danmarks Naturfredningsforening og Dyrenes Beskyttelse. *Sådan ligger landet – Tal om landbruget 2017,* 2018.

Descola, Philippe. "Modes of being and forms of predication". *HAU: Journal of Ethnographic Theory* (2014) 4,1: 271–280.

Duus, Søren Duran. "Henning Larsen-team vinder 219.000 kvm stor træbydel på Amager". <https://estatemedia.dk/dk/2019/12/05/henning-larsen-architects-vinder-bydelsprojekt-paa-219-000-kvm-paa-amager-faelled> (Accessed March 2024).

Ejrnæs, Rasmus. *Natur.* Aarhus: Aarhus University, 2013.

Ejrnæs, Rasmus. *Den uendelige have.* Aarhus: Aarhus Universitetsforlag, 2016.

Ejrnæs, Rasmus. "Natur for naturens skyld". Interview in *Verdens Skove* with Jonas Kragh Madsen, 21 March, 2016.

Ejrnæs, Rasmus. "Det er egoistisk kun at se ulven som en fjende". *Altinget,* 26.2.2018.

Ejrnæs, Rasmus, Jesper Bladt and Camilla Fløjgaard. "Rewilding som planmål i Antropocæn". *Tidsskrift for Kortlægning og Arealforvaltning* (2017) 123,48: 35–46.

Eliade, Mircea. *Myth and Reality.* New York: Harper Torchbooks, 1963.

Ethnographic Machines. *Amager Fælledsagen på Facebook.* <https://medium.com/@EthnographicMachines/amager-fælledsagen-på-facebook-mere-end-flygtige-likes-og-60c8ffc562d3> (Accessed May 2021).

Faubion, James D. *An Anthropology of Ethics.* Cambridge: Cambridge University Press, 2011.

Fink, Hans. "Et mangfoldigt naturbegreb". In: P.W. Agger, A. Reenberg, J. Læssøe and H.P. Hansen (ed.) *Naturens værdi: Vinkler på danskernes forhold til naturen.* Copenhagen: Gad, 2003.

FN-forbundet. FN vedtager global aftale om at beskytte dyr og planter. <https://www.fnforbundet.dk/nyheder/2022/fn-vedtager-global-aftale-om-at-beskytte-dyr-og-planter> (Accessed March 2024).

Foucault, Michel. "Of Other Spaces: Utopia and Heterotopias". *Diacritics* 16,1 (1986): 22–27.

Frederiksen, Karl Erik. *Troldtøjets Sand samt andre vandrehistorier fra Tibirke og Arresøs opland.* Helsinge Forlaget, 2000.

Frederiksen, Signe, Finn N. Rasmussen and Ole Seberg. *Dansk flora.* Copenhagen: Gyldendal.

Friis, Christian. "Vejby-Tibirke selskabet. Manglende omsorg for vores område". *TisvildeNyt* (2017) 25,6: 14–15.

Gad, Tue. *Helgener.* Copenhagen: Rhodos, 1971: 128–131.

Gagliano, Monica. *Thus Spoke the Plant: A Remarkable Journey of Groundbreaking Scientific Discoveries and Personal Encounters with Plants.* Berkeley: North Atlantic Books, 2018.

Gan, Elaine, Anna Tsing, Heather Swanson and Nils Bubandt. *Arts of Living on a Damaged Planet. Ghosts and Monsters of the Anthropocene.* Minneapolis: University of Minnesota Press, 2017.

Garff, Joakim. *Søren Kierkegaard: A Biography.* Princeton: Princeton University Press, 2005.

Gausset, Quentin, Karina H.B. Jensen and Julia B. Hunt. *ViGør – Fortællinger fra den grønne frontlinje.* Forlaget Ingefaer, 2019.

Gell, Alfred. "Technology and magic". *Anthropology Today* (1988) 4,2: 6–9.

Gelsted, Otto. *Tibirke Bakker.* Copenhagen: Arthur Jensens Forlag, 1941.

Gjerris, Mickey and Cecilie Rubow. *Naturens sprog. Historier fra virkeligheden om fortryllelse.* Copenhagen: Eksistensen, 2018.

Gregersen, Niels Henrik. "Tre slags panenteisme: et forsøg på en begrebsafklaring". *Dansk Teologisk Tidsskrift* (2009) 72,4: 282–302.

Gregersen, Niels Henrik. "Deep Incarnation: Opportunities and Challenges". In: Niels Henrik Gregersen (ed.) *Incarnation. On the Scope and Depth of Christology.* Augsburg Fortress, 2015.

Gribskov Kommune. *New Nordic Coast,* Gilleleje. <https://fishingzealand.dk/wp-content/uploads/new-nordic-coast.pdf> (Accessed March 2024).

Grønkjær, Niels. *Den nye Gud. Efter fundamentalisme og ateisme.* Copenhagen: Eksistensen, 2015.

Hammer, Everett. "Here's to Unsuicide: An interview with Richard Powers". *Los Angeles Review of Books.* 7 April, 2018.

Hansen, Morten D.D. "Vi, som inhalerede". In: Mickey Gjerris and Cecilie Rubow (ed.) *Naturens sprog. Historier fra virkeligheden om fortryllelse.* Copenhagen: Eksistensen, 2018.

Hansen, Morten D.D. "Når naturen fortryller os". 1: 2. *Vildspor,* Radio4. <https://www.radio4.dk/program/vildspor/?id=nr-naturen-fortryller-os-12_ep_09_05_20> (Accessed March 2024).

Haraway, Donna. *The Companion Species Manifesto: Dogs, People, and Significant Otherness.* Chicago: Prickly Paradigm Press, 2003.

Haraway, Donna. *When Species Meet.* Minneapolis: University of Minnesota Press, 2008.

Haraway, Donna. *Staying with the Trouble: Making Kin in the Chthulucene.* Durham and London: Duke University Press, 2016.

Harding, Garrett. "The Tragedy of the Commons". *The Social Contract*: [1968] (2001): 26–35.

Hartigan, John. "How to Interview a Plant: Ethnography of Life Forms". *Care of the Species: Races of Corn and the Science of Plant Biodiversity*. Minneapolis: University of Minnesota Press, 2017.

Hastrup, Kirsten. *A Place Apart: An Anthropological Study of the Icelandic World*. Oxford: Oxford University Press, 1998.

Hastrup, Kirsten. "Icelandic Topography and the Sense of Identity". In Michael Jones and Kenneth R. Olwig (eds.): *Nordic Landscapes: Region and Belonging on the Northern Edge of Europe*. Minneapolis, London: University of Minnesota Press, 2008.

Hedegaard, Lotte. *Iron Age Myth and Materiality: An Archaeology of Scandinavia AD 400–100*. Florence: Routledge, 2011.

Henare, J.M., Martin Holbraad and Sara Wastell. *Thinking Through Things: Theorising artefacts ethnographically*. Milton Park: Routledge, 2006.

Herbener, Jens-André. *Naturen er hellig. Klimakatastrofe og religion*. Copenhagen: Informations Forlag, 2015.

Hoffmeyer, Jesper. *7 ting vi plejer at tro på*. Copenhagen: Tiderne Skifter, 2017.

Hundeide, Michael T. *Ornitologisk praksis som persepsjon av naturen. Om naturopplevelse, kunnskapservervelse og naturhistorisk entusiasme*. Department of Social Anthropology. Oslo: University of Oslo, 2013.

Hyltoft, Ole. *Livet ved havet*, Hovedland, 2015.

Haaning, Aksel. *Naturens lys. Vestens naturfilosofi i højmiddelalder og renæssance 1250–1600*. Copenhagen: C.A. Reitzels Forlag, 1998.

Haaning, Aksel. *Den dobbelte arv. Kapitler om natur og spiritualitet, kristendom og historie samt Antikrist: Problemet om det onde*. Copenhagen: C.A. Reitzels Forlag, 2005.

Ingold, Tim. *The Perception of the Environment: Essays on Livelihood, Dwelling and Skill*. London: Routledge, 2000.

Ingold, Tim. *Correspondences*. Cambridge: Polity Press, 2020.

IPBES (2019): *Global assessment report on biodiversity and ecosystem services of the Intergovernmental Science-Policy Platform on Biodiversity and Ecosystem Services*. In: E.S. Brondizio, J. Settele, S. Díaz and H.T. Ngo (eds.). Bonn: Germany, 2019.

IPCC (2023): *Climate Change 2023: Synthesis Report. Contribution of Working Groups I, II and III to the Sixth Assessment Report of the Intergovernmental Panel on Climate Change* (Core Writing Team, H. Lee and J. Romero (eds.). IPCC, Geneva, Switzerland.

Ishøy, Martin. *Klimaklar kristendom. Miljøteologiske begrundelser*. Copenhagen: Forlaget Anis, 2009.

Jarløv, H.C. *Danmarks berømteste helligkilde.* Vejby-Tibirke Selskabet (1990): 2–11.

Jensen, Ole. *På kant med klodens klima. Om behovet for et ændret klima.* Copenhagen, Forlaget Anis, 2011.

Johansen, Bo Thyge. "Sortspættereden i Asserbo Plantage 2019". *Pandion* (2020) 10.

Johansen, Jens Christian V. "Holy springs and Protestantism in early modern Denmark: A Medical Rationale for a Religious Practice". *Medical History* (1997) 41: 59–69.

Jorden kalder. <https://krogerup.dk/lange-ophold/hovedfag/jorden-kalder> (Accessed May 2021).

Jørgensen, Dorthe. "Etik og transcendens". 1. *omtanke. Større end omskæring.* November 2018.

Jørgensen, Dorthe. "Menneskets modtagelighed for tro". In: Kjeld Slot Nielsen and Sanne B. Thøisen (eds.) *Midt i en medietid. Digitalisering og medialisering i religion, filosofi og kunst.* Copenhagen: Eksistensen, 2020.

Kallestrup, Louise Nyholm. *I pagt med djævelen. Trolddomsforestillinger og trolddomsforfølgelse i Italien og Danmark efter Reformationen.* Copenhagen: Forlaget Anis, 2009.

Kelly, Paul, Chloë Williamson, Ailsa G. Niven, Ruth Hunter, Nanette Mutrie and Justin Richards. "Walking on sunshine: Scoping review of the evidence for walking and mental health". *British Journal of Sports Medicine* (2018) 52: 800–806.

Kierkegaard, Søren. *Journalen AA:6. Den 29de Juli, 1835.*

Kleres, Jochen and Åsa Wettergren. "Fear, hope, anger and guilt in climate activism". *Social Movements Studies* (2017) 16: 507–519.

Kohn, Eduardo. *How Forests Think: Toward an Anthropology Beyond the Human.* Berkeley: University of California Press, 2013.

Krøijer, Stine. "Revolution is the way you eat: Exemplification among left radical activists in Denmark and in anthropology". *Journal of the Royal Anthropological Institute* (2015) 21, S1: 78–95.

Krøijer, Stine. "Træer og andre(s) arter i Amazonas". *Tidsskriftet Antropologi* (2021) 83: 155–176.

Krøijer, Stine and Cecilie Rubow. "Enchanted Ecologies and Ethics of Care". *Environmental Humanities* (2022) 14,2.

*Ny løsning for Ørestad Fælled Kvarter.* <https://www.kk.dk/sites/default/files/agenda/1f95148f-6282-40f1-b522-0a9f6f90de7e/52551052-dca0-4bbc-9d18-1e3ca871775f-bilag-1.pdf> (Accessed March 2024).

Lambek, Michael. "Living as if it mattered". In: Lambek, Michael, et al. *Four Lectures on Ethics: Anthropological Perspectives,* HAU, 2015.

Lange, Sidsel Brøndum. "Biologer frygter ukritisk forskning i biodiversitet". <https://videnskab.dk/miljo-naturvidenskab/biologer-frygter-ukritisk-forskning-i-biodiversitet> (Accessed May 2021).

Langendorf, Ida Nielsen. *Sommerfuglemøder. Et eksplorativt studie af møder mellem sommerfugle og mennesker.* Master's thesis. Department of Sociology, University of Copenhagen, 2020.

Latour, Bruno. *We have Never been Modern.* Harvard University Press, 1993.

Latour, Bruno. "To modernize or to ecologize? That's the question". In: N. Castree and B. Willems-Braun (eds.) *Remaking Reality: Nature at the Millennium.* London and New York: Routledge (2012): 221–242.

Latour, Bruno. "Waiting for Gaia. Composing the common world through art and politics". In: Albena Yaneva and Alejandro Zaera-Polo (eds.) *What is Cosmopolitical Design?* Farnham: Ashgate, 2015.

Latour, Bruno. *Down to Earth: Politics in the New Climatic Regime.* Polity Press, 2018.

Le Guin, Ursula K. The Compass Rose. Panther, 1984Lidegaard, Mads. *Myte og sagn.* Copenhagen: Gyldendal, 2007.

Lien, Marianne. *Becoming Salmon: Aquaculture and the Domestication of a Fish.* Oakland: University of California Press. 2015.

Liep, John. "Luftbåren *kula.* Danske feltornitologers tilegnelse af fugle". *Tidsskriftet Antropologi* (1996) 33: 5–19.

Liisberg, Bering. *Domina Helena. Sagn og Historie fra Tisvilde.* Copenhagen: Nyt Nordisk Forlag, 1919.

Liselunds Laboratorium Møn. *Kastanjeforsamlingen. Deltagerbaseret laboratorium.* Oktober 2021. <https://liselundlaboratorium.org/oktober> (Accessed March 2024).

Lovejoy, Arthur. *The Great Chain of Being: The Study of the History of an Idea.* New York: Harper & Brothers, [1936] 1964.

Lovelock, James. The Revenge of Gaia. London. Penguin, 2007..

Luckmann, Thomas. *The Invisible Religion: The problem of religion in modern society.* New York: Macmillan Publishing, 1967.

Luckmann, Thomas. "Shrinking Transcendence, Expanding Religion?" *Sociological Analysis* (1990) 51, 2: 127–138.

Luhrmann, T.M. "The Art of Hearing God: Absorption, Dissociation, and Contemporary American Spirituality". *Spiritus: A Journal of Christian Spirituality* (2005) 5,2: 133–157.

Lund, Lars. "En cikorie er ikke blot en cikorie". *Fyens Stiftstidende*, 1.8.2010. <https://fyens.dk/artikel/en-cikorie-er-ikke-blot-en-cikorie> (Accessed March 2024).

Löfgren, Orvar. *On Holiday: A History of Vacationing.* Berkeley: University of California Press, 1999.

Löfgren, Orvar. "Motion and Emotion. The Microphysics and Metaphysics of Landscape Experiences in Tourism". In: Alf Hornborg and Gísli Pálsson (eds.) *Negotiating Nature: Culture, Power, and Environmental Argument.* Lund: Lund University Press.

Laage-Thomsen, Jakob and Anders Blok. "Civic Modes of Greening the City? Urban Natures In-between Familiar Engagement and Green Critique". *Local Environment: The international journal of justice and sustainability* (2020) 25,2: 162–178.

McDonald, David. "The Etymology of 'Jizz', revisited". *Canberra Bird Notes,* (2016) 41,2: 113–117.

McLoughlin, Eimear. "Knowing Cows: Transformative mobilizations of human and non-human bodies in an emotionography of the slaughterhouse". *Gender, Work & Organization* (2018) 26,3: 322–342.

Madsen, Stig Toft. "Den taksonomiske taktstok". *Tidsskriftet Antropologi* (2021) 83: 25–50.

Massey, Doreen. *For Space.* Los Angeles: Sage, 2005.

Michaelsen, Anders S., Johanne Bak, Biomedia and Lars Andersen. *Vidensindsamling Natur 2013, Amager Fælled.* Biomedia, 2013.

Ministry of Food, Agriculture and Fisheries *Danmarks nationale skovprogram* (National Forest Plan), 2018. <https://mfvm.dk/fileadmin/user_upload/ MFVM/Nyheder/Danmarks_nationale_skovprogram_2018.pdf> (Accessed May 2021).

Ministry of Climate, Energy and Utilities . *Borgerting på Klimaområdet.* kefm. dk/klima-og-vejr/borgertinget. (Accessed May 2021).

Mols Laboratory Research Station. *Welcome.* <https://www.naturhistoriskmuseum.dk/visit>

Moor, Joost de, Michiel De Vydt, Katrin Uba and Mattias Wahlström. "New Kids on the Block: taking stock of the recent cycle of climate activism". *Social Movement Studies,* 2020.

Morton, Timothy. *Dark Ecology.* New York, Chichester: Columbia University Press, 2016.

Morton, Timothy. *Being Ecological.* Pelican Books, 2018.

Moselund, J.E. et al. *Den danske rødliste.* <https://bios.au.dk/raadgivning/natur/ redlistframe/soeg-en-art> (Accessed March 2024).

Munck, Jørgen. User profile on netfugl.dk <https://www.netfugl.dk/profiles. php?id=showprofile&profile_id=58> (Accessed March 2021).

Myers, Natasha. *How to grow livable worlds: Ten (not so easy) steps for life in the Planthroposcene,* 2021. <https://www.abc.net.au/religion/natasha- myers-how-to-grow-liveable-worlds:-ten-not-so-easy-step/11906548> (Accessed March 2024).

Nairn, Karen. "Learning from Young People Engaged in Climate Activism: The Potential of Collectivizing Despair and Hope". *Young* (2019) 25,5: 435–450.

Naturbasen. "Gransanger". <https://www.naturbasen.dk/art/591/gransanger> (Accessed March 2021). [En tilsvarende engelsk side?]

Natural History Museum, Aarhus. *Rewilding på Molslaboratoriet*. <https://www.naturhistoriskmuseum.dk/molslaboratoriet/rewilding-på-molslaboratoriet/spørgsmål-og-svar> (Accessed March 2021).

Neimanis, Astris. *Hydrofeminisme: Eller, om at blive en krop af vand*. Laboratory for Aesthetics and Ecology, 2018.

Ohrt, Hans et al. *Naturkortlægning på delområder af Amager Fælled*. Report to the City of Copenhagen, 2018.

Olsen, Martin Lyngbæk, Katrine Falk Lønstrup and Daniel Bue Lauritzen. "Her er resultatet af folketingsvalget 2019". Altinget. <https://www.altinget.dk/artikel/183360-her-er-valgresultatet> (Accessed March 2014).

Ortner, Sherry B. "Is Female to Male as Nature is to Culture?" *Feminist Studies*, (1972) 1, 2: 5–31.

Ott, W.R. "Human Activity Patterns: A Review of the Literature for Estimating Time Spent Indoors, Outdoors, and in Transit". In: *Proceedings of the Research Planning Conference on Human Activity Patterns*. EPA National Exposure Research Laboratory, Las Vegas (1989) 3–1 – 3–38.

Pálsson, Gísli. "Human-environmental relations: Orientalism, paternalism and communalism". In: Philippe Descola and Gísli Pálsson (eds.) *Nature and Society: Anthropological Perspectives*. London and New York: Routledge, 1996: 63–81.

Paulli, Simon. *Flora Danica*, 1648.

Pedersen, Bo Bang. "Helene Klint og Kyst – en mosaik om naturen og kystsikringen". *Vejby-Tibirke årbog 2017*: 109–123.

Pers, Michael. "Tro og kildevand". *Bibliotek for læger* (1999) 191: 318–332.

Pontoppidan, Erik. "Det Fierde Capitel. Om nogle særdeles Jord- Leer- og Farve-Arter, Samt Alun, Vitriol, Salt, Svovel og deslige Mineralier, saa vidt noget deraf hidindtil Hos os er opdaget". *Den Danske Atlas*, Tome I,. Book 2, 1769.

Powers, Richard. *The Overstory: A Novel*. New York. W. W. Norton & Company.

Rappaport, Roy A. "Ritual Regulation of Environmental Relations among a New Guinea people". *Ethnology* (1967) 6,1: 17–30.

Reiter, Gry Inger. "Her er debattens superliga". *Politiken*, 22.12.2017.

Ries, Nancy. "Potato Ontology: Surviving Postsocialism in Russia". *Cultural Anthropology* (2009) 24: 181–212.

Ritzau. "Grønne organisationer jubler: Klimamål er historiske". <https://jyllands-posten.dk/politik/ECE11454438/groenne-organisationer-jubler-klimamaal-er-historiske> (Accessed May 2024).

Robbins, Joel. "What is the matter with transcendence? On the place of religion in the new anthropology of ethics". *Journal of the Royal Anthropological Institute* (2016) 22: 767–808.

Robbins, Paul. *Lawn People: How Grasses, Weeds, and Chemicals Make Us Who We Are*. Philadelphia: Tempe University Press, 2007.

Rogers, Douglas. "Oil and Anthropology". *Annual Review of Anthropology* (2015) 44: 365–380.

Rosa, Hartmut. *The Uncontrollability of the World*. Polity Press, 2020.

Rosa, Hartmut. *Resonance: A Sociology of Our Relationship to the World*. Polity Press, 2019.

Rosiek, Jan. *Danmark, Gurre, stranden. Steder i dansk litteratur*. Copenhagen: U Press, 2015.

Rubow, Cecilie. *Hverdagens teologi. Folkereligiøsitet i danske verdner*. Copenhagen: Forlaget Anis, 2000.

Rubow, Cecilie. "Bagom transcendens". *Kritisk Forum for Praktisk Teologi* (2021) 163.

Rubow, Cecilie. "The Indoor People's Enchanted Ecologies". *Environmental Humanities* (2022) 14, 2.

Rubow, Cecilie. "Three Ecologies in Danish Eco-Theology". Wyller, Trygve, et al., editors. *Redeeming the Sense of the Universal: Scandinavian Creation Theology on Politics and Ecology*. Göttingen: Vandenhoeck & Ruprecht, 2024. 251–262.

Rubow, Cecilie. "The Weird Magic of Becoming Ecologically Aware". *Journal for the Study of Religion, Nature and Culture* (2025), 286–306.

Rømer, Lars Christian Kofoed. *Tales in an Underground Landscape: Anthropological Excursions in the Danish Island of Bornholm*. PhD Thesis, Department of Anthropology, University of Copenhagen, 2018. Danish Healthy Food Council, The. *De officielle Kostråd – godt for sundhed og klima*. <https://raadetforsundmad.dk/viden/publikation/de-officielle-kostraad> (Accessed March 2024).

Sandbeck, Lars. *Fantasiens Gud. Den teologiske vending mod det mytisk-poetiske sprog hos Amos Niven Wilder, Peter Kemp og Johannes Sløk*. Copenhagen: Eksistensen, 2006.

Sandbeck, Lars. *Den gudløse verden. Ateisme og antireligion i en postkristen æra*. Copenhagen: Eksistensen, 2020.

Scharff, William. "Et gaardmandshjem, Tisvilde". *Danske Hjem*, 1953. Dansk Folkemindesamling 19 February 1962.

Schmedes, Frej Pries and Elisabeth Friis. "Byggeri på Amager Fælled bliver aldrig grønt, selv om arkitekterne påstår det. Læserbrev". *Information*, 18 December, 2019.

Schmitz, Hermann. *Kroppen* (The Body). Aalborg Universitetsforlag, 2017.

Schmitz, Hermann. *New Phenomenology: A Brief Introduction*. Mimesis International, 2019.

Seberg, Ole and Signe Frederiksen. "Hvorfor ændres klassifikationer?" *Urt* (2007) 31,1: 36–45.

Sjørslev, Inger. *Ting. I nære og fjerne verdener*. Aarhus: Aarhus Universitetsforlag, 2013.

Smidt, Claus M. *Tisvildes trylleri*. Nivågaards Malerisamling, 1990.

Smith, Jonathan Z. "A Pearl of a Great Price and a Cargo of Yams: A Study in Situational Incongruity". *History of Religions* (1976) 16,1: 1–19.

Steffen, Will et al. "Trajectories of the Earth System in the Anthropocene". *Proceedings of the National Academy of Sciences* (2018) 115.

Stoltze, Michael. *Danmarks Naturfredningsforening vil hellere slå på landmændene end beskytte naturen*. <https://www.information.dk/debat/2017/04/danmarks-naturfredningsforening-hellere-slaa-paa-landmaendene-beskytte-naturen> (Accessed March 2024).

Stuckrad, Kocku von. *A Cultural History of the Soul. Europe and North America from 1870 to the Present*. New York: Columbia University Press, 2022.

Svenningsen, Jesper. *Seks år af et liv. Johan Thomas Lundbye. Dagbøger om tro, skæbne, kunst og kærlighed. Kilder til dansk kunsthistorie*. Copenhagen: Ny Carlsbergfondet. Strandberg Publishing, 2018.

Taylor, Bron. *Dark Green Religion: Nature Spirituality and the Planetary Future*. Berkeley: University of California Press, 2010.

Taylor, Charles. "What is Human Agency?" *Human Agency and Language: Philosophical Papers 1*. Cambridge: Cambridge University Press, 1985.

Taylor, Charles. *Sources of the Self: The Making of the Modern Identity*. Cambridge: Harvard University Press, 1989.

Thiele, J.M. *Prøver af Danske Folkesagn*. Brødrene Thieles Forlag, 1817.

Thorsen, Andreas. "Engang vrimlede det med hybenhjerter, viltre svaler og brede bøge i den danske sang. Så hvor forsvandt digte om naturen hen?" 8.9.2019. <https://www.zetland.dk>.

Thurfjell, David. *Granskogsfolk. Hur naturen blev svenskarnas religion*. Stockholm: Nordstedts, 2020.

Thurfjell, David, Cecilie Rubow, Atko Remmel and Henrik Ohlsson. "The Relocation of Transcendence: Using Schutz to Conceptualize the Nature Experiences of Secular People". *Nature and Culture* (2019) 14, 2: 190–214.

Tsing, Anna L. *Friction: An Ethnography of Global Connection*. Princeton: Princeton University Press, 2005.

Tsing, Anna L. *The Mushroom at the End of the World*. Princeton: Princeton University Press, 2015.

Tsing, Anna L., Jennifer Deger, Alder Keleman Saxena, and Feifei Zhou. *Field Guide to the Patchy Anthropocene: The New Nature* (p. 1). (Function). Kindle Edition. *Field Guide to the Patchy Anthropocene. The New Nature*. Stanford University Press, 2024

Tvermoes, Liv, Anne Marie Rubin, Per Grønlykke, Peter Fogh, Lene and Svend Kierkegaard. *Fiskerlejet i Tisvildeleje*. In collaboration with Grundejerforeningen for Tisvilde og Omegn, (Owners Association in and around Tisvilde), n.d.

Tybjerg, Jonathan. "Hver femte unge dansker tror, en rødspætte er en fugl. Hvad mister vi, når vi mister sproget for naturen?" 30.9.2019.

Tønder, Lars. *Om magt i den antropocæne tidsalder*. Copenhagen: DJØF Forlag, 2020.

Vacher, Marc. "Consuming Leisure Time". *Social Analysis* (2011) 55,2: 45–61.

Veng, Adam, Magnus Juhl and Cecilie Rubow. "Montage. Frej og den store vandsalamander". *Tidsskriftet Antropologi* (2021) 83: 91–100.

Wamberg, Jacob. "Between Paradise and the Anthropocene Garden: Views of nature in and outside the arts 1600–2017". In: Erlend G. Høyersten, Anne Mette Thomasen, Jacob Vengberg Sevel and Anette Vandsø: *The Garden: End of Times, Beginning of Times*, 2017: 19–39.

Weisdorf, Matti. *For the Love of the Living: A Rubber-boot Quest for the Biocene in Aarhus, Denmark*. PhD dissertation. Department of Anthropology. University of Copenhagen.

Willig, Rasmus and Anders Blok. *Den bæredygtige stat*. Copenhagen: DJØF Forlag.

Wolf, Jakob. *Krop og atmosfære. Hermann Schmitz' nye fænomenologi*. Copenhagen: Eksistensen, 2017.

Wolf, Jakob. "Transcendensen i følelserne". *Kritisk Forum for Praktisk Teologi* (2021) 163.

Yinon, M. Bar-On, Rob Phillips and Ron Milo. "The biomass distribution on Earth". *PNAS* (2018) 19 June (115).

* 9 7 8 8 7 7 5 9 7 2 5 7 9 *